The

BOOKLOVER'S
GUIDE
to the
MIDWEST

A LITERARY TOUR

The
BOOKLOVER'S
GUIDE
to the
MIDWEST
A LITERARY TOUR

GREG HOLDEN

CLERISY PRESS

Published by Clerisy Press
Printed in the United States of America
Distributed by Publishers Group West
First edition, first printing

For further information, contact the publisher at:

Clerisy Press
P.O. Box 8874
Cincinnati, OH 45208-0874
CLERISY PRESS   www.clerisypress.com

Library of Congress Cataloging-in-Publication Data

Holden, Greg.
    The booklover's guide to the Midwest : a literary tour /
By Greg Holden. ~ 1st ed.
        p. cm.
    ISBN-13: 978-1-57860-314-5
    ISBN-10: 1-57860-314-5
    1. Literary landmarks—Middle West—Guidebooks. 2. Middle
West—Intellectual life—Guidebooks. I. Title.

PS144.M53H65 2009
810.9'977~dc22

                                                2009020554

Cover designed by Kelly N. Kofron
Interior designed by Donna Collingwood

The p'   ·ss: pp. 9, 15, 55,
29, 3   **810.9977 HOL**   , 183, 185, 187,
188,   **Holden, Greg**   250, 263, 270
         The booklover's guide to
The ɟ   **the Midwest : a literary**   nons: pp. 8, 25,
48, 1   **tour**

Othe·   ¡0—George Ade
Mem   69 & 70—Ross
Lock **35340635273922**   **Aug 10** yne Birthplace,
115—The Amana Heritage Society, 131—Guttenberg Public Library, Guttenberg, Iowa,   177—Loome Theological Booksellers, 181—Terri Schocke, 235—Robert L. Liebold, 245—National First Ladies Library

The rest of the photos courtesy of the author

Dedication

*T*o my mother and father

Acknowledgments

*E*very book is a team effort. The authors you read about in this book benefited from working with editors, agents, spouses, assistants and many others who furthered their knowledge or helped prepare their work for publication. I could not have assembled this book without the help of many people as well.

First and foremost is Jack Heffron of Clerisy Press, who first saw potential in this idea and who guided it patiently through many twists and turns to fruition. Also at Clerisy I had the support of Richard Hunt, Donna Poehner, and Howard Cohen. And the intrepid interns Lissa Kramer and Kara LeNoir helped gather many of the illustrations.

Many museum staff members and literary mavens contributed photos and other information. They include Robert Liebold, Joyce Lyng, Les Roberts, Ross Lockridge III, Sarah Levar, Gary Goodman, Sandra Barron, Karen Minto, David Oyerly, and Ronald Wallace.

My own personal team includes my agent, Neil Salkind, and the staff at Studio B Productions, and my longtime assistant, book lover, and friend Ann Lindner.

Table of Contents

The

BOOKLOVER'S
GUIDE
to the
MIDWEST

A LITERARY TOUR

Introduction

The Booklover's Guide
to the Midwest

"*We* unconsciously catch the tone of every house in which we live, and we are influenced by surroundings nearer and closer still than the climate of the country which we inhabit."

–*Sarah Orne Jewett*

I have always been fascinated with places where writers grew up and gained the life experiences that later would become the material for their work. In college, I majored in both English and writing, and over the next decade or so I published a fair number of books myself. One of those books, which appeared in 2000, is *Literary Chicago*. It presents walking and driving tours of my hometown, as well as profiles of current writers, lists of bookstores, and other venues writers haunt.

I always wanted to expand this travelogue to include areas throughout the Midwest that were either claimed by writers as a home base or that have claimed writers as cultural attractions. For instance, Gene Stratton-Porter created an enclave for herself and her family in Indiana that she named Limberlost Farm. There she conducted nature studies and wrote novels that drew from the material she gathered from nature, such as *Song of the Cardinal* and *A Girl of the Limberlost*.

Just as fascinating to me are towns like West Salem, Wisconsin. Each September, West Salem holds a festival to commemorate a novelist and memoirist most of the world has nearly forgotten. Hamlin Garland was born in West Salem and lived there until he was eight. He later lived in Chicago, New York, and many other locales, but returned each summer to his home in West Salem. The festival that honors him is called "Garland Days," and the 2006 event included a rummage sale, a silent auction, and a display of antique cars arranged in Garland's backyard. A cake decorated with an image of Garland was served at the Hamlin Garland House, which is a National Historic Landmark. West Salem is just one of many Midwestern towns that uses the legacy of a writer who lived there as an attraction to boost the local economy.

In *The Booklover's Guide to the Midwest*, I'll take you to the homes where writers lived and worked and to the towns that keep their memories alive today.

Why a Midwest Literary Tour?

In urban centers like Chicago, New York, and San Francisco, many historic sites related to famous writers are within walking distance of one another. Why drive around the Midwestern countryside from one small town to another, looking at a few historical plaques or markers along the way?

The reason is evident if you're exploring the winding roads of the Spoon River Valley on a sunny October afternoon, heading from a country festival to visit the grave of Ann Rutledge, the girl Abraham Lincoln once loved, at the Petersburg cemetery. Recalling the opening lines of Edgar Lee Masters's *Spoon River Anthology* as you drive, makes the trip far more than a hunt for the perfect piece of rhubarb pie:

> Where are Elmer, Herman, Bert, Tom and Charley,
> The weak of will, the strong of arm, the clown, the
> boozer, the fighter?
> All, all, are sleeping on the hill.
>
> One passed in a fever,
> One was burned in a mine,
> One was killed in a brawl,
> One died in a jail,
> One fell from a bridge toiling for children and wife~
> All, all are sleeping, sleeping, sleeping on the hill.

Living in the Midwest has given myriad writers a unique depth of character. Their surroundings are what formed their identity and their very soul. A driving tour through their literary and physical landscape gives you a representative picture of America itself.

Who This Book Is For

I consider myself a literary pilgrim: I love planning trips to locations where I can track down the settings used by my favorite authors and visit the homes where these writers once lived and worked. This book will appeal to both the committed and casual literati who want something more from a trip than recreation, hotels, and shopping. Take it along on a vacation or weekend getaway as your practical guide to the highways, roads, towns, and events that will reveal the literary history that you seek.

My hope is that it will also have wider appeal to travelers who appreciate our cultural heritage and enjoy uncovering the layers of meaning and history in the small towns, parks, and rural settings where writers found inspiration and solace. While some families speed down interstates on their way to amusement parks, others are late to a birthday or anniversary celebration with relatives. If you're hurrying from Chicago to Detroit or from Milwaukee to Minneapolis, it's easy to overlook the ecology and history of the heartland—but not if you're willing to get off the beaten path.

Looking through the eyes of the Midwest's great writers will lead to an appreciation and understanding of what life is really like in the heartland. Whether you visit a mansion in a thriving metropolis or a shack at the deadend of a dirt road, you'll find a rich literary history often overlooked by tourists and locals alike.

Retrace the steps of writers and the characters they've created. Walk down the actual Main Street that novelist Sinclair Lewis described in his famous novel of the same name. See Laura Ingalls Wilder's "Little House in the Big Woods" and "Little House on the Prairie." Stroll among the gravestones from which poet Edgar Lee Masters took the names for his *Spoon River Anthology*. Get lost in the same cave where Tom Sawyer and Huck Finn explored.

You'll find many environmentalists here, including novelist Wallace Stegner and Aldo Leopold, author of *A Sand County Almanac* and the father of the modern environmental movement. In northern Michigan, you can travel in the footsteps of Ernest Hemingway, who spent many summers with his family in Petoskey and later commemorated the area in his Nick Adams stories. Other poets and writers put you in touch with Native Americans and the great expanse of the prairie.

If you love to seek out Andrew Carnegie libraries, don't believe for a minute that Midwestern literature can only be found on dusty shelves. Writers are anywhere there is an audience. You can listen to the tall tales in the Burlington, Wisconsin, annual Liars' Club contest, for example. This guide lists plenty of sites for special festivals and poetry slams. In regard to the latter, I brake for coffee shops that cater to writers.

The Booklover's Guide to the Midwest will also direct you to plenty of bookstores. Who could pass up a chance to visit the only bookstore with a castle inside of it: the Canterbury Bookstore in Madison, Wisconsin. Even if you can't visit all the places described in this book, you'll enjoy reading about them. And once you arrive at a destination that you love, you're bound to find other interesting things to see and do nearby. Who knows, maybe a few years from now someone will be looking for sites that inspired you to do your own writing. With *The Booklover's Guide to the Midwest* in one hand and a road atlas in the other, you're ready for a journey into literary history.

chapter one

Illinois

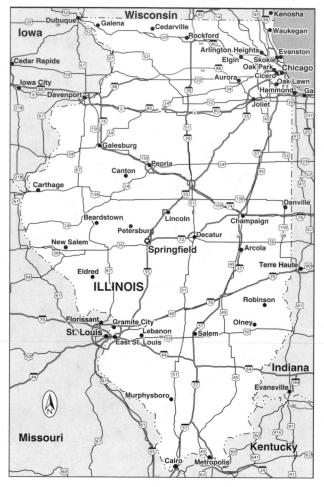

Driving Tours

1. The Galesburg-Spoon River Tour

2. The Galena-Northwest Illinois Tour

3. The Oak Park Tour

4. The I-94 and North Shore Tour

5. The Springfield-Lincoln Country Tour

6. I-57: From Champaign to Cairo

7. Chicago

*I*t's not just the land of Lincoln: Illinois was the birthplace of Carl Sandburg, Ernest Hemingway, Nelson Algren, black poet Gwendolyn Brooks, and Latino writers Ana Castillo and Sandra Cisneros. Surprisingly, it's the final resting place of Russian-born anarchist and author Emma Goldman, who asked to be buried in a suburban Chicago cemetery next to the "martyrs" executed after the Haymarket Riots. And I was born here and have spent all my life here, too. Illinois has inspired many writers. In 1842, Charles Dickens enjoyed a stay in a little inn with a view of the prairie in a southern Illinois town. He observed:

> There lay stretched before my view, a vast expanse of level ground unbroken, save by one thin line of trees, solitude and silence reigning paramount around.

The Chicago area itself is great for walking tours. You can walk past the homes in Oak Park where Edgar Rice Burroughs wrote many of the books in his *Tarzan, the Ape-Man* series. You can visit Oz Park, which is dedicated to L. Frank Baum, who wrote *The Wonderful Wizard of Oz* in 1900 when he and his family were living in Humboldt Park. You can enjoy the Poetry Slam, a public poetry reading competition held in a former 1920s speakeasy. And you can spend days exploring wonderful bookstores, attending readings, and retracing the steps of famous writers and the characters they created all around the city. An overwhelming number of sites in the state are in the city of Chicago itself. But in keeping with this book's nature as a series of driving tours, I'll start with a series of drives around the state and finish up with walks around the city itself.

Edgar Rice Burroughs' bookplate

The Galesburg-Spoon River Tour

►Galesburg

The Carl Sandburg birthplace in Galesburg is located just a mile from the freight train yards where the writer's father worked for less than a dollar an hour as an assistant blacksmith. A visitor to the tiny home (now the Carl Sandburg Historic Site) at 331 East Third Street allows you to enter the life of a poor working-class family of the late nineteenth century. You wonder: How could they all fit into a place that is smaller than my garage? Sandburg's later sympathy for labor issues and his inspiration for poems about working-class people undoubtedly began as he watched his father

Carl Sandburg

trudge home down Third Street, exhausted at the end of his long day's hard labor.

At first, Sandburg was resistant to setting his birthplace up as a memorial, but eventually he came around to the idea. In fact, he visited the home and old friends several times before his death in 1967. Today, the Sandburg birthplace is also notable for the museum that was created when the home next door was purchased. The barn-museum contains exhibits about the writer's life and is used for a literary festival each year, as well as for regular meetings of historical and literary groups. The effort to turn the house into a shrine is the doing of the state of Illinois and the group of local townspeople who saved the home, the nonprofit Carl Sandburg Historic Site Association.

Between the little house and the much bigger museum out back, you'll find an interesting literary walk. First of all, there's a big rock in the backyard. Sandburg named his 1948 novel *Remembrance Rock* after the rock in the yard of his birthplace in Galesburg. Although he lived on a farm named Connemara in North Carolina near the end of his life, he requested that he and his wife be buried beneath Remembrance Rock. There's a winding path of stones on which quotations from Sandburg's work are inscribed.

Carl Sandburg Birthplace
311 Third Street, Galesburg, Illinois 61401
309-342-2361
www.sandburg.org

Note: At the time this book was written the house was closed due to budget deficits in the state of Illinois. Check the Web site to see if tours are being offered again or if the museum has reopened.

Galesburg is served by both the Santa Fe and Burlington train lines, and trains are an integral part of life here. As you drive over the train tracks in Galesburg, envision nineteen-year-old Carl hopping a freight train to live the life of a hobo and see the country. In his book *Always the Young Strangers* he writes of leaving "with my hands free, no bag or bundle, wearing a black-sateen shirt, coat vest, and pants, a slouch hat," hoping to meet "many young strangers" along the way.

The Sandburg family wasn't living in the house on Third Street at the time. Sandburg grew up in a number of progressively larger homes around town; they are privately owned and not open to the public.

At the Central Congregational Church, 60 Public Square, in 1901, Sandburg heard Booker T. Washington lecture and listened to his first symphony concert. A *Life* magazine article from 1953 showed a picture of Sandburg sitting on a stage in the church, a guitar on his lap.

It's worth a quick drive through the nearby Knox College campus (near Cherry Street and South Streets) just to see Old Main, the only site of the seven Lincoln/Douglas senatorial debates that remains much the same as it was in 1858. Lincoln, Douglas, and other dignitaries had gathered in the building, but when they tried to get to the debate platform they found that the door was blocked. So they climbed out the window, prompting Lincoln to say, "At last I've gone through college." But you should also know that in addition to Carl Sandburg, other authors who attended Knox College (some when it was called Lombard College) include writers of speculative, children's, and comedic literature such as Jack Finney, Eugene Field, and Sherwood Kiraly. Knox College is still known for its outstanding program in creative writing.

►The Spoon River Valley

One of the most pleasant driving trips I've ever taken occurred during the Spoon River Valley Scenic Drive Fall Festival. This event, held during the first two weeks in October, draws nearly one hundred thousand people every year. But because the sites are so spread out, you don't feel like you're in a traffic jam—unless you're trying to go to a particularly good garage sale. And the scenery is gorgeous. About eighteen towns participate, including Farmington, London Mills, Smithfield, Cuba, Bernadotte, and Ipava. The map at www .spoonriverdrive.org/map.htm suggests you start at London Mills.

Spoon River Valley Scenic Drive
P.O. Box 525, Canton, Illinois 61520
309-647-8980
info@spoonriverdrive.org

Seeing the countryside and standing in the cemetery while reciting the opening lines of Edgar Lee Masters' *Across Spoon River* makes the trip far more than a weekend drive in search of the perfect piece of rhubarb pie (not that there's anything wrong with that):

> Where are Elmer, Herman, Bert, Tom and Charley,
> The weak of will, the strong of arm, the clown, the boozer,
> the fighter?
> All, all, are sleeping on the hill.
>
> One passed in a fever,
> One was burned in a mine,
> One was killed in a brawl,
> One died in a jail,
> One fell from a bridge toiling for children and wife—
> All, all are sleeping, sleeping, sleeping on the hill.

Many of the characters in *Spoon River Anthology* have been identified as former residents of the towns included on the scenic drive and as persons buried in Oak Hill Cemetery or in Oakland

Cemetery in Petersburg. Masters died in New York City, but he was buried according to his wishes in the cemetery outside his hometown of Petersburg, near the grave of Ann Rutledge (Abraham Lincoln's first love) and others he made famous in his *Spoon River Anthology*.

Masters was born in Garnett, Kansas, in 1868; he grew up in Petersburg, and at age twelve his family moved to Lewiston, where he went to high school and was first published in the *Chicago Daily News*. He wrote plays; books of poetry; novels; and biographies of Abraham Lincoln, fellow Illinois poet Vachel Lindsay, and Walt Whitman.

Masters' boyhood home in Petersburg is only slightly bigger than Sandburg's first home in Galesburg. It's charming in that it fits in so well with the surrounding neighborhood; there's no big gift shop, parking lot, or even a huge sign out front. You park on the street and walk in, just as he must have done countless times himself.

Edgar Lee Masters Memorial Museum
Eighth and Jackson, Petersburg, Illinois 62675

Edgar Lee Masters' boyhood home, now a museum

217- 632-7013
Memorial Day through Labor Day
Tuesday through Saturday
10:00 a.m. to noon and 1:00 p.m. to 3:00 p.m.

Although the area embraces its identity today in welcoming tourists, residents of communities lining the Spoon River were often not flattered by their portrayal in the writings of Masters and disapproved of his own marital history. In turn, he described them as narrow-minded and hypocritical.

Carl Sandburg fans have their chance to sneak a peek at the colorful leaves the same October weekends by way of the Knox County Scenic Drive, 309-343-2485. In either case you'll get historic sites, demonstrations, craft shows, and kids' stuff, but if you choose the latter you'll also treat your tummy to ham and beans, corn chowder, and pies at the 1870s Glisson School and Walnut Grove Farm.

▶Granite City

This town along the Mississippi River is part of the greater St. Louis area. One of its native sons, Robert Olen Butler (1945–   ), is a 1993 Pulitzer Prize winner for *A Good Scent from a Strange Mountain*. Butler served in Vietnam from 1969 to 1971; this story collection focuses on the lives of Vietnamese immigrants in Louisiana.

▶Beardstown

The Beardstown Ladies, a group of fourteen women whose ages ranged from forty-four to ninety, formed "The Beardstown Ladies' Investment Club" in 1983. The club still exists, although it can now be described as a cautionary tale for publishers as well as writers. At first, they attracted attention for returns on investment of more than 23 percent per year. Together, they wrote a bestseller called *The Beardstown Ladies' Common-Sense Investment Guide.*

Today, however, the ladies are probably about as well respected as James Frey (1969–   ), who was found to have made up much of what was in his supposed memoir *A Million Little Pieces* and later excoriated on Chicago's own *Oprah Winfrey* show. Following a tradition of big city muckraking, *Chicago* magazine asserted in 1998 that the Beardstown Ladies' rate of return was worse than previously reported (around 9 percent). Further investigation resulted in a class action lawsuit against their publisher (Hyperion, a division of Disney), which settled the case by offering to anyone who was unhappy with the Beardstown Ladies that they would swap the faulty guidebook for some of their other books.

Other than that, this is a typical Illinois town with a River Museum (in a restored opera house at 121 South State Street) and a courtroom used by Abraham Lincoln (he defended Duff Armstrong here in the famous "Almanac Trial.") In addition to the operating courtroom, you can see gun and arrowhead collections at the Beardstown Museum (101 West Third Street).

▶ Carthage

The next time an editorial really annoys you, remember what happened to Joseph Smith (1805–1844) after he ordered a newspaper destroyed. Smith was the founder of Mormonism and the translator of the *Book of Mormon*. Accused of treason, he and his brother Hyrum were jailed in Carthage where they were killed by a mob. You can tour the jail and see what's supposed to be a bloodstain on the floor left by Smith. Then watch a video at the Historic Carthage Jail and Visitor Center (217-357-2989) at 307 Walnut Street. Contact the Nauvoo Tourism Office (217-453-6648 or 877-628-8661) for more places to visit related not only to the Mormons, but also to the American Indians, Icarians, and pioneers.

For a unique, tasty treat, head for Baxter's Vineyards/Winery (217-453-2528) for blue cheese like you'll find nowhere else.

▶ New Salem

Many New Salem residents moved to Petersburg, which had been surveyed by Abraham Lincoln (1809–1865) in 1836, after it became the seat of Menard County in 1839. For details, visit the Menard County Historical Museum at Seventh and Jackson Streets. Visitors to the area won't want to miss Lincoln's New Salem State Historical Site (217-632-4000) where there is one original building (where Lincoln, an inveterate book-hugger, studied at night). Many other houses and shops, a school, a sawmill, and the Rutledge Tavern have been reconstructed to look as they did in the 1830s when Lincoln was a resident. If you're there in the summer, you might want to catch a performance at the outdoor theater (217-632-5440 or 800-710-9290).

The Galena-Northwest Illinois Tour

The area in the far northwest corner of the state is a popular destination for vacationers who come for antiquing and sightseeing. After the flat country in the north central part of the state, you take Route 20 west and begin to see hilly farmland. It's an area marked by scenic drives, along which you can follow in the steps of some famous Americans who wrote about their exploits in some best-selling books.

▶Cedarville

The Episcopal Bishop of Washington invited author and social activist Jane Addams (1860-1935) to be interred next to Woodrow Wilson in the National Cathedral. Jane preferred the family plot in Cedarville, where she was born and raised. The house Addams's father built in 1854 is still there, and you can see why living in the most prominent house in the village prompted her to realize the "inequities of the human lot." The house is privately owned and not open to the public.

Jane Addams

Addams recalled her idyllic childhood in Cedarville, speaking of "a scene of rural beauty, unusual, at least, for Illinois. The prairie around the village was broken into hills, one of them crowned by pine woods...My stepbrother and I carried on games and crusades which lasted week after week, and even summer after summer, as only free-ranging country children can do."

Addams's most famous book is *Twenty Years at Hull House*, in which she describes the origin and activities of the famous settlement house that served immigrants on Chicago's Near West Side. Exhibits at the Cedarville Area Historical Society, which is located in a former school built in 1889, include artifacts from the period before Jane moved to Chicago. It has a schedule of special events that often feature authors. Jane loved to play on the banks of Cedar Creek, which ran through her property, and often wrote about her early appreciation for nature. So I'm sure she, like many collectors, would also be impressed with the Cedarville Art Glass Company, a gallery-like shop that features the work of Daniel Edler. And the Jane Addams Children's Book Award has been presented annually since 1953 to the book that best promotes peace, social justice, and world community. In case you haven't guessed, I'm in love with Jane Addams.

Cedarville Area Historical Society
450 West Second Street, Cedarville, Illinois 61013
815-563-4485
May through October
Saturday and Sunday
1:00 p.m. to 4:00 p.m.

Cedarville Art Glass Company
100 N. Stephenson. Cedarville, Illinois 61013
815-563-4601
www.edlerstudio.com

►Galena

Before the Civil War, future general and president Ulysses S. Grant (1822–1885) worked in Galena as an assistant in his father's leather shop. Late in life, he was left penniless through the failure of a brokerage firm, but his *Personal Memoirs*, completed while dying of throat cancer, brought his family nearly five-hundred thousand dollars. (The book was written for Mark Twain's publishing company, and Twain gave Grant generous royalties that helped his family.) You can tour the Ulysses S. Grant Home State Historical Site, but that's only the beginning. Galena, which was once the largest Mississippi River port north of St. Louis and the center of trade for the upper Mississippi lead mine region, has some of the finest period architecture in the Midwest. And Main Street contains at least one rare bookstore among its many craft shops and fine restaurants.

Fall is an especially good time to visit this scenic town. In early October you can attend the Galena County Fair, which includes Irish dancers, live music, and crafts.

Main Street Fine Books & Manuscripts
206 North Main Street, Galena, Illinois 61036
815-777-3749
http://msfb.wcinet.com

▶ Murphysboro

Murphysboro is the home of writer Kent Haruf (1943–   ), author of best-selling novel *Plainsong*. The town is located on the Southern Illinois Treasure Trail, a scenic drive that winds through seven towns that, although they may be small in population, are big on antiques—anything from china to claw-foot tubs.

The Oak Park Tour

Oak Park, a suburb just west of Chicago, is rich with literary history. It's also a pretty town with architecturally significant houses, a few designed by former resident Frank Lloyd Wright (1867–1959). Walks around Oak Park can be given a literary focus that takes into account the many writers who have lived here in the past century.

Oak Park seems to really value its older residences, and there are so many sites within walking distance of one another. This makes it perfect for walking around town. And some famous writers' homes are within a few blocks of one another.

I suggest that you park your car on Lake Street, on the street or in one of the parking garages. Imagine, for instance, that it's 1910, and you're taking a walk down Lake Street near Oak Park Avenue. Let's say you are standing on Lake Street in front of Scoville Park.

Scoville Park war memorial

To your left, you see the First Congregational Church, where Hemingway was baptized in 1899. Then you can take a walk up the hill and through Scoville Park, where you might see young Hemingway and his sister sledding. Today, there's a statue with his name added to a list with other World War I veterans.

The Write Inn

Turn the corner and walk north on Oak Park Avenue. You pass a little hotel called the Write Inn, which is a good place to stay if you are going to spend time in the area if you don't mind an old-fashioned Murphy bed that pops out of the wall. (If you're hungry, you can eat at the inn's restaurant, Hemmingway's Bistro.)

The Write Inn
211 North Oak Park Avenue, Oak Park, Illinois 60302
708-383-4300
www.writeinn.com

Across the street, you see a huge building with big columns, which is the site of the Hemingway Museum. You can purchase combined admission here for the museum and the Hemingway birthplace down the block. The museum contains some of Hemingway's notebooks and something he might not want to have on display—the "Dear Ernest" letter from the nurse he loved in Italy after being wounded in World War I, and who served as the model for the woman in A *Farewell to Arms*.

Ernest Hemingway Museum

Ernest Hemingway Museum

200 North Oak Park Avenue, Oak Park, Illinois 60302
708-848-2222
www.ehfop.org
Sunday through Friday, 1:00 p.m. to 5:00 p.m.
Saturday, 10:00 a.m. to 5:00 p.m.

Down the street, at 228 North Oak Park Avenue, you come to the home of the Reverend William E. Barton (1861–1930). In 1910, he was the pastor of the First Congregational Church. He's also the author of several books about Abraham Lincoln. Most notably, in 1924 he wrote a two-volume *Life of Abraham Lincoln* that was considered the leading study of Lincoln before Carl Sandburg usurped that claim. In the late teens, by the way, Sandburg moved from Chicago to Maywood, which is not so far from here. Reverend Barton's son, Bruce Barton (1886–1967), would eventually become much more famous than the reverend. Bruce Barton founded the advertising agency BBDO and wrote a famous book about Jesus Christ called *The Man Nobody Knows*. He served two terms in the U.S. Congress in the 1930s.

Few, if any, original furnishings remain in the Ernest Hemingway birthplace at 339 North Oak Park Avenue, but restoration is based on old photographs. Hemingway's father was a physician and delivered Ernest himself in a second-floor bedroom on July 21, 1899. Hemingway is widely reported to have disliked his hometown and never visited it after 1930, but the town has since embraced his legacy as a historical attraction, creating a splendid museum down the street from the birthplace.

Hemingway as a young man

Another novelist recently wrote a novel while working in Hemingway's attic. Oak Park novelist Bill Hazelgrove gained even more notice for the residence when he wrote his own novel *Mica Highways* in the home's attic. "For a writer, it's like writing in a church," he commented.

Every year on the English holiday of Boxing Day, December 26 (a holiday the Hemingway family observed), the Hemingway Readers Theatre holds a production and party with English tea and refreshments. The event takes place at the birthplace, which is decorated for the season.

Hemingway told a little fib about this house when he wrote an article for *Esquire* magazine in 1935. You can see that he, like me, was given to complaining about his hometown and how it became developed over the years. Hemingway used to go hunting by the river just west of here, and he remembers it in this article:

> You can remember the miracle it seemed when you hit
> your first pheasant when he roared up from under your
> feet to top a sweet briar thicket and fell with his wings
> pounding and you had to wait till after dark to bring him

Hemingway's birthplace

into town because they were protected, and you can feel
the bulk of him still inside your shirt with his long tail up
under your armpit, walking into town in the dark along
the dirt road that is now North Avenue where the gypsy
wagons used to camp when there was prairie out to the
Des Plaines river where Wallace Evans had a game farm
and the big woods ran along the river where the Indian
mounds were.

I came by there five years ago and where I shot that pheas-
ant there was a hot dog place and filling station and the
north prairie...was a subdivision of mean houses, and in
the town, the house where I was born was gone and they
had cut down the oak trees and built an apartment house
close out against the street. So I was glad I went away from
there as soon as I did.

As you can see, Hemingway's birth house is still here after all, as well as some oak trees.

The Ernest Hemingway Foundation of Oak Park/
Ernest Hemingway Birthplace

339 North Oak Park Avenue, Oak Park, Illinois 60302
708-848-2222
See the above museum information for details

A fine house used to stand at 325 North Oak Park Avenue that was occupied by Edgar Rice Burroughs in 1918–1919. This fine house once had a third-floor ballroom.

Born in Chicago in 1875, Burroughs tried and failed at several businesses before deciding to write pulp fiction. At the time Hemingway was growing up a few doors down, Burroughs was a successful writer. He wrote many books in the Tarzan series as well as a series of *John Carter of Mars* books. He lived in several residences in Oak Park, including 700 Linden Avenue.

Turn the corner at Iowa and walk west to Kenilworth

Book cover from Burroughs' first Tarzan book

Avenue, and you will find the stucco house where Hemingway lived from 1906 to 1919 at 600 North Kenilworth Avenue. His bedroom was in the middle of the three dormer windows on the second floor. In 1928, Hemingway's father, suffering from depression, shot himself in this house. It's a private residence and not open for tours.

Walk north past the Oliver Wendell Holmes Elementary School, 508 North Kenilworth Avenue, where Hemingway might have played on the playground along with a young boy named Carl Rogers (1902–1987). Three years younger than Hemingway, Rogers would grow up to be a famous psychotherapist and the author of one of the most famous books of psychology, *On Becoming a Person*. At 414 Augusta, there's the home that Edgar Rice Burroughs moved into a few years later, just after he published a book called *Tarzan of the Apes*.

Head a few blocks west to Forest Avenue, turn south, and you come to Frank Lloyd Wright's studio and home where he lived with his family. Wright left his family in 1909 to go to Europe with another woman. One of the tenants in the apartments in the early years of the twentieth century was Charles MacArthur (1895–1956)—a young reporter who would later become a well-known playwright and screenwriter. He and Ben Hecht would later collaborate on *The Front Page*. The home and studio are open for tours.

Frank Lloyd Wright Home and Studio
951 Chicago Avenue, Oak Park, Illinois 60302
708-848-1976
www.wrightplus.org

To return to the starting point of this tour, walk west on Chicago Avenue to Forest, and walk south to Lake Street. Lake Street is one of the big commercial areas in Oak Park, and if you continue to walk west, you'll find plenty of restaurants. Before you get there, you might want to stop in at the main branch of the Oak Park Public Library. Ask Information Services for access to the Hemingway Collection, a room that contains books about the author and his family, and five binders containing photos donated by Hemingway friends and family. The library also contains a Local Authors Collection that recognizes Oak Park writers.

Oak Park Public Library
834 Lake Street, Oak Park, Illinois 60301
708-383-8200
www.oppl.org/main

You'll also find a good independent bookstore, Barbara's, a few blocks west on Main Street. It frequently holds readings and signings by authors.

Barbara's Bookstore
1100 Lake Street, Oak Park, Illinois 60301
708-848-9140
www.barbarasbookstore.com

In the midst of all these literary accolades about Oak Park, there's a monkey wrench. Leave it to Cicero, Oak Park's neighbor to the south, to claim Hemingway as its own native son. Words are important to writers and, if you're going to split hairs and depend on technicalities, a resident of Cicero is likely to point out that Oak Park was not incorporated until late 1901. Hemingway was born in 1899—technically in Cicero Township. But the location where he was not only born but also grew up is clearly Oak Park. In fact, he attended Oak Park/River Forest High School, where he studied English and wrote for the school newspaper.

Other alums of the same high school include the poet Charles Simic (1938–), novelist James Park Sloan (1945–), and mystery writer Barbara Mertz (1927–). Alex Kotlowitz is a current resident and Jane Hamilton (1957–) grew up in Oak Park as well. So Oak Park's literary history is hardly a thing of the past.

The I-94 and North Shore Tour

▶ Waukegan

Ray Bradbury, one of the greatest science-fiction writers of the twentieth century, was born in this northern Illinois city on August 22, 1920. In some of the stories and novels he set here, he called it "Green Town." Waukegan is an especially good place to go if you want to spend the day on the beach at Illinois Beach State Park in nearby Zion. It's a good place to drink the water if you want to be a writer, too; one local author, Diane Ackerman (1948–), estimates that more than eighty people who lived in Waukegan at one time or another have become writers.

Although the small house at 11 South St. James in Waukegan where Bradbury was born is not open to the public, you can visit the library at 128 North County Street and view a collection of his books and newspaper articles. Events are frequently held in a room named for him. Actually, the small Carnegie library where he developed his love of books and wrote about so vividly in *Dandelion Wine* and *Something Wicked This Way Comes* has been preserved, and this much larger facility is its replacement. The original library, built in 1903, is at 1 North Sheridan Road.

Bradbury is still an active presence in his hometown, an instance of a town and a writer sharing mutual respect and affection. Bradbury returned to Waukegan in 1990 for the dedication

Ray Bradbury

of Ray Bradbury Park, 99 North Park Avenue. He also returned in 1996 for the Ray Bradbury's Dandelion Wine Waukegan Fine Arts Festival. And every year the Waukegan Public Library holds an annual Ray Bradbury writing contest.

In October, you can attend the Bradbury Storytelling Festival, held in the Genesee Theatre in Waukegan. Find out more at www .bradburystorytellingfestival.org.

Waukegan Public Library
128 North County Street, Waukegan, Illinois 60085
847-623-2041
www.waukeganpl.org

Waukegan's other famous resident, the comedian Jack Benny (1894–1974), is honored with a statue downtown and with a middle school that is named for him. He was one of the most popular entertainers in the Golden Age of Radio and the star of his own TV show as well. He wrote an autobiography, but never published it. His daughter Joan completed it, and it appeared in 1990 as *Sunday Nights at Seven: The Jack Benny Story*.

Ward Just, a highly respected author of fifteen novels and many short stories, was born in Waukegan in 1935. He began his career as a reporter for the newspaper his family owned, the *Waukegan News-Sun*. He was a correspondent for *Newsweek* and the *Washington Post* before leaving journalism to write fiction full-time.

Local author Diane Ackerman lived in Waukegan until age eight and fondly recalls experiences with the Waukegan Public Library bookmobiles in her childhood. (You can read her essay about bookmobiles on the library's Web site, www.waukeganpl.org/community/ localauthor.asp?LaID=2.) She also wrote about the town in the introduction to her 1991 novel *The Moon by Whale Light*.

Eleanor Taylor Bland (1944–   ) wasn't born in Waukegan, but has chosen to make it her home and works it into her fiction. She serves on the library board, teaches writing classes, and presents awards for the Ray Bradbury Creative Writing Contest. She is an active mystery writer who has published thirteen novels in the Marti MacAlister Mystery series. Her fictional town of Lincoln Prairie is a combination of Waukegan and other neighboring towns, North Chicago and Zion. She weaves real-life locations into her stories, including the Carnegie Library, Genesee Theatre, and the old Waukegan Hotel. In an interview, she said, "I work as much about the local scene into the books as possible. I enjoy it as much as the locals."

The Springfield-Lincoln Country Tour

▶ Lincoln

This small town was the birthplace of William Maxwell (1908–2000), the highly respected editor of J. D. Salinger and other contributors to the *New Yorker* magazine. His 1980 novel, *So Long, See You Tomorrow*, won the American Book Award.

▶ Eldred

Charles Dickens (1812–1870) visited the farm that is now called Hobson's Bluffdale during his 1842 tour of the states. A friend of his, the scholar John Russell, owned the farm at the time. Now you can go there to start your own novel or to get inspired while horseback riding, boating, swimming, going on hayrides, helping out with collecting eggs, feeding animals, and baling hay. You'll also enjoy the 1828 John Russell House. My children and I spent a few days there, and we enjoyed walking through the comfortable old place with long plank wooden floors and bookcases full of dusty artifacts, some of which look like they could date to Dickens's time. The family that owns the farm serves huge country breakfasts and other meals at long tables where you can eat with with other guests. In the spring, the nearby hills are a good place for Morel mushroom hunting.

Bluffdale Vacation Farm
RR1, Eldred, Illinois 62027
217-983-2854
www.bluffdalevacationfarm.com

▶Lebanon

While Charles Dickens (1812–1870) was visiting nearby St. Louis, he expressed a desire to see an American prairie before leaving the Midwest. He was driven thirty miles into Illinois to see Looking Glass Prairie. Of his stay at the Mermaid House in Lebanon, he said: "In point of cleanliness and comfort it would have suffered by no comparison with any village alehouse, of a homely kind, in England."

This short visit lives on in the charming town of Lebanon; every April, an event called Dickens Days celebrates the great writer's visit to the Mermaid House. The inn itself has been restored; it's believed to be haunted. Some have said Dickens's stay at the inn provided some inspiration for his famous story *A Christmas Carol*.

In his book *Blue Highways*, William Least Heat-Moon (1939–) mentions the town as "a brick street village where Charles Dickens spent a night at the Mermaid Inn." The inn is open by appointment only.

The Mermaid House
114 St. Louis Street, Lebanon, Illinois 62254
618-537-8420

▶Springfield

Poet Vachel Lindsay (1879–1933) wrote of his house at 603 South Fifth Street (217-524-0901) in Springfield: "Everything begins and ends there for me." This was, indeed, literally true: the poet was

Vachel Lindsay

born in the house in 1879 and died there in 1931 at age fifty-two. In between, he spent years tramping the country, exchanging his poetry for room and board. The home has the distinction of being the last place where Abraham Lincoln, a frequent subject of his literary works, stayed before moving to Washington, D.C., to assume the presidency. Lindsay took his own life, but his true cause of death was covered up and said to be from a heart problem until Edgar Lee Masters published a biography of Lindsay in 1935.

Lindsay wrote frequently of Springfield. Here is one example:

Springfield Magical

In this, the City of my Discontent,
Sometimes there comes a whisper from the grass,

"Romance, Romance—is here. No Hindu town
Is quite so strange. No Citadel of Brass
By Sinbad found, held half such love and hate;
No picture-palace in a picture-book
Such webs of Friendship, Beauty, Greed and Fate!"

In this, the City of my Discontent,
Down from the sky, up from the smoking deep
Wild legends new and old burn round my bed
While trees and grass and men are wrapped in sleep.
Angels come down, with Christmas in their hearts.
Gentle, whimsical, laughing, heaven-sent;
And, for a day, fair Peace have given me
In this, the City of my Discontent!

He and Abraham Lincoln are both buried in Oak Ridge Cemetery (217-789-2340), the second most visited cemetery in the country and the largest in Illinois. For good luck, don't forget to rub the nose on Lincoln's bust.

If I were to pick two don't-miss Abraham Lincoln highlights (and don't forget that he was also an amazing writer of everything from poetry to speeches), they would be the Abraham Lincoln Presidential Library and Museum (217-782-5764) on North Sixth Street between Madison and Washington Streets and the Lincoln Home National Historic Site (217-492-4241) on North Eighth Street and Jackson Streets. But Springfield is lousy with other interesting places, and I never pass up an opportunity to go through the Dana-Thomas House State Historic Site (217-782-6776) designed by Frank Lloyd Wright at 301 East Lawrence Avenue.

Springfield is as good as any place to talk about another passion of mine: Route 66, immortalized by John Steinbeck (1902–1968) in *Grapes of Wrath* as "The Mother Road." Nor was Steinbeck the first or last to celebrate the highway in books, songs, movies, and that great 1960s television show. The route from Chicago to Los Angeles was over twenty-four hundred miles in length, and more than four hundred miles of historical highway are left for you to explore in Illinois. In Springfield, for example it retained its four lanes and is now the Dirksen Parkway. Keep your eye out for original gas stations, motels, and restaurants. Once you get bitten by the bug, I wouldn't be surprised if you followed the Neon Parade to the World's Largest Sock Hop, which is part of the International Route 66 Mother Road Festival in Springfield each and every September. I encourage you not to pass up the Joe Rogers Chili Parlor for the, um, chili. But at the Cozy Dog Drive-In you'll get more than a hot dog on a stick. That tasty treat was invented by Edwin S. Waldmire, who was born in Petersburg in 1916 and opened his first restaurant when he was a student at Knox College in Galesburg. Not only was he an avid reader and collector of books, but he always encouraged others to read by lending out his books. Bob, one of his five sons, will eventually transfer his father's library to a memorial nature sanctuary in Arizona. But they were still there the last time I went to Springfield. Bob is also planning to keep his promise to his dad to publish *The Story of Ed Waldmire and His Book,* an assemblage of Paine's *The Age of Reason,* Twain's *Captain Stormfield's Visit to Heaven, Jefferson's Bible,* and Eisenhower's *Farewell Address.*

Another place to look for a book is Prairie Archives, although owner John Paul has been known to tell customers, "We have everything but what you want." In addition to 250,000 rare, used, and new books, Paul stocks collectibles and the inevitable T-shirt offerings. The most popular is inscribed: "Abraham Lincoln: They'd have to shoot me to get me back to Springfield."

I-57: From Champaign to Cairo

This drive certainly brings to mind Dickens's comment about the flatness and solitude of the Illinois countryside. As you approach the southern part of the state, however, the landscape changes dramatically. At the very southern end of the state, you'll find the home of Superman.

►Champaign

Elaine Palencia (1946–   ) of Champaign, is the author of several novels, short stories, reviews, and poetry. Her short story collection, *Small Caucasian Woman,* set in Kentucky, was nominated for the PEN/Faulkner Award. She has also published a book of poems entitled *Taking the Train.*

▶ Danville

Susan Wittig Albert (1940–   ) was born in Danville. She has authored the now famous Nancy Drew books. Some of her other novels are *Rueful Death: A China Bayles Mystery, Rosemary Remembered, Hangman's Root,* and *Witches' Bane.*

▶ Arcola

This town is a central location for one of the Amish communities in the Midwest. Accordingly, many folks come here for the Illinois Amish Interpretive Center and Amish Country Tours (217-268-3599) at 111 South Locust Street. In addition to the quilts and crafts of the Amish, you can find samples of brooms made with the broomcorn that Arcola is famous for.

Of literary interest to those who still enjoy a bedtime story is the Raggedy Ann and Andy Museum at 110 East Main Street. Johnny Gruelle (1880–1938), creator of Raggedy Ann and Andy, was born in Arcola in 1880, and you'll find his artwork here as well as plenty of collectibles. As the doting dad of two daughters, I have a soft spot for these dolls; see more under Indianapolis in the Indiana chapter.

Nearby Rockome Gardens (217-268-4106) will help you continue your trip into the nostalgic agrarian past with its old-fashioned ice-cream parlor and quirky displays. They also sell more locally made goods and offer rock and floral gardens, specialty shops, and buggy rides.

▶ Robinson

James Jones (1921–1977) was born and raised in this small town near Springfield. He won commercial success and literary fame with *From Here to Eternity* (1951), an army novel set in Hawaii just before the Japanese attack on Pearl Harbor. The Crawford County Historical Museum has artifacts and exhibits of local interest, while the Military Museum and Memorial Wall is housed in a remodeled railroad depot.

▶ Olney

One significant bit of writing in Olney was a city ordinance giving white squirrels the right of way on any city street. A twenty-five dollar fine is inflicted on any motorist unlucky enough to run over an albino, a variety that is officially counted each year. But another native son was partial to birds, writing books with titles such as *Birds of Middle and North America* and *Color Stands and Color Nomenclature*. A replica of the front porch of his summer cottage is on the grounds of the Robert Ridgway Memorial Arboretum and Bird Sanctuary, along with his grave marked by a granite boulder with a bronze plaque with birds sculpted on it. Only a larger arboretum in Japan is said to have more plant species.

If you get nervous without visiting a library every day or two, check out the McCoy Memorial Library in McLeansboro. It is listed in the National Register of Historic Places and has antiques and fireplaces galore. The Saline County Area Museum (618-253-7342), which includes furnished historic buildings moved here from around the area, is also a popular attraction.

►Salem

If you'd like a taste of local history before you glimpse the arch of St. Louis, take a side trip to Salem. It is proud to be the birthplace of orator and writer William Jennings Bryan (1860–1925), with his statue by Gutzon Borglum (who also did Mount Rushmore), his former home (the Silas Bryan Farm) at 408 Broadway (618-548-2222), and his birthplace (which is now a museum and is near the library that also bears his name).

John Thomas Scopes, the defendant in the "Monkey Trial" in which Bryan was the prosecutor, also grew up in Salem. There's a nice walking tour of other historic architecture, including Max Crossett's Cafe. Others may be impressed that this is a former stagecoach station, but I can't get over the fact that they sold their original recipe for Miracle Whip Salad Dressing to Kraft Foods in 1931 for three hundred dollars. In my opinion, that recipe is some writing worthy of note.

►Metropolis

Self-proclaimed hometown of fictional movie and cartoon character Superman, Metropolis has the only official Superman phone booth where you can actually speak with the Man of Steel. His fifteen-foot statue greets visitors to the Super Museum at 517 Market Street (618-524-5518). The local newspaper is called the *Daily Planet*. If

William Jennings Bryan

that's not enough to make you want to visit, there are numerous festivals with various themes held throughout the year. The Curtis House Museum (618-524-5720) is open Sunday afternoons or by appointment, and you can soak up more history (and festivals) connected to Fort Massac, which dates to Spanish explorer Hernando de Sota in the early 1540s.

▸Cairo

Writers and book people love libraries. For a library with atmosphere, you'll really love the Cairo Public Library at 1609 Washington Avenue. It boasts a rare Tiffany grandfather clock and artwork, including a painting by Raphael. You can see more historical displays at Magnolia Manor (27th Street and Washington Avenue) and the U.S. Custom House Museum (14th Street and Washington Avenue).

Cairo, which (as you can guess) is named for its resemblance to that other town in Egypt, is built on a peninsula and protected by a huge levee. Being at the confluence of the Ohio and Mississippi Rivers made it an attractive military post during the Civil War, and Ulysses S. Grant used it as a base to launch his decisive campaigns against Forts Henry and Donelson. In *Blue Front*, Martha Collins (1940–   ) dissects a horrific lynching that took place here. Cairo is also mentioned in poetry by Dave Etter (1928–   ), although his most well-known book is entitled *Alliance, Illinois*.

Charles Dickens, who seems to have visited just about every notable place in the Midwest on his single tour of the states in 1842, stopped in Cairo too. He boarded a steamboat for a ride down the Mississippi to St. Louis.

Chicago

On Super Bowl Sunday not long ago, a friend and I avoided all the bars filled with sports fans and headed to a former speakeasy called the Green Mill. This venerable place on Broadway Avenue is home to the Poetry Slam, a poetry competition that has become a national phenomenon. We were thrilled by the many poets who came onstage, and we even wrote our own poems too.

This is the kind of event literate, book-loving people can experience on a regular basis in Chicago. No matter what neighborhood you're in, chances are you'll find a bookstore of some sort, even if it's a specialty shop like a comic book store or an outlet for religious books and spiritual objects. For many years, I took my daughters to music lessons at the Fine Arts Building on South Michigan Avenue. We walked past studios marked by plaques indicating where Harriet Monroe started the magazine *Poetry*, and where Frank Baum and John McCutcheon created the *Wizard of Oz* books.

Not only that, but if you look closely as you drive the city streets, you'll pass homes with little green metal markers in front of them labeled Chicago Tribute. If you park and read the notes on the markers, you'll discover that famous people once lived in the homes. Many of them are writers.

On a quiet side street, you pass the home where Carl Sandburg wrote many of his early poems while raising his young family. You can see the apartment building where Margaret Anderson and her female companion strolled naked, looking at the lake and playing the piano. There's the apartment in a once gritty, working-class neighborhood where Nelson Algren wrote about gritty, working-class people. You'll find the apartment where Ernest Hemingway lived before heading for Europe. Drive Division Street, which Studs Terkel celebrated in one of his early collections of interviews. And all over the city you'll find coffee shops where you can read, write your own works of literature, or listen to writers share their work.

Chicago Writers' Homes

▸Nelson Algren, 1758 West Evergreen

Nelson Algren (1909–1981) was born in Michigan, but he is regarded as the quintessential Chicago writer, thanks to works such as *Chicago: City on the Make*. Algren lived in several different parts of Chicago, but he is forever associated with Wicker Park, the neighborhood around Division Street where many of his most famous stories and novels are set.

If you look both ways as you cross one of three very busy streets—Ashland Avenue, Division Street, and Milwaukee Avenue—you make your way to a little traffic island that's right in the middle of this extremely busy intersection. On warm days, you can sit on a bench and watch the traffic go by and listen to the water cascading over the Nelson Algren fountain, which is one of the few monuments in Chicago erected to one of its own writers.

Algren lived at 1958 West Evergreen for a full sixteen years, from 1959 to 1975, and you can see this apartment today. There's a Chicago Tribute marker in front of the building, and the street has one of those honorary street sign names calling it Nelson Algren Avenue. Mike Royko (1932–1997) led a campaign to have the street renamed, and it took years to do so, because the local residents didn't want to have their addresses changed. So it was eventually renamed with one of those brown street signs.

In 1967 Algren's apartment was broken into, which prompted him to get a permit for a .38 revolver. When he left Chicago for New Jersey in March of 1975 he held a garage sale here. He auctioned off his furniture, even his dishwasher. The *Chicago Tribune* reported that he sold old copies of *Playboy* magazine at two dollars each with his signature on the cover atop the torsos of the women pictured in the magazine. Someone paid $150 for a poker table on which Algren claimed he battled through successive card games with two tough guys who became models for characters in *The Man With the Golden Arm.*

Algren is best known as the writer of novels like *The Man With the Golden Arm* and *A Walk on the Wild Side.* The romance between Simone de Beauvoir and Nelson Algren still gets a lot of attention. This is an indication of how Chicago's famous writers are still part of its legacy and artistic milieu. A few years ago, Chicago's Lookingglass Theatre produced *Nelson Algren: For Keeps and a Single Day.* A play called *Nelson and Simone* was staged at the Live Bait Theater. At the time they met, Algren was living in a ten-dollar-a-month cold-water flat on Wabansia Avenue, a block or two east of Ashland Avenue. De Beauvoir was visiting Chicago, and Algren's current girlfriend, Mary Guggenheim, thought she needed someone to show her around town. She suggested that Algren act as her tour guide. He met de Beauvoir at the Palmer House downtown and took her on a tour of Chicago's lowlife, beginning with skid row on Madison Street. They were immediately attracted to one another, despite their widely different backgrounds and interests, and Miss Guggenheim was soon out of the picture. They would be on-and-off lovers for the next decade. The place where they met for many of their trysts is gone, but you can stand next to a city parking facility and look under the Kennedy Expressway and imagine that they're there, having a drink at his little wooden writing table.

▶ Ernest Hemingway, 1239 North Dearborn

After their wedding in northern Michigan in 1921 (see the Michigan chapter), Ernest Hemingway (1899–1961) and his first wife Hadley moved into an apartment in the top floor of this building. At the time, the neighborhood was a run-down Bohemian area frequented by writers like Carl Sandburg and Sherwood Anderson. The latter (who is profiled in the Ohio chapter) befriended Hemingway and urged him to go to Paris. Hadley found the apartment depressing, and they moved to Paris in December 1921. A plaque in front of the building identifies it as "The Hemingway Apartment."

►Harriet Monroe, 543 North Wabash

Every day, Harriet Monroe (1860–1936) would walk from 543 North Cass Street, which is now called Wabash Avenue, to the offices of the literary magazine she founded, which is simply called *Poetry*. This became one of the most highly regarded literary publications in the country, and it published writers such as T. S. Eliot, William Carlos Williams, W. B. Yeats. *Poetry* still exists and it has its offices in the Newberry Library, 60 West Walton. It was an assistant editor at *Poetry* who got a young poet named Carl Sandburg hooked up with his publisher, Alfred Harcourt of Harcourt Brace & Company.

►Carl Sandburg, 4646 North Hermitage Avenue

Carl Sandburg's (1878–1967) house at 4646 North Hermitage is located on a quiet street in the city's Andersonville neighborhood. Sandburg made his first trip to Chicago in 1896 where he was excited by glimpses of "the trolley cars, the teamsters, the drays, buggies, surreys, and phaetons." When he moved to Chicago from Milwaukee in 1912, he took a second-floor apartment in this house with his wife and baby daughter. He commuted from here to downtown, where he worked at a succession of magazines and newspapers while writing the poems that would be collected in his first book, *Chicago Poems*. This book includes the famous poem "Chicago," where he describes the city as:

> Hog Butcher for the World,
> Tool Maker, Stacker of Wheat,
> Player with Railroads and the Nation's Freight Handler,
> Stormy, husky, brawling,
> City of the Big Shoulders...

For a time, Sandburg worked in the Loop at *Systems* magazine, the same place that employed Edgar Rice Burroughs who wrote the Tarzan series. Sandburg was known for being a sober, serious sort. Supposedly, a playful colleague at the *Chicago Daily News*, where Sandburg worked as a movie reviewer and reporter, once hired an out-of-work actor to dress up as Abraham Lincoln and wait for Sandburg on a street corner on the way home from the *News* building. When Sandburg appeared, Lincoln walked toward him, tipped his hat and remarked, "Evening, Mr. Sandburg." Without missing a beat, Sandburg simply said, "Evening, Mr. Lincoln."

▸ Studs Terkel, 650 West Castlewood Drive

When I was growing up, I listened every chance I could to Studs Terkel's (1912–2008) radio program, which ran on local radio station WFMT for several decades. On it, Terkel talked to politicians, performers, artists, and average people. His books were also built around interviews, and Terkel is famed as an oral historian. His works include *Division Street America*, *Working*, and *The Good War*.

Ben Hecht residence

Terkel was born on the Near West Side in a hotel and was a lifelong Chicago resident.

▸Ben Hecht, 5210 South Kenwood Avenue

When you're in Hyde Park, the home of President Barack Obama and the University of Chicago, don't miss seeing the fine residence of Chicago newspaperman, playwright, novelist, and screenwriter Ben Hecht (1893–1964) at 5210 South Kenwood Avenue. He lived here in the early 1920s, around the time he was publishing the *Chicago Literary Times* and what is generally agreed to be his best novel, *Erik Dorn*.

▸Edgar Lee Masters, 4853 South Kenwood Avenue

Another house worth a look is the former home of Edgar Lee Masters (1868–1950) at 4853 South Kenwood. Its grandeur befits his prestige in the 1910s as a successful lawyer and partner in the legal firm of Clarence Darrow. Like the present-day lawyer/novelist Scott Turow, Masters labored in his spare time on the poems that would make him famous and that were eventually collected under the title *Spoon River Anthology*. Turow, by the way, can still recall the moment that he discovered the impact of reading. He claims that on a car trip with his mother he realized what a "No Parking" sign meant, which gave him an extraordinary feeling of independence, competence, and power.

Edgar Lee Masters' home

President, author, and Chicagoan Barack Obama

▶Barack Obama, 5046 South Greenwood Avenue

Don't try to get too close to this home, which is closely guarded by the U.S. Secret Service. At times when President Obama (1961–) is at home, the whole block is guarded at either end by police, and getting anywhere near it is pretty much out of the question.

When Obama purchased this Georgian revival mansion, there were rumors of a shady deal, because it was purchased for less than the asking price and, allegedly, with the assistance of now-indicted fundraiser Antonin Resko.

I mention Obama not because of this or because he is president, but because he is the author of two best-selling and very readable memoirs, *Dreams From My Father* and *The Audacity of Hope*. For more than a decade, Obama taught in the University of Chicago Law School, and his wife, Michelle, worked for the University as well.

▶ Margaret Anderson, 837 West Ainslie Street

In the 1920s, the apartment building with the two identical towers was right on the lakefront. Lake Shore Drive hadn't been created with landfill as yet. This was the home where a young woman named Margaret Anderson lived. Margaret Anderson (1886–1973) started a literary magazine called *The Little Review* in 1914. This magazine, which had offices in the Fine Arts Building on South Michigan Avenue, gained literary fame as the first publication to publish James Joyce's controversial novel *Ulysses*.

In 1915, when she ran out of funding for *The Little Review*, rather than fold the magazine, she opted to save money by closing her office and going to live in a tent on the Lake Michigan beach near Lake Bluff. Her tent was furnished with Oriental carpets, paintings, and a piano. Writers like Sherwood Anderson and Ben Hecht would come out to visit her on the beach. As you can tell, Anderson always wanted to live as close to the water as possible. She lived in the apartment at 837 West Ainslie with her co-editor and lesbian lover, Jane Heap. She spent most of her time soaking—in the bathtub, though, not in the lake. She writes in her memoir:

> For me there was a room and bath like a dream of spring—
> pale green walls, wisteria hangings, a pink rug, a large yellow
> lamp, a blue lake…It was widely separated from the rest
> of the apartment. If one locked door didn't insulate me, I
> could entrench myself behind two, in the bathroom. I could
> spend my home life bathing.

After the death of her father, she and her mother had a fight, and her mother took almost all the furniture in the apartment. All that was left were two beds, two knives, two forks, two spoons. Anderson and Heap decided this made the apartment "marvelous… nude as the day it was built. Nothing but the lake and the stars in the windows…" But one thing was missing: she rented a Mason and Hamlin piano in exchange for an ad in *The Little Review*. She writes: "We spent the afternoon pacing the empty apartment in order to burst suddenly into the living room and be startled by it standing there against the windows and the lake."

▶James T. Farrell, 7136 South East End Avenue, 7046 South Euclid Avenue, 2023 East 72nd Street

One of the most famous Chicago novels, or series of novels, is the *Studs Lonigan* trilogy, written by James T. Farrell (1904–1979), who grew up in South Shore and Washington Park, two neighborhoods near the University of Chicago. In 1928, he was living in a flat on the second floor of the building on 72nd Street.

Farrell used to walk across Washington Park to the University to take classes in Cobb Hall or hang out at the C-Shop. He wrote the story "Studs" for an advanced composition class taught by James Weber Linn, who was a novelist himself.

One day in the late 1920s, Farrell sat with a friend named Mary Hunter on the grass near Botany Pond where he made the first outline of the book that would grow out of his short story. "In a sense, Studs Lonigan was born that afternoon," he later recalled.[1]

James T. Farrell residences on East 72nd Street (above) and East End Avenue (right)

▶ Lorraine Hansberry, 5330 South Calumet Avenue

Lorraine Hansberry (1930–1965), the author of the famous play *A Raisin in the Sun*, lived here from 1930 to 1938, and her stay was not always a happy one. After her family moved to this neighborhood, which was predominantly white at the time, there was controversy. Eventually, the family was evicted on the grounds that existing racial codes were being violated.

▶ The Marx Brothers, 4512 South King Drive

I realize that the Marx brothers aren't known for their literary works, but I love the fact that they grew up in Chicago and lived in a fine house on King Drive. Groucho wrote a memoir called *Groucho and Me*, and Harpo authored a memoir with the title *Harpo Speaks*.

▶ Saul Bellow, 5805 South Dorchester

Saul Bellow (1915–2005), the author of such novels as *Herzog*, *The Adventures of Augie March*, and *Mr. Sammler's Planet*, is listed as liv-

Saul Bellow's residence

ing in this apartment building in a 1973 University of Chicago directory. He taught in the Committee on Social Thought at the University.

Other Notable Chicago Writers

▶L. Frank Baum, 1667 North Humboldt Boulevard

One of the best-known authors who lived in Chicago was someone you don't often associate with this city: L. Frank Baum (1856–1919), the author of *The Wizard of Oz* books. Yet, Baum wrote his first and most successful books when he lived in Chicago. He wrote *The Wonderful Wizard of Oz* while living at 1667 North Humboldt Boulevard. Unfortunately, the house was torn down many years ago.

▶Gwendolyn Brooks, 4334 South Champlain

Gwendolyn Brooks (1917–2000), grew up here, but her house no longer exists. She was named Poet Laureate of the State of Illinois in 1968 and received an American Academy of Arts and Letters Award among many other honors.

▶Edna Ferber, 1642 East 56th Street

Unless they happen upon another Chicago Tribute sign, most people don't realize that the author of *Show Boat*, *So Big*, and many other novels lived here in Chicago for many years. Edna Ferber (1887–1968) lived in an apartment near the lakefront with her mother at 1642 East 56th Street. In a letter, she alluded to the beauty that erupts every spring after a grim Chicago winter, as well as less pleasant aspects of urban life:

> The lake's going on as usual, and things are green (you don't know what that means after six months of brownstone fronts) and burglars tried to break in last night, and it's the same old Chicago.[2]

▶Sterling Plumpp

Of the city where he has chosen to live since 1962, Sterling Plumpp (1940–) says: "Chicago is the place where I found the space to begin my lifelong search for self and purpose." Plumpp, who is a professor and associate head of the department of African-American Studies at the University of Illinois in Chicago, loved hearing the blues singers who played in clubs on the South Side in the 1960s and 1970s. His fourteen books include collections of poetry such as *Ornate with Smoke*. He is the recipient of the Richard Wright Literary Excellence Award and the Carl Sandburg Prize for poetry.

▶Frank Norris

Frank Norris was born in Chicago in 1870. Although he spent most of his life in San Francisco, he wrote one novel about his birthplace called *The Pit: A Story of Chicago*. This book exposed corrupt manipulation of the grain markets in the trading pit of the Chicago Board of Trade. The novel opens with a scene about one hundred years ago as the upper crust of Chicago's society waits outside the Auditorium Theatre at 430 South Michigan Avenue to attend an opera:

> At eight o'clock in the inner vestibule of the Auditorium Theatre by the window of the box office, Laura Dearborn, her younger sister Page, and their aunt...were still wait-

Chicago native and novelist Frank Norris

ing for the rest of the theatre-party to appear. A great, slow-moving press of men and women in evening dress filled the vestibule from one wall to another. A confused murmur of talk and the shuffling of many feet arose on all sides, while from time to time, when the outside and inside doors of the entrance chanced to be open simultaneously, a sudden draught of air gushed in, damp, glacial, and edged with the penetrating keenness of a Chicago evening at the end of February.

▶Ring Lardner

Short story writer and sportswriter Ring Lardner (1885–1933) was born in Niles, Michigan, and came to Chicago in the 1910s to work on newspapers as a reporter and sportswriter. He was most famous as the author of short stories like "You Know Me, Al," and the author of a column in the *Tribune* called "In the Wake of the News." He lived in an apartment on North Buena Avenue in 1918.[3]

▶Richard Wright, 3743 South Indiana Avenue

Novelist Richard Wright (1908–1960) lived at several locations on the South Side; all have been torn down. At this location, he had his own room in a rundown mansion called "La Veta," where he worked on his stories. He went on to write *Black Boy*, *Native Son*, and many other works.

Literary and Book-Related Venues

▶The Newberry Library, 60 West Walton Street

This library on the city's Near North Side is a great resource for anyone researching family history or for literary research. There is a small bookstore inside near the entrance; once a year, a huge book sale is held at which you can get good buys on used books.

The library stands in front of Bughouse Square. This is traditionally where leftists and other activists get up on soapboxes and speak about injustices in society and other causes. When the well-known Chicago author Studs Terkel died in 2008, a memorial was held on this site, and his ashes were scattered here. It was one of Terkel's favorite places.

►Oz Park

The name of Oz Park recognizes the fact that the creator of the Land of Oz lived in Chicago at the time. There's a statue of the Tin Man at Webster and Lincoln, and a yellow brick road path in the park itself. Oz Fest is held every year just east of the lagoon.

►6 North Michigan Avenue: Mystery Writer's Death Scene

Everyone loves a good mystery, and that includes the readers of the mystery writer Eugene Izzi (1953–1996), author of novels such as *The Criminalist* and *Bad Guys*, who apparently lived in fear. He had equipped his condominium with two burglar alarms and a guard dog. He claimed he had been beaten up "by people who knew their business." On December 7, 1996, the body of the forty-three-year-old author was found hanging outside his office in Room 1418 of this building. At the time he was wearing a bulletproof vest with $481 and a pair of brass knuckles in his pocket. A .38 caliber revolver lay on the floor of the office. The case was ruled a suicide, but friends of Izzi's say he had just signed a three-book contract with Avon Books and that he had no reason to take his own life.

►Gross Park, Henderson and Paulina

Have you heard the story about the Chicago real estate developer who claimed he was responsible for writing the famous play *Cyrano de Bergerac*? His name was Samuel Eberly Gross, and this park sits in the middle of a neighborhood that was once called Gross Park. Samuel Eberly Gross built ten thousand houses around the city and suburbs. In 1896, he also wrote a romantic comedy called *The Merchant Prince of Cornville*. He had 250 copies of this work printed and handed them to friends and acquaintances. He also submitted the play to the Porte Street St. Martin Theater in Paris, which held the work for a while and then returned it.

The actor-manager of the theater, Constant Coquelin, was a friend of the French playwright Edmond Rostand. When Rostand's masterpiece *Cyrano de Bergerac* appeared, Gross was outraged. Both his play and Rostand's featured a character with a prominent nose. Both works also contained a scene in which the "nosy" protagonist stood under a balcony impersonating a less witty but more attractive lover.[4]

He charged that Coquelin had aided Rostand in stealing the most essential aspects of *The Merchant Prince of Cornville* and threatened to file a court injunction seeking to block any American performance of *Cyrano*. When *Cyrano* came to Chicago with Sarah Bernhardt and the same Coquelin in the principal roles, depositions were taken, including one from Rostand himself, who argued that "there are big noses everywhere in the world."[5] Gross decided not to file his injunction. He professed to be as eager to see *Cyrano* as anyone in the theater-going public. In May 1902, Judge Christian C. Kohlsaat issued an injunction in U.S. District Court declaring Gross to be "the author of Cyrano's being." Gross was awarded nominal damages of one dollar.

▶ Harpo Studios, 1058 West Washington Boulevard

In terms of book publishing, this is hallowed ground. Harpo Studios is the home of the Oprah Winfrey Show. It is the only television studio owned by an African-American woman. Winfrey has a popular book club, and when she picks a book for the club, publishers usually go back and print an extra 750,000 copies. You can sit in on an Oprah show for free; call 312-591-9222 for reservations.

▶ Fine Arts Building, 410 South Michigan Avenue

In the early part of the twentieth century, the Fine Arts Building was a hub of literary activity. One of the nicest features of the building is the fact that the elevators are still "manned" by real men, just as they were a century ago. If you ride up to the tenth floor, you'll walk past studios once occupied by architect Frank Lloyd Wright and *Chicago Tribune* columnist/cartoonist John McCutcheon, an author in his own right. A publishing house occupied another studio. In yet another, illustrator William Denslow used to meet with L. Frank Baum, the author of *The Wizard of Oz* books. Walk down the stairs to the ninth floor and in Room 917 you can see the office of *The Little Review*, edited by Margaret Anderson. *The Little Review* published James Joyce's *Ulysses* and many other famous writers. In another office, you might overhear a meeting of a group of artists and writers who called their group The Little Room; they included Harriet Monroe, editor and founder of *Poetry* magazine.

▶ Cliff Dwellers Club, 209 South Michigan Avenue

The Cliff Dwellers is a private club for writers, architects, musicians, and others associated with fine arts organizations in Chicago. Since it was founded as the Attic Club in 1907, the Cliff Dwellers has counted many famous writers among its members. The name of the club comes from a novel of the same name by Henry Blake Fuller.

The club holds an annual Bloomsday Festival on June 16 in honor of James Joyce's monumental novel *Ulysses*, which chronicles the events in the life of character Leopold Bloom in Dublin on June 16, 1904. On March 1, 1914, Irish poet William Butler Yeats was honored by *Poetry* magazine at a famous banquet held in the Cliff Dwellers' quarters.

In the club, you'll find a statue called *Bird Girl* by Sylvia Shaw Judson. This is the original mold of the statue that was used on the cover of the best-selling 1994 novel *Midnight in the Garden of Good and Evil* by John Berendt.

▶ Willis Tower (formerly Sears Tower), Franklin and Adams Streets

The top-floor observatory in the tower, which is still the world's second-tallest building, is a must-see for first-time visitors to Chicago. A mural called "The Sights and Soul of Chicago" includes the likenesses of Chicago writers such as Ernest Hemingway and Ana Castillo, among others.

▶ Goethe Memorial, Diversey Parkway and Stockton Drive

Here at the north end of Lincoln Park, you can view the monument to the German poet Wolfgang von Goethe done by Herman Hahn in 1913. On the wall behind the sculpture, you'll find a likeness of Goethe and a quotation from his most famous poem, "Faust."

▶ William Shakespeare Statue, Near Belden Avenue and Cannon Drive

Just across Cannon Drive from the Lincoln Park Zoo, there's a statue of the English playwright and poet William Shakespeare that was done by William Ordway Partridge. It was bequeathed to the Chicago Park District in 1893 by Samuel Johnson, president of the Chicago City Railroad Company. When the city was figuring out where to put the statue, they were attracted to this location by the presence of an English-style perennial garden, which is commonly called Grandmother's Garden, and this was considered a fitting site for the statue. The garden is just to the south of the statue.

▶ Eugene Field Memorial

You can't see it unless you walk through the Lincoln Park Zoo to the east side, near the lagoon, but there's a nice memorial to poet Eugene Field next to the small mammal house in the zoo.

▶ Hans Christian Andersen Statue

The statue of Hans Christian Andersen by John Gelert is just west of the zoo and about a block south of the main entrance on Cannon Drive. It shows Andersen with a swan, which recalls the author's famous story "The Ugly Duckling."

▶ Schiller Statue

The statue near the west entrance to the Lincoln Park Zoo is of the German poet Johann Christoph Friedrich von Schiller. It was cast in Germany and brought here in 1886. He's the author of the poem "Ode to Joy," which Beethoven set to music in his Ninth Symphony.

▶ Abraham Lincoln Statue, Behind Chicago History Museum, 1601 North Clark Street

Impress your children by pointing out the statue of Abraham Lincoln just east of the Historical Society and telling them that President Lincoln was a published poet. The statue was completed in 1887 by August Saint-Gaudens, who visited Lincoln several times during his lifetime and also paid his respects when Lincoln was lying in state after he was killed. So it's a very realistic work of art. Carl Sandburg, who lent his name to the massive housing project located just north of here—Sandburg Village, quoted a poem that Lincoln wrote, called "My Childhood Home I See Again":

> I've heard it oft, as if I dreamed,
> Far-distant, sweet, and lone;
> The funeral dirge it ever seemed
> Of reason dead and gone.

To drink its strains, I've stole away,
All silently and still,
Ere yet the rising god of day
Had streaked the Eastern hill.

▸LaSalle Bank Theatre, 22 West Monroe Street

This famous old theater, formerly known as the Shubert Theatre, was the site of a revival of the musical *Chicago* in 1997. *Chicago* was first produced in 1975 with choreography by Bob Fosse (a Chicagoan himself). The original drama on which the musical was based dates to 1926 when Maurine Watkins wrote it as an assignment for her Yale University drama class.

▸Lottie's Pub

You can have a shot and a beer at a pub that Algren frequented, Lottie's Pub, at 1925 West Cortland, which is now a sports bar, but which still has stairs that lead down to the basement. In Algren's day, the upper part of the facility used to be a grocery store, while the basement was a drinking hole.

▸Hyde Park

Hyde Park gets its name from London's famous park of the same name. The World's Columbian Exposition of 1893 was held here, and the Museum of Science and Industry is the only building that remains from that event. The Exposition was the setting for the book *The Devil in the White City: Murder, Magic, and Madness at the Fair that Changed America* by Erik Larson.

Until Barack Obama, a longtime Hyde Park resident, was elected president, Hyde Park wasn't a well-known part of the city, unless you lived on the South Side or attended the University of Chicago, which dominates the neighborhood. Novelist Philip Roth (1933–   )attended the university and set part of his 1962 novel *Letting Go* on campus. The main character is a teacher at the university: "I walked to the University through the crackling weather and the virgin snows, and arrived at Cobb Hall feeling as righteous, as American, as inner-directed as a young Abe Lincoln."[6]

Langston Hughes

Hyde Park is the residence of writers such as poet Elizabeth Alexander (1962–   ), novelists Richard Stern (1928–   ) and Rosellen Brown (1939–   ), and mystery writers Sara Paretsky (1947–   ) and Arizona Stone Dale (1962–   ). Saul Bellow attended the undergraduate college in the 1930s and subsequently taught in the university's Committee on Social Thought before leaving for Boston University in 1993. It's also a nice place to take a walking tour of the campus and surrounding neighborhood, where you can find a number of literary sites.

Poet Langston Hughes (1902–1967) once taught at the University of Chicago Laboratory Schools, 1362 East 59th Street.

O'Gara and Wilson

Powell's Books

▶Bookstores on 57th Street

The stretch of 57th between Kimbark and Harper is a booklover's paradise. One of the great bookshops is 57th Street Books, which has a terrific children's section and frequently holds author readings. O'Gara and Wilson moved to 1311 East 57th a few years ago from what was considered to be the oldest bookstore location in the city a few blocks west. Powell's Books is a huge used bookstore at 57th and Harper.

57th Street Books

Locations that Appear in Literary Works

▶ Grant Park

East of Michigan Avenue between Roosevelt Road and Randolph Street

Norman Mailer, in his book about the 1968 Democratic Convention, *The Siege of Chicago*, looked from his hotel room window in the Chicago Hilton to see thousands of protestors camped out in Grant Park near Balbo Drive. A famous photo was taken of young people crowding around (and on) the statue of John A. Logan across from Ninth Street.

▶ Monadnock Building

53 West Jackson Boulevard

This building, built in 1890, is one of the city's earliest skyscrapers and was designed by Daniel Burnham and John Wellborn Root.

In her V. I. Warshawski mystery novel *Blood Shot,* Sara Paretsky has Warshawski meet a reporter in a bar called the Golden Glow, which is supposed to be located on the ground floor of this building.

▶Fisher Building
343 South Dearborn

Carl Sandburg, who worked downtown as a reporter for the *Chicago Daily News* as well as for other newspapers, was inspired by skyscrapers. In his poem "The Skyscraper Loves Night," he writes:

> One by one lights of a skyscraper fling their checkering cross work on the velvet gown of night.

▶Union Park
1501 West Randolph Street

This historic park dates back to 1853. In the 1910s, black residents began moving to the area, and Union Park became a rare integrated area. In 1892, Theodore Dreiser lived near Union Park while working at a now-defunct newspaper called the *Chicago Globe.*

In Dreiser's novel *Sister Carrie,* he has Carrie Meeber live "in sin" with Drouet in his three-room apartment facing the park:

> Drouet had taken three rooms, furnished, in Ogden Place, facing Union Park, on the West Side. That was a little, green-carpeted breathing spot, than which, to-day, there is nothing more beautiful in Chicago. It afforded a vista pleasant to contemplate. The best room looked out upon the lawn of the park, now sear and brown, where a little lake lay sheltered. Over the bare limbs of the trees, which now swayed in the wintry wind, rose the steeple of the Union Park Congregational Church, and far off the towers of several others.

You can still see the Union Park Congregational Church, built in 1869, at 60 North Ashland Avenue. The original founders were abolitionists; the original wooden chapel that stood here before the church was built was a way station on the Underground Railroad.[7]

▸ St. John Cantius Church
825 North Carpenter

This beautiful old church plays a role in the Nelson Algren novel *Never Come Morning*. A poor woman in the story named Steffi Rostenkowski has a realization:

> Night after night she heard the iron rocking of the bells of St. John Cantius. Each night they came nearer. Till the roar of the Loop was only a troubled whimper beneath the rocking of the bells. "Everyone lives in the same big room," she would tell herself as they rocked, "But nobody's speakin' to anyone else, 'n nobody got a key."

▸ Chicago Cultural Center
Randolph Street and Michigan Avenue

This building functioned as the city's main public library when it was first constructed. In the novel *Studs Lonigan*, Studs meets his girlfriend Catherine on the steps of the library. They walk south on Michigan Avenue, and the street appears "like a fog of electricity and mist between the massive piles of stone."

▸ Art Institute of Chicago, 111 South Michigan Avenue

When he lived in Chicago, Ernest Hemingway used to visit the Art Institute to see paintings by Paul Cezanne that inspired him. You can still see these paintings today. In Willa Cather's novel *Lucy Gayheart*, she sees a singer she is in love with, Clement Sebastian, come out of the art museum, which seems "perpetually flooded with orange-red sunlight...Sebastian came out of the building at five o'clock and stopped beside one of the bronze lions to turn up the collar of his overcoat, light a cigarette, and look vaguely up and down the avenue before he hailed a cab and drove away."

▸ Chicago Stock Exchange Trading Room
Art Institute, Columbus Drive between Randolph and Madison Streets

The original Trading Room of the Chicago Stock Exchange, built in 1893–1894 and designed by Louis Sullivan and Dankmar Adler, is preserved on the east side of the Art Institute. The Stock Exchange

Lincoln Park Zoo

is an important location in Frank Norris's novel *The Pit: A Story of Chicago*. You can walk around the Trading Room and think of the activity that once went on there, as described by Norris: "Endlessly, ceaselessly the Pit, enormous, thundering, sucked in and spewed out, sending the swirl of its mighty central eddy far out through the city's channels."

▶Lincoln Park Zoo
2001 North Clark Street

The farm in the zoo is described near the end of Jane Hamilton's novel *A Map of the World*. After going through a major domestic ordeal in Wisconsin, a farm family is forced to leave and they move to Chicago, where the husband has to make quite a step down from running his own farm and caring for his Golden Guernsey cows. The wife explains:

> He manages the dairy animals in the Lincoln Park Zoo in Chicago now, what we laughingly call "the herd."...The six cows are Holsteins, a word nothing at all like Golden

Guernsey, a word you cannot say without looking as if you're masticating.

▶Wolf Point
Chicago River near the Orleans Street Bridge

This point of land, where the North Branch of the Chicago River separates from the South Branch, played a central role in a book called *Wolf Point: An Adventure in History* by Leonard Dubkin. The narrator, a businessman working in the nearby Merchandise Mart, travels back in time to discover the role Wolf Point played in Chicago's history.

▶The Dalton Home in *Native Son*
4605 South Drexel Boulevard

In Richard Wright's novel *Native Son*, the protagonist, Bigger Thomas, comes to a house at this address in a predominantly white neighborhood to ask for a job. He is afraid to walk in this well-to-do neighborhood, so he brings a knife. He ends up inadvertently killing Mary Dalton in the house by smothering her with a pillow.

Literary Events

▶Printers Row Book Fair
Dearborn Street between Polk and Congress

Every June, the several-block stretch of Dearborn Street known as "Printers Row" is blocked off to vehicle traffic and turned into a book festival. Booksellers line the streets; famous writers give readings in Dearborn Street Station, 47 West Polk. Festival attendees can enjoy music at the event.

Be sure to stop in Sandmeyer's Bookstore, 714 South Dearborn, 312-922-2104, a good independent bookstore.

My Favorite Bookstores

Chicago is filled with bookstores, and it would be impossible to list them all in one place. I prefer to mention a few that I frequent and can personally recommend.

Abraham Lincoln Book Shop, 357 West Chicago Avenue, 312-944-3085, features artifacts associated with the Great Emancipator, along with rare books.

The Art Institute of Chicago Bookstore, 111 South Michigan Avenue, 312-443-3535, is a great place to shop for cards, posters, journals, and of course, books about artists.

Barbara's Bookstore, Navy Pier, 700 East Grand Avenue, 312-222-0890, is a refuge amid the bedlam of this tourist attraction. Other Barbara's stores, such as the one at 1350 North Wells, are worth visiting as well.

Bookworks, 3444 North Clark Street, contains a good selection of records and CDs as well as good used books.

Borders Books, Music & Café, 150 North State Street, 312-606-0750, has a coffee shop with a nice view of State Street. The Borders at 830 North Michigan Avenue has an even better view of the Water Tower and North Michigan Avenue, if you are lucky enough to find a table near the window.

Chicago Rare Book Center, 56 West Maple Street, 312-988-7246, contains lots of rare books related to Chicago.

Gallery Bookstore Limited, 923 West Belmont Avenue, 773-975-8200, is tiny, cramped, mazelike, and thoroughly wonderful. It smells the way a used bookstore should.

The Newberry's A. C. McClurg Bookstore, 60 West Walton Street in the Newberry Library 312-255-3520. The name is taken from a famous store at the Fine Arts Building that was frequented by famous Chicago writers.

Occult Bookstore, 1579 North Milwaukee Avenue, 773-392-0995, contains strange, offbeat, and downright weird books about spirituality, religion, magic, the occult, and everything in between.

O'Gara and Wilson, Ltd., 1311 East 57th Street, 773-363-0993, is a classic used bookstore with a few antiques as well. There are old magazines, postcards, and other ephemera.

Powell's Book Store, 1501 East 57th Street, 773-955-7780, is simply one of the best and biggest used bookstores in the city. Bargain books are in the basement.

Sandmeyer's Bookstore, 714 South Dearborn Street, 312-922-2104, is a quiet refuge in the South Loop; have a burger at Hackney's across the street.

Seminary Co-Op Bookstore, 5757 South University Avenue, 773-752-4381, is in the basement of a church, and is a fantastic resource for new books, textbooks, and lots of scholarly works.

Women and Children First, 5233 North Clark Street, 773-769-9299, has a great children's section and hosts readings by writers.

Endnotes

1 Farrell, James T. *Reflections at Fifty*, p. 59.

2 Gilbert, Julie Goldsmith. *Ferber: A Biography of Edna Ferber and Her Circle*, p. 401.

3 Lardner, Ring, and Clifford M. Carruthers, *Letters of Ring Lardner* (Orchises Press, 1995), 120.

4 Emmett Dedmon, *Fabulous Chicago* (New York: Random House, 1953), p. 216.

5 Dedmon, p. 218.

6 Roth, Philip. *Letting Go*, p. 230.

7 Chiat, Marilyn Joyce Segal, *The Spiritual Traveler—Chicago and Illinois* (2004: Hidden Spring), 149.

chapter two

Indiana

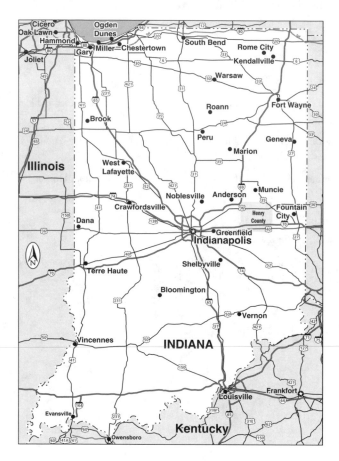

Driving Tours

1. Following I-70: From the "Hoosier's Nest" to the Banks of the Wabash

2. I-65: From the "Aesop of Indiana" to the banks of the Muscatatuck

3. I-69: From Middletown, USA to "The Falstaff of Detectives"

4. I-74: The Ben-Hur Tour

5. I-80/90: From "Hulman" to Wildflower Woods

6. I-27 from Richmond to Uncle Tom's Refuge

7. Highway 24: Peru and Roann

8. Highway 41: Vincennes

$\mathcal{T}$raveling into Indiana, you travel into the past. The interstate highways that crisscross the state take you from summer resorts and urban sprawl back to the agrarian landscape where you can walk in the steps of the state's many famous writers. Moving off the beaten path, you encounter a small-town Midwest that harkens back to the days of horse-drawn carriages, town squares, and farms. That sense of tradition and "good old days"—and the clash with industrialization and modern mobility—is what helped create the so-called "golden age" of Indiana literature in the late nineteenth and early twentieth centuries and what continues to inspire writers today.

Indiana has a rich literary history. The state was second only to New York in the number of published authors when the Indiana Society of Chicago was founded in 1905. George Ade, James Whitcomb Riley, Booth Tarkington, Meredith Nicholson, and George Barr McCutcheon were among those associated with the society in its early years. In a 1947 study, the Indiana Historical Society found that Hoosier authors ranked second only to New Yorkers in the number of best-sellers produced in the previous forty years.[1] The study goes on to affirm that writers during Indiana's literary heyday catered to readers who preferred idealized traditional values and wanted an escape from a fast-changing world.

Indiana is the place to go when you are tired of the modern world and are looking for safety in the past. You might be bored on the interstate as you drive for hours seeing nothing but farms, billboards, and the occasional antique mall. But the moment you get off the superhighway and into the countryside, you discover all sorts of hidden treasures. You'll find the two-story "Cabin in the Wildflower Woods" where Gene Stratton-Porter lived. You can hug her favorite oak tree and walk through the gardens and ponds she designed. You'll find the ornate "study" created by the author of *Ben-Hur*, which combines Romanesque, Byzantine, and Greek architectural styles. You'll walk on the sidewalk past Kurt Vonnegut's home, carefully stepping around handprints he made along with his family.

As the humorist George Ade wrote, Indiana is not like the rest of the Midwest:

> Indiana has a savor not to be detected in Ohio. It is decidedly un-Michigan-like. Although it tinges off toward Illinois on the west and Kentucky on the south, the community is neither nebulous nor indefinite. It is individual.

> . . . Forty or fifty years ago the native son who went travelling owned up to an indefinite residence somewhere between Chicago and Louisville. To-day the Hoosier abroad claims Indiana fervently, hoping to be mistaken for an author.[2]

Around Indiana's boundaries, nothing is flat and simple. And many Hoosier writers hail from the edges of the state—from the Wabash River Valley, from the hilly countryside near the Ohio River, from the forests and lakes near the Ohio border. Other writers reside in the state's college towns—Bloomington, South Bend, Lafayette, Muncie, Terre Haute—where you can get a taste of "Hoosier hospitality" in independent bookstores and coffee shops. You have to seek out sites associated with Indiana's writers, but getting there is half the fun as you sample some great family restaurants and quirky museums on the way.

▶ Following I-70: From the "Hoosier's Nest" to the Banks of the Wabash

The key word to keep in mind as you hurtle down I-70 through Indiana is *Hoosier*. You are now in the *Hoosier* State. I can hear what you're asking: What, exactly, is a Hoosier, and where did the term come from?

Two writers who lived near I-70, in fact, were dubbed "The Hoosier Poet" in their careers. Although he worked for most of his life as a clerk in various public offices in Richmond, John Finley (1797–1866) wrote the poem "The Hoosier's Nest." It contains the following inspiring lines about the state:

> Blest Indiana! in thy soil
> Are found the sure rewards of toil,
> Where honest poverty and worth
> May make a Paradise on earth.

"The Hoosier's Nest" was originally published in the *Richmond Palladium* newspaper in 1830. A Hoosier, according to the poem, is a humble man who works hard to support his family:

> Not thus the honest son of toil,
> Who settles here to till the soil,
> and with intentions just and good,
> Acquires an ample livelihood:
> He is (and not the little-great)
> The bone and sinew of the State.

Finley originally spelled the word "Hoosher" and later changed it to "Hoosier." After the poem was reprinted in the *Indianapolis Journal* on January 1, 1833, a toast was offered at a Jackson Day dinner on January 8, 1833, to "The Hoosher State of Indiana." But Finley didn't bother to explain the term. The Web site of the state of Indiana (www.in.gov/rde/xfw/in_core/hs.xsl/faqs.htm) presents several possible origins, none of which is terribly flattering. One claims that settlers would answer a knock at the door in thick country dialect: "Who's yere?" The second Hoosier Poet, James Whitcomb Riley, speculated that Indiana settlers were so vicious that chunks of noses and ears frequently would be bitten off in tavern fights. When the dust settled, the inquiry would be: "Whose ear?" (In case you're wondering, boxer Mike Tyson, infamous for biting off a piece of an opponent's ear, hails not from Indiana but from Brooklyn, New York.)

If you stop off at Richmond, you won't find any trace of the homes where Finley lived. There are other things to see in Richmond, though. By the time you get there, a new museum to commemorate the Gennett Recording Studios may be open. Gennett played an important role in the birth of jazz; Hoagy Carmichael, a native of Indiana, recorded the first version of "Stardust" there.

Also in Richmond is the beautiful campus of Earlham College. The highest point in Indiana (all of 1,257 feet above sea level) is in nearby Bethel.

If you are looking for a place to eat in Richmond, try Little Sheba's (175 Fort Wayne, 765-962-2999) or the Olde Richmond Inn (138 South Fifth Street, 765-962-2247).

▶Henry County/Raintree County

The novel *Raintree County*, which was called "The Great American Novel" when it was published in 1948, is one of the best-known works to use Indiana as a setting. The geographic region known as Raintree County is fictitious, but Ross Lockridge (1914-1948) based it on Henry County. Get off I-70 at Exit 131 and head south to the town of Straughn, which was called Waycross in the novel. Henry County was the home of Lockridge's ancestors. As a boy, the main character of the novel, John Shawnessy (who is based on Lockridge's grandfather John Wesley Shockley), traveled down the fictional Shawmucky River in search of Paradise Lake. On the way, he got stuck in the Great Swamp. The Shockley home is on Route 40 in Straughn, on the south side of the road about two-thirds of the way through town.

The novel tells the story of how Raintree County got its name: when the country was first being settled by pioneers, a preacher passed through, saying he had had a vision of heaven as "a green land full of fruit-bearing trees and pleasant waters." The preacher planted a seed that grew into a raintree, and the land around it became known as Raintree County. The novel follows Shawnessy's search for the raintree, which, he believes, is the Tree of Knowledge. Shawnessy loves to spend time by the Shawmucky River, escaping the demands of the world to write.

John Wesley Shockley, the grandfather of Ross Lockridge, was the inspiration for the main character of *Raintree County*.

▶Greenfield

If you are traveling between Richmond and Indianapolis, you can take either the interstate or, if you're not in a hurry, the much more scenic National Road (US Highway 40). This highway goes directly through Greenfield (which is just three miles south of Exit 104 on I-70).

Greenfield is proud to be known as the birthplace of the second Hoosier Poet, James Whitcomb Riley (1849–1916), who is remembered today as the creator of the character Little Orphan Annie. A Riley festival has been held in Greenfield each fall (www.rileyfestival .com) for decades, featuring a Parade of Flowers, art and quilt exhibits, and pumpkins. Riley's work is the inspiration for a different theme each year. In 2008 the theme was "Our Hired Girl," based on the poem of the same name:

> Our hired girl, she's 'Lizabuth Ann;
> An' she can cook best things to eat!
> She ist puts dough in our pie-pan,
> An' pours in somepin' 'at's good and sweet,
> An' nen she salts it all on top

John Wesley Shockley was a schoolmaster in Straughn, Indiana.

With cinnamon; an' nen she'll stop
An' stoop an' slide it, ist as slow,
In th' old cook-stove, so's 'twon't slop
An' git all spilled; nen bakes it, so
It's custard pie, first thing you know!

Residents of Greenfield are not alone in enthusiastically embracing their favorite son. Another Indiana writer, George Ade, said the following about Riley:

Our beloved Riley of Indiana once in a while consented to recite his poems in public. He had a genius for character acting. As a storyteller he was delightful beyond all description. Whenever he appeared on a rostrum, the auditorium was jammed with well-dressed people leaning forward. His readings brought him many dollars and gave happiness to the kind of "folks" for whom he had an affection.[3]

If this whets your appetite for more things James Whitcomb Riley, be sure to visit the festival. If you can't make the festival, you can still visit the home, which was built by Riley's father in 1850.

Riley Birthplace and Museum
250 West Main Street, Greenfield, Indiana 46140
317-462-8539
April to November
Closed Sunday and holidays

▶Indianapolis

Back on the road, as the tall buildings of Indianapolis loom to the west, you might contemplate topics covered in a 1900 book called *The Hoosiers* by a once-famous writer named Meredith Nicholson (1866–1946). It's a series of essays on the state of Indiana, its citizens, and their way of life. Nicholson was born in Crawfordsville, Indiana, but in an essay called "Indianapolis and American Culture," he wrote of the state's capital city:

> Indianapolis is not like other cities of approximately the same size. It is not the native who says so, but the visitor from abroad, who is puzzled by a difference between the Hoosier capital and Kansas City, Omaha, and Denver, or Minneapolis and St. Paul. . . . The distinguishing quality of Indianapolis is its simple domesticity. The people are home-loving and home-keeping. In the early days, when the town was a rude capital in the woods, the people stayed at home perforce; and when the railroad reached them they did not take readily to travel. . . . The more the Hoosier travels, the more he likes his own town.[4]

Nicholson described Indianapolis as a "neighborly and cosy town," a phrase that aptly describes the communities inhabited by two utterly different writers, Booth Tarkington and Kurt Vonnegut.

▶ Booth Tarkington

Booth Tarkington (1869–1946) wrote extensively about what could be described as a "lost world." He described the experiences of middle-class Americans in the middle of the country who were in the middle of a great change—the Industrial Revolution. It was a nostalgic world, looking back from the post World War I era to a quieter, simpler time in which men wore stove-pipe hats, callers to a house were ushered into the "parlour," and hostesses kept "open

Booth Tarkington

house" on New Year's Day. Of all the writers of his time, Booth Tarkington most accurately interpreted the American scene from the beginning of the century through the twenties as the average American saw it.

Tarkington was a prolific writer who churned out manuscripts over a wide span of time, beginning with *Monsieur Beaucaire* (1900) and ending with *The Show Piece* (1947), with some sixty-three volumes in between that were very popular when they were published. But these days, Tarkington is remembered—when he is remembered at all—for his two Pulitzer Prize winning novels that both were turned into movies. *The Magnificent Ambersons* (1919) was directed by Orson Welles as his follow-up to *Citizen Kane*, and *Alice Adams* (1922) became one of the first starring vehicles for Katherine Hepburn when it was released in 1935. Much of the action in *The Magnificent Ambersons* consists of sleigh rides up and down National Avenue. There is still a National Avenue today, just north of the University of Indianapolis and just south of I-65.

In a May 2004 article in the *Atlantic Monthly*, novelist Thomas Mallon cites these two novels as being the only ones Tarkington wrote that are worthy of consideration. But *Penrod* gave its name to a type of child, and was also a big hit in its day. Note: *Penrod* and many other books of its era may be offensive to today's readers because of the frequent use of the "n" word.

Tarkington grew up in Indianapolis in a house at 1100 North Pennsylvania that his mother called Barley Bright, which was destroyed when I-65 was constructed in 1972. During his later years, Tarkington and his wife Susanah spent about half of each year at 4270 North Meridian Street and the other half at Seawood, the home they developed at Kennebunkport, Maine. As you pass the house with the gate and the brick posts with carvings of cherubs on top of each, you can imagine Tarkington garbed in his bathrobe putting into practice his tips for writers who work long hours. He wrote to a friend:

> I've worked out a sort of system. I live in bathrobes. Nothing of anything from outside gets by to my workroom. That's the first requisite. About two o'clock they bring me beef-tea and coffee. I get into some clothes at six, don't eat heavily, and am back at seven, bathrobe again. I have a pencil machine and sharpen about three dozen every night; write on a draughtsman's drawingboard, tilted, a card-table at my elbow.

▶ *Kurt Vonnegut, Jr.*

Kurt Vonnegut, Jr., was born on Armistice Day, November 11, 1922, in Indianapolis. Revisiting his birthplace in 1986 to deliver the annual McFadden Memorial Lecture, Vonnegut told a North Central High School audience: "All my jokes are Indianapolis. All my attitudes are Indianapolis. My adenoids are Indianapolis. If I ever severed myself from Indianapolis, I would be out of business. What people like about me is Indianapolis."[5] In nearly all Vonnegut's books, there is at least one character from Indianapolis.

As a student at Shortridge High School he was a writer and editor for the *Shortridge Daily Echo,* the first high school daily newspaper in the country. Vonnegut began his education at the Orchard School, which was elite and private. But after family finances nosedived during the Depression he was put in the James Whitcomb Riley Public School, which was near his family's home at 4401 North Illinois Street. Impressions of a later occupant, Indianapolis architect Vaughn Hickman, were featured in an article entitled "Living with History." Hickman takes care to preserve the Vonnegut family monogram in the leaded glass and the handprints of the entire Vonnegut family, including Kurt Sr. and Jr., in the cement walk behind the home. A photo of Hickman and his wife taken with

Vonnegut during an impromptu visit is also proudly displayed. The *Indianapolis Business Journal* printed another description of the house on October 25, 2004, called "A Place with History: Vonnegut's Past Still Part of Butler-Tarkington Home." On Palm Sunday in 2007, a ceremony was held at the home, led by an Indianapolis librarian. (Vonnegut's book *Palm Sunday* [1981] includes vivid observations of his hometown in what could be called an "autobiographical collage.") Vonnegut died in April 2007, two weeks before he was scheduled to visit Indianapolis as part of the city's "Year of Vonnegut" festivities.

Palm Sunday includes an account of Vonnegut's frustration in trying to get the *Indianapolis Star* to run an obituary for another Indianapolis writer, Janet Flanner, who was the Paris correspondent for the *New Yorker*. Like Vonnegut, Flanner was a member of the prestigious American Academy and Institute of Arts and Letters. To learn more, visit www.bsu.edu/ourlandourlit/Literature/Authors/flannerj.htm.

▶ *James Whitcomb Riley*

James Whitcomb Riley's home—or rather, the house where he lived for twenty-three years as a guest of the families who actually owned it—is located in the Lockerbie neighborhood of Indianapolis. During your tour, you can view his writing, his desk, a portrait of his dog, and his top hat and cane, among other things.

Perhaps the best thing about the museum is that it is associated with the Riley Children's Foundation, which was created in the poet's honor following his death. Children from around the world seeking medical care stay at the James Whitcomb Riley Hospital for Children.

James Whitcomb Riley Museum Home
528 Lockerbie Street, Indianapolis, Indiana 46202
For group reservations: 317-631-5885
www.rileykids.org/museum
Tuesday through Saturday, 10 a.m. to 3:30 p.m.
Sunday, noon to 3:30 p.m.

James Whitcomb Riley Museum Home

▶ John Gruelle

A talented cartoonist, John (Johnny) Gruelle (1880–1938) worked at the *Indianapolis Star* and other newspapers in Cleveland and New York. Although he was born in Arcola, Illinois, he can certainly be considered a Hoosier because his parents moved to Indianapolis that same year.

The story goes that one day Gruelle found a faceless rag doll in his attic. He drew a face on the doll, called it Raggedy Ann, and gave it to his daughter Marcella. The doll became Marcella's constant companion. *Raggedy Ann Stories* was published in 1918, and by 1938 three million copies had been sold—more than any children's book since *Alice in Wonderland*. Gruelle wrote forty other children's books, many describing the adventures of the doll that has become part of American culture. It was a stroke of marketing genius that Gruelle had patented Raggedy Ann's design in 1915.

►Terre Haute

Theodore Dreiser

If you get to the western edge of Indiana near the Illinois border, it's worth the ten-minute drive from Exit 3 on I-70 to visit Terre Haute. Theodore Dreiser (1871–1945) was born in a house that still stands at the southwest corner of 12th and Walnut in Terre Haute. It's a private home, and you'll find nary a plaque or other marker. This seems rather odd in light of the fact that writing such novels as *Sister Carrie* and *An American Tragedy* made Dreiser into one of the greatest and best-known Indiana writers. But what's even more strange is that there is a birthplace and museum in Terre Haute dedicated not to him but to his older brother, Paul Dresser (more about Paul later).

One of ten children born to a poor German immigrant, Dreiser had a childhood plagued by unhappiness and poverty. His fiction does not mention Indiana; in his nonfiction works such as *A Hoosier Holiday* and *Dawn*, however, he writes about his home state with a mixture of nostalgia and ambivalence. He is said to have lived in a house of prostitution in Evansville, Indiana, for instance—a house run by a woman named Sally, for whom Paul wrote a song called "My Gal Sal."

Terre Haute borders on the Wabash River, a body of water that inspired not bucolic nostalgia in the writer but a sense of fear. Theodore Dreiser writes in *A Hoosier Holiday:*

> I had been made fearful by my brother Rome, who once
> took my brother Al, my sister Trina and myself out in a
> small boat upon the Wabash River, a to me mysterious,
> ominous and most uncertain body or thing which had
> motion, and hence life, maybe. I think I must have been
> overawed by its quantity and movement as well as its differ-
> ence from solid earth. At any rate, there it was, strange and
> fearsome. And then when a stern-propelled steamboat, of
> no doubt minute size but to me enormous, came into view
> around a bend and after passing, left in its wake a ripple
> which rocked our small craft, I was panic-stricken.[6]

▶ *Paul Dresser*

Paul Dreiser (1857–1906), who changed his name to Dresser when he went on stage, penned the Indiana state song, "On the Banks of the Wabash." The chorus of this song takes a more peaceful view of the river:

> Oh, the moonlight's fair tonight along the Wabash,
> From the fields there comes the breath of new mown hay.
> Thro' the sycamores the candle lights are gleaming,
> On the banks of the Wabash, far away.

Why is there a Paul Dresser historical site and not a Theodore Dreiser site in Terre Haute? "He's more in tune to Terre Haute," said the lady on the phone, speaking of Paul Dresser.

Paul Dresser Memorial Birthplace
First Street and Dresser Drive, Terre Haute, Indiana 47802
812-235-9717

Paul Dresser Memorial Birthplace

▶ *Eugene Debs*

Another reason to go to Terra Haute is to visit the house where Eugene Debs (1855–1926) lived with his wife, Kate, from 1890 until his death in 1926. Debs ran for U.S. president five times on the Socialist Party ticket, receiving a million votes in 1920 even though he was still in prison for having made an antiwar speech in 1918. Ever the writer, his scathing indictment of prison life was entitled *Walls and Bars*.

Eugene Debs earned a place in history books because he was a notable labor leader, but he gets extra minutes of fame because he was the hero of Kurt Vonnegut. A character in Vonnegut's 1982 novel *Deadeye Dick* is given the name Eugene Debs Metzger. Also in Vonnegut's 1990 novel *Hocus Pocus*, the main character Eugene Debs Hartke is named for the labor leader. A quote from Debs appears several times in the book: ". . . while there is a lower class, I am in it, and while there is a criminal element, I am of it, and while there is a soul in prison, I am not free."

The home of Socialist and labor leader Eugene V. Debs

Eugene V. Debs House

451 North Eighth Street, Terre Haute, Indiana 47807
812-232-2163
www.eugenevdebs.com
Wednesday through Sunday, 1:00 to 4:30 p.m.

I-65: From the "Aesop of Indiana" to the banks of the Muscatatuck

▸Brook

As you leave the steel mills of Gary and head south on I-65, ask your traveling companions the following: Who wrote the first play about football? Who had three shows that were hits on Broadway at the same time? Who directed ten films and wrote a hundred movie scripts? Who built a full-scale golf course and country club on the land surrounding his Indiana home, where he hosted presidents such as Theodore Roosevelt and William Howard Taft? Whose home, tucked just outside a tiny town with a population of 1,062 between I-65 and the Illinois border, is crammed with art and antiques that he collected in trips around the world and is on the National Register of Historic Places?

Answer: George Ade (1866–1944). George Who? Get off I-65 and head west on IN Highway 16 toward the town of Brook, and listen to George Ade's amazing story. (The house is two miles east of Brook on IN 16.) Ade was born in Kentland, Indiana, on February 9, 1866, one of seven children. While at Purdue University he became a member of the Sigma Chi fraternity, an organization he supported generously in later years.

Ade was one of the most popular writers in America, with admirers who included Mark Twain and literary critic William Dean Howells. Why, then, is Ade nearly forgotten today? That may be because he never wrote a best-selling novel and because he wrote in slang dialect that is outdated. His *Fables in Slang* recall Aesop's fables, and paint a picture of colorful characters in the changing society of the early twentieth century. He is brilliant with humorous observations, as well as aphorisms.

Before the days of blogs, newspaper columns were popular venues. Ade began writing in 1890 for the *Chicago Morning News*, which later became the *Chicago Record*. In 1901, he wrote the first

George Ade in his study

John T. McCutcheon

note

At Purdue, Ade met the cartoonist John T. McCutcheon (1870-1949), who later became well known for his work with the *Chicago Tribune* and the cartoon "Injun Summer." He also illustrated the first edition of L. Frank Baum's *The Wonderful Wizard of Oz*, as well as other books in the Wizard of Oz series. He illustrated Ade's collection of columns, *Stories of the Streets and of the Town*.

Broadway-style musical (a musical that tells a single narrative story): *The Sultan of Sulu*. The musical grew from a story idea given to him by John McCutcheon, who heard about the real-life Sultan of Jolo on a trip abroad. Ade also wrote the first American play about football. The last act of *The College Widow* includes a college football play. In 1904, Ade was the first playwright to have three plays running simultaneously on Broadway: *The College Widow*, *The County Chairman*, and *The Sho-Gun*.

Ade used money from his work and real estate investments to build a palatial estate on twenty-four hundred acres of Newton County land, called Hazelden Farm. It included a golf course and country club, landscaped gardens, a pool, a garage, a greenhouse, and a caretaker's house. The parties he hosted, including an annual gathering for local children, were the stuff of legends. In 1908, William Howard Taft launched his presidential campaign at a picnic Ade threw for twenty-five thousand supporters. A rally also was held for Theodore Roosevelt in 1912 during his campaign with the Bull Moose Party. Soldiers and sailors who visited Hazelden after World War I were made especially welcome.

But all the comforts of Hazelden didn't make Ade a homebody. He circled the globe twice and visited China and Japan four times. The house is filled with an amazing number of artifacts, many collected on his trips to China, India, and Tibet. Among other treasures are a Grecian urn and a Waterford crystal punch bowl.

Today, Hazelden is owned by Newton County and is maintained by a group of volunteers, the George Ade Memorial Association. "There is no one there full-time, but you can contact one of the board members and we will take people through by appointment," says association member Mike Davis. "We put together at least one major event at the house each year. We did one on his Asian collection, highlighting all the stuff he collected in China and Japan. We once did a reading of a couple of Ade's fables there. They're very humorous when you read them aloud."

Why do Davis and other members of the association continue to devote themselves to a long-dead Indiana writer who is not well remembered? "It's a sense of place," he explains. "Here is a guy who grew up in modest means in Newtown County and went on to win that kind of acclaim. Whenever I meet with a group of our local students, they tell me, 'I can't wait to get out of here.' It's probably what every small-town kid across the world says. Here is a wonderful example of that. George Ade took his upbringing in Newton County and wove it into a wonderful career."

Ade's career on Broadway was short-lived. Beginning in 1905, a series of plays failed. But also in 1905, he co-founded (along with John McCutcheon and Edward M. Holloway) the Indiana Society of Chicago. In a 2005 book by Sesh Heri, *The Wonder of the Worlds*, Ade was a character along with Nikola Tesla, Mark Twain, and Harry Houdini, who pursued Martian agents who had stolen a powerful crystal from Tesla at the World's Columbian Exposition in Chicago in 1893.

If you visit Hazelden today, you'll find on one side of the home, Hazelden Country Club, the golf course he had built, and on the

George Ade's home, Hazelden. Ade suggested the site of its construction in his will "since everyone knows the only place you can find a doctor is on a golf course."

The Indiana Society of Chicago is still active and holds an annual dinner. You can find out more about the group at www.indianasocietyof-chicago.org/html/aboutus.html.

other, the George Ade Health Care Center. The home is not open regular hours, but you can arrange for a tour by writing to the George Ade Memorial Association (P.O. Box 102, Kentland, Indiana 47951) or by calling Mike Davis (219-474-3339) or Newton County (219-474-6081).

▶West Lafayette

As you get back on I-65 and head south toward Lafayette, home to Purdue University, you won't be leaving the influence of Ade totally behind. The Ross-Ade football stadium was partially paid for by—you guessed it—George Ade.

▶*John Philip Sousa*

You'll find the John Philip Sousa Museum at 601 New York Street, in West Lafayette. Wait a minute, you may be thinking, Sousa (1854–1932) is the composer best known for military marches such as "The Stars and Stripes Forever." It's true that on November 9, 1927, he visited Purdue to present a sterling silver loving cup to its marching band. But "The March King" also wrote some of the most bizarre novels of the twentieth century.

A case in point is the 1902 novel *The Fifth String*. In it a young violinist makes a deal with the devil for a magic violin with five strings, each of which can be used to excite an emotion. They include Pity, Hope, Love, and Joy, but the fifth string is Death and can be played only once before causing the player's own death. Because his brilliant career cannot console him for his inability to win the love of the woman he desires, he plays upon the Death string at his final concert.

In 1905, Sousa published the book *Pipetown Sandy*, which included a satirical poem titled "The Feast of the Monkeys." Animals attending a lavish party are forced to watch the King of Beasts, the lion, eat the entire feast. At the end of his gluttony, the lion explains, "Come all rejoice, You've seen your monarch dine." Sousa called the poem "nonsense verse," but there was definitely an egalitarian tone to it.

In 1920, he wrote a forty-thousand-word story called *The Transit of Venus* about a group of misogynists. They form the Alimony Club and, as a way of temporarily escaping the society of women, embark on a sea voyage to observe the transit of Venus. The captain's niece, however, has stowed away on board and soon wins over the men.

▶ William H. Gass

William H. Gass (1924–   ) was for many years a professor at Purdue University. He is the author of novels such as *Omensetter's Luck* and *In the Heart of the Heart of the Country*. If you want to learn more, visit www.bsu.edu/ourlandourlit/Literature/Authors/GassWH.html.

▶ Vernon

Jessamyn West

Author Jessamyn West (1902–1984) was born in the tiny town (population 318) of Vernon, Indiana, and left the Hoosier state shortly thereafter. But this didn't stop her from writing about Indiana all her life. Comparing herself to other authors who created fictional universes, she remarked, "I write about [Indiana] because knowing little about it, I can create it." Just as remarkable as West's attraction to Indiana is the devotion to Jessamyn West the author by Jessamyn West the librarian, who wrote to her namesake at the age of eleven, and began an ongoing correspondence. You can read more at www.jessamyn.com/jessamyn/jess.html.

According to Wikipedia, the first Jessamyn West was a second cousin of Richard Nixon. She wrote *The Secret Look*, a book of poems, many collections of short stories, travel books, and reminiscences. Her most famous book is *The Friendly Persuasion*, a story that describes Quaker farm life in the mid-1800s. The nearby Muscatatuck River still provides drinking water to North Vernon, and canoes can be launched at the town park in Vernon. The novel begins:

> Near the banks of the Muscatatuck where once the woods had stretched, dark row on row, and where the fox grapes and wild mint still flourished, Jess Birdwell, an Irish Quaker, built his white clapboard house.

▶ Bloomington
Ross Lockridge

Ross Lockridge was born in Bloomington on April 25, 1914, and his work is steeped in Midwestern history and Hoosier folklore. His father, a historian, was known as "Mr. Indiana," and young Ross accompanied him on trips throughout the state. He planned to write his doctoral dissertation at Harvard University on Walt Whitman, but what came out was his family history. It follows the story of John Shawnessy in a mythical county that is based on nineteenth-century Henry County, Indiana. After five years, he had a twenty-pound manuscript, which he lugged to the offices of Houghton Mifflin. Prior to its publication, the novel became a Book-of-the-Month Club selection, and the 1,060-page story was excerpted in *Life* magazine. When it was published on January 5, 1948, it received good reviews. But just two months later, Lockridge, who was suffering from depression, committed suicide. The next day his only novel was named the number one bestseller in the country.

(You can read more about *Raintree County* earlier in this chapter, in the I-70 tour.)

Indiana novelist Ross Lockridge

I-69: From Middletown, USA to "The Falstaff of Detectives"

Just a few miles east of Exit 41 on I-69, you head into the town of Muncie, Indiana. Doesn't it look like Anywhere, USA, the quintessential American city? You're not the first person to entertain such an idea. Muncie, in fact, was singled out for fame in 1929, when the sociologists Robert and Helen Lynd chose it as the subject of their book *Middletown: A Study in Modern American Culture.*

Middletown was the study of a "typical" American city and how its residents were coping with the rapid changes of the twentieth century. Today, Muncie can accurately describe itself as "the most thoroughly studied community of its size in the nation," according to James Connolly, director of the Center for Middletown Studies. The Center is part of Ball State University in Muncie. Talk show host David Letterman hails from Muncie, as does Jim Davis, the creator of the Garfield comic strip.

▶ *Emily Kimbrough*

Muncie has embraced its native daughter, Emily Kimbrough, the co-author (with Cornelia Otis Skinner) of *Our Hearts Were Young and Gay*, a reminiscence of their trip to Europe in the 1920s. She was a writer, lecturer, editor, and radio host.

Born in 1899, Kimbrough grew up at 715 East Washington Street. An Emily Kimbrough Historic District has been created in Muncie's East End in an effort to preserve a historic area of Queen Anne and other Victorian homes where the author grew up. In *How Dear to My Heart* (1944) she wrote vividly of this area:

> The lamp on the newel post lighted with a wax taper held high in the winter dusk. The gas fire which burned against an asbestos shield in my grandfather's den. The used carbon from the street corner lamps that made a good chalk for marking hopscotch squares. The street cry of fresh lye hominy and horseradish. And the squeak of wagon wheels on the snow. I shall not, I know be accurate, because I shall not even try to verify my memories.

An annual Festival and Historic Home Tour is held in the district each September. You can find out more about the Emily Kimbrough Historic District at www.muncie-ecna.org/ecna/kimbrough.php.

If you're in the mood for an offbeat attraction, visit Robinson's Jar Museum at North Wheeling Avenue and East Cowing Drive (765-282-9707). It's a private museum that claims to have one of the greatest collections of fruit jars in the United States.

▶ Marion

Marie Webster

Marie Webster (1859–1956) is hardly a household name—that is, unless someone in your household loves quilting. Webster, who lived most of her life in Marion, wrote the first book dedicated solely to the history of the quilt: *Quilts, Their Story, and How to Make Them*, published in 1915. She created many classic quilt patterns with colorful names like Sunbonnet Lassies, Pink Rose, and White Dogwood.

When you enter Marion, just west off Exit 47 on I-69, head for the Quilter's Hall of Fame. Housed in Webster's own home, it is the only National Historic Landmark that honors a quilter.

Quilter's Hall of Fame
926 South Washington Street, Marion, Indiana 46953
765-664-9333
www.quiltershalloffame.net
Wednesday through Saturday, 10 a.m. to 3 p.m.
April to mid-December

▶ Noblesville
Rex Stout

If you knew you would be forever known for just one fictional character, would you write? For most authors, the answer is probably yes. Rex Stout (1886–1975) created many characters and wrote a series of mysteries that was named Best Mystery Series of the Century at the 2000 Boucheron World Mystery Convention. But Stout is best known as the creator of the "Falstaff of detectives," Nero Wolfe.

Nero Wolfe was a larger-than-life character in many ways. He was a big eater, so it was logical that he was physically large and slow moving. In fact, he rarely left his home, but spent his time lavishing attention on orchids. But his mind was amazingly perceptive, and he solved crimes with the power of his prodigious brain. He and his faithful assistant, Archie Goodwin, first appeared in 1934 in a novel called *Fer-de-Lance*. Stout continued to write Nero Wolfe mysteries and many other works until his death in 1975. His protagonist lives on in the hearts and minds of many fans. For example, the Wolfe Pack is a group that meets regularly in New York.

Stout was born in this little town just north of Indianapolis, but not long after his birth, the family moved to Kansas. From there he traveled extensively through Europe, so there isn't much trace of Indiana in his writings . . . certainly not of Noblesville. Stout held very liberal beliefs—a stark contrast to another former resident Noblesville. The American Fascist William Dudley Pelley settled in Noblesville in 1942. But shortly after arriving, he was charged with high treason and sedition and later sentenced to fifteen years in prison. When he was released early (in 1950) he returned to Noblesville and published metaphysical and political books and journals. In 1995 a local builder found a trunk in an abandoned barn that contained sashes, hoods, and more than one thousand membership cards and dues receipts from a local chapter of the Ku Klux Klan. The materials were donated to the Hamilton County Historical Society.

►Kendallville
Philip Appleman

Kendallville is the home of a contemporary author who writes about Indiana. The poetry of Philip Appleman (1926–   ) is often tinged with nostalgia for his childhood in Indiana.

I-74: The Ben-Hur Tour

►Crawfordsville

This town is well worth a detour from I-74; it is associated with three well-known Indiana writers: Maurice Thompson, General Lew Wallace, and Meredith Nicholson.

Maurice Thompson (1844–1901), whose most famous novel was *Alice of Old Vincennes*, lived much of his life in Crawfordsville with his wife (who was also named Alice). His novel *A Banker of Bankersville* is a semi-autobiographical account of a man's return to Crawfordsville after a long period of travel. He writes:

> All the country around Bankersville was extremely fertile and under high cultivation, so that one might drive for miles in any direction, over some one of the many fine gravel roads, between broad fields and always in sight of big red barns and comfortable farm-houses. It was a region of corn, wheat, oats, blue-grass, fat cattle and rotund hay-stacks, as well as a paradise of healthy brown-faced youths and rosy-cheeked, bouncing lasses.[7]

Thompson and his wife lived in the house his wife inherited in the 1890s, which he named Sherwood Place. Here he became friends with one of Crawfordsville's other noted authors, General Lew Wallace.

▶ *General Lew Wallace*

Without a doubt, the single biggest attraction in Crawfordsville, and one of Indiana's most notable sites devoted to a writer, is the General Lew Wallace Study and Museum. Lew Wallace (1827–1905) was an eclectic person, and his "study" reflects his many interests. Besides being a general in the Civil War, he was a lawyer, legislator, and governor of the New Mexico Territory.

When I approached the site late one afternoon just before closing time, I was impressed by the tall brick wall around the estate. I expected to see a grandiose mansion. Instead, I saw a parking lot, a visitor center, beautiful gardens and grounds, and a small red brick building in the center of the property. This "study" built by Wallace is where he lived and worked. He had once written that he wanted to build a "study" where he could "bury himself in a den of books," and that's just what he did. His one great novel, *Ben-Hur: A Tale of the Christ*, is long and tedious and does not make for scintillating reading. But it sold extremely well when it was published in 1880 and gained several new leases on life when it was made into a play and then into several movies. The chariot race scene in the 1959 version with Charlton Heston is particularly memorable. *Ben-Hur* gave the general the financial means to build a bizarre temple in Crawfordsville.

The women of Crawfordsville have ensured that the study is cared for and promoted as a scenic attraction. A women's group called Community House purchased the study in 1941 and gave it to the city as a museum. Today, the Lew Wallace Study Preservation Society maintains the property, holds an annual Lew Wallace Festival, and markets its mission energetically on the Web and in print.

The study doesn't have many windows, but it is topped with a dome and a raised skylight. A Grecian-style frieze runs around the dome and depicts characters from Wallace's novels. A gate emulating one in an old French abbey leads visitors to a tree-shaded area,

note
While in Crawfordsville, be sure to visit the rotating jail at 225 North Washington Street. The two-story structure was constructed on a huge turntable that made the jail cells turn around the guards; that way the guards didn't have to get up to check on them. The jail had to be turned by hand; supposedly, many sheriffs made their wives turn the handle. The last inmates were housed there in 1972; it's now called the Old Jail Museum. Call 765-362-5222 for hours, or visit www.oldjailmuseum.net

Lew Wallace's ornate "study"

and above looms a forty-foot Italian-style tower. Today, the study holds costumes used in the 1959 production of *Ben-Hur*, as well as old cannonballs, swords, and other artifacts of war collected by Wallace. He was also a painter, and the study contains examples of his work that include images of the men who were convicted of assassinating President Abraham Lincoln in the trial over which he presided as a military judge. In 1885, Wallace was sent by President Garfield to Turkey, where he visited many of the places he depicted five years before when writing *Ben-Hur*. He found his descriptions to be accurate in every detail and saw no need to change a single word in his book.

General Lew Wallace Study & Museum
200 Wallace Avenue, Crawfordsville, Indiana 47933
765-362-5769
www.ben-hur.com

▶ *Meredith Nicholson*

Meredith Nicholson (1866–1947) was born in Crawfordsville and traveled extensively throughout the state. The son of a Civil War veteran, he was fascinated by the Civil War and by Indiana—both of which found their way into his books. One of his best-known works is *A Hoosier Chronicle*, published in 1912. He wrote proudly of his home state:

> The Hoosier, pondering all things himself, cares little what Ohio or Illinois may think or do. He ventures eastward to Broadway only to deepen his satisfaction in the lights of Washington or Main Street at home. He is satisfied to live upon a soil more truly blessed than any that lies beyond the borders of his own commonwealth.[8]

▶ Shelbyville

Charles Major (1856–1913) was born in Indianapolis and later moved to Shelbyville. He wrote ten novels in all, most of which described the pioneer period with a focus on the power of nostalgia. The first was published in 1898, and *Rosalie* appeared posthumously in 1925. *The Bears of Blue River* (1901) is entertaining to adults and children alike.

After the remarkable success of his book *When Knighthood Was in Flower* (1898), he retired from his law practice and maintained an office for the sole reason of having a quiet place to write. We should all be so lucky. Today, you'll find the Charles Major Education Center and Charles Education Manor in Shelbyville. There is a historical marker at the site of his home, 38 North Harrison Street.

▶Dana

The Quonset Hut and Ernie Pyle

A Quonset hut is a prefabricated enclosure of galvanized steel and iron that was used widely by the U.S. military during World War II. It's a fitting name for a museum dedicated to the most famous correspondent of that war. Ernie Pyle was born on a farm near Dana in 1900 and studied journalism at Indiana University. Writing from the point of view of the common soldier not only made him beloved by the troops but also won him the Pulitzer Prize in 1944. He was killed by machine gun fire on Ie Shima, an island near Okinawa, on April 18, 1945. It is touching to be able to compare Pyle's boyhood home with an actual Quonset hut and to view some World War II items that are associated with Pyle and others that were donated by members of the community.

Ernie Pyle State Historic Site
P.O. Box 338, 120 West Briarwood Avenue, Dana Inidana 47847-0338
www.in.gov/ism/StateHistoricSites/ErniePyleHome/index.aspx
765-665-3633

The Ernie Pyle State Historic Site is located one mile north of US 36 on IN 71.

I-80/90: From "Hulman" to Wildflower Woods

▶Hammond

If you take the Chicago Skyway out of the big city and head toward Indiana, you'll quickly come to the town of Hammond. Jean Shepherd (1921–1999) was born in Chicago but grew up in Hammond at 2907 Cleveland Street in the Hessville neighborhood. He attended Warren G. Harding Elementary School near his home and graduated from Hammond High School in 1939. Shepherd not only wrote about Hammond in *A Christmas Story* and other books, but he also talked about it extensively on the radio. Shepherd is, in fact, regarded as one of radio's greatest storytellers and entertainers. He hosted "The Jean Shepherd Show" on station WOR in New York for many years. Sometimes his forty-five-minute radio monologues included readings from authors such as Indiana's own George Ade, who lived not far from him.

Jean Shepherd's childhood home in Hammond

At WOR, Shepherd had a devoted following of "Night People" who loved his broadcast. One of his radio pranks was book related: Fed up with what he regarded as a flawed method for choosing best-sellers, he told his listeners to fan out all over the Big Apple, asking bookstores for a book with the title *I, Libertine.* So many requests were made that the book made the *New York Times* Best Seller List. The problem was that the book didn't actually exist. After building word-of-mouth demand, Shepherd found a publisher and invented a story to go along with the book, hiring writer Thomas Sturgeon to create it. He then posed on the back cover as the book's fictitious author, Frederick R. Ewing.

Shepherd also appeared in the movie *A Christmas Story,* which he narrates. He is the man in the department store who tells young Ralphie that the end of the line to see Santa Claus is actually much farther away. The movie was not actually filmed in Hammond and the name of the fictional town is Hulman, but there are references to Harding School (where Ralphie gets his tongue stuck to the flagpole), Cleveland Avenue, and the nearby town of Griffith that make it clear what setting Shepherd had in mind.

Warren G. Harding Elementary School has been rebuilt since Shephard attended.

▶Miller
Nelson Algren and Simone de Beauvoir

The town of Miller is located on Lake Michigan just east of Gary and just west of the Indiana Dunes National Lakeshore. Sometimes, you might hear the town called Miller Beach. Near the beach itself, you find a group of small cottages. Imagine that it is the 1950s, and two of the world's most celebrated writers, Nelson Algren and Simone de Beauvoir, have chosen one of those cottages for a romantic tryst.

Algren was madly in love with the French writer, who was still married to the philosopher Jean-Paul Sartre; he dreamed of one day marrying de Beauvoir, but alas, it never happened. A playwright named John Susman turned their romance into a drama entitled "Nelson and Simone," which was staged by Chicago's Live Bait Theater in 2000.

There is a story that conversations between the two about the plight of women helped de Beauvoir write her most famous book: when de Beauvoir complained that she was having difficulty putting the plight of women into context, Algren suggested that she think about women the same way that white Americans thought about African-Americans. The result was the book, *The Second Sex*, which is considered a seminal work in the feminist movement.

▶Ogden Dunes: Home of "Diana of the Dunes"

A woman named Alice Gray, who became known as "Diana of the Dunes," decided to leave Chicago and live a free life in the Indiana Dunes on the shore of Lake Michigan. She originally lived in an abandoned shack near the town of Miller. Gray was inspired by Lord Byron's poem called "Solitude," which goes:

> To sit on rocks, to muse o'er flood and fell,
> To slowly trace the forest's shady scene,
> Where things that own not man's dominion dwell,
> And mortal foot hath ne'er or rarely been;
> To climb the trackless mountain all unseen,
> With the wild flock that never needs a fold;
> Alone o'er steeps and foaming falls to lean;
> This is not solitude, 'tis but to hold Converse with
> Nature's charms, and view her stores unrolled.

Gray became celebrated in the *Chicago Examiner* and other publications as a free spirit who bathed regularly in the lake and dried herself off by running nude up and down the beach, to the delight of local fishermen. But she did not have complete solitude. She met a man named Paul Wilson who had moved into another shack in the area, and they were eventually married. They lived in a shack called the Wren's Nest at Ogden Dunes.

You can read more about Diana of the Dunes in a wonderful essay by David Hoppe called "Child of the Northwest: Alice Gray and 'Diana of the Dunes.'" You'll find a link to the essay and more information about Alice at www.spicerweb.org/Miller/MillerHistory/DianaoftheDunes.aspx.

▶Chesterton

L. Frank Baum

The interstate highway goes through the charming town of Chesterton at Exit 31. Head north, and you'll reach the Indiana Dunes National Lakeshore. This scenic area is the favored location of many who have summer homes near the lake. L. Frank Baum, the author of *The Wonderful Wizard of Oz* series of books, had a home here as well in the early part of the twentieth century.

Baum may have lived in Chicago when he wrote the early Oz books, but the nearby town of Chesterton celebrates the fact that

L. Frank Baum

Baum once lived here near Lake Michigan. Baum's son, in fact, established the International Wizard of Oz Club in this area. Every fall, the city holds a Wizard of Oz festival. Actors who played the Munchkins in the original Wizard of Oz movie with Judy Garland have attended the festival, which attracts as many as one hundred thousand visitors. At the time I was writing this, the annual Wizard of Oz festival

The Tin Man, one of Baum's most famous creations

was auctioning off dinner with the "Lollipop Kid" and his wife. At any time of year, you can view artifacts from the 1939 movie in the museum. The Wizard of Oz Fantasy Museum and Yellow Brick Road Shop closed December 31, 2008, but the town still holds the Wizard of Oz Festival. For more information on the festival, visit www .ozfestivalchesterton.com and www.yellow brickroadonline.com.

►Warsaw

If you exit I-80-90 around Elkhart and head south toward Goshen, you'll find the highway that leads south to Warsaw. The town of Warsaw was named for the capital of Poland in honor of the Polish-American patriot and Revolutionary War hero Thaddeus Kosciusko and was home to two well-known writers. The nineteenth-century writer and satirist Ambrose Bierce (1842–1914) lived here, as did novelist Theodore Dreiser. Bierce is best-known for his story "An Occurrence at Owl Creek Bridge." He attended Warsaw High School. In his seventies, he joined Pancho Villa's army in Mexico, and disappeared without a trace; his place and date of death are unknown.

Dreiser wrote about Warsaw and the surrounding area vividly in his book *A Hoosier Holiday*. In the book, he recounts a road trip back to Indiana with the artist Franklin Booth made twenty-six

Theodore Dreiser

years after he left the state. His family lived in Warsaw, he says, "in a comparatively large brick house set in a grove of pines."[9] He also wrote of the surrounding countryside:

> In grey or rainy weather the aspect of the whole place was solemn, historic. In snowy or stormy weather, it took on a kind of patriarchal significance. When the wind was high these thick, tall trees swirled and danced in a wild ecstasy. When the snow was heavy they bent low with their majestic plumes of white. Underneath them was a floor of soft brown pine needles as soft and brown as a rug. We could gather basket upon basket of resiny cones with which to start our morning fires.[10]

Dreiser's kind words about Warsaw are surprising, given all that happened to him and his family there. Fleeing Chicago, the Dreisers came to Warsaw to escape debt collectors. On the positive side, Theodore went to school, where he met a young female teacher who encouraged him to read. He fell in love both with the teacher and with books. Was this the person he was referring to when he wrote:

> The first girl who ever kissed me and the first girl I ever ventured to kiss were at Warsaw. Would not that cast a celestial light over any Midwestern village, however homely?[11]

Later, he speaks of the "bevy of attractive girls" who lived in Warsaw. He also delights in revisiting a home where the family lived, remembering:

> In my day there was a bed and a dressing stand and mirror in each of these rooms, quite double the size of the other two, a square reading table of cheap oak by which I used to sit and work at times, getting my lessons. In the main it was a delight to sit here of a hot summer day, looking out on the surrounding world and the trees, and reading betimes. Here I read Shakespeare and a part of Macaulay's "History of England" and Taine's "History of English Literature" and a part of Guizot's "History of France." I was not an omnivorous reader—just a slow, idle, rambling one—but these rooms and these books, and the thought of happy days to come, made it all a wonder world to me. We

had enough to live on. The problem of financing our lives was not as yet distracting me. I longed for a little money, but not much, and life, life, life—all its brilliant pyrotechnic meanings—was before me, still to come.[12]

But his sisters were the subject of scandal: One ran off with a bar employee who had stolen thirty-five hundred dollars from his employer; the other became pregnant as a result of an affair with the son of a wealthy family.

Warsaw was not kind to its famous resident: Dreiser's books were not only banned, but *burned*, by the local library. This was while Dreiser was still alive. Supposedly the trustees objected to the content of the books, which was considered not only obscene but (shudder) leftist. Perhaps they were reacting to Dreiser's 1931 book *Tragic America*, in which he railed against the wealth and power of the church in this country.

▶ Rome City
Gene Stratton-Porter

If you leave I-80/90 at Exit 121 and drive south on IN Highway 9 for about twenty miles, you'll come to Rome City, the second home of the nature writer and novelist Gene Stratton-Porter (1863–1924). The "Cabin in Wildflower Woods," as she called it, is a two-story frame structure with exterior cedar logs situated on the aptly named Sylvan Lake that was built in 1913. Porter moved here from Geneva, Indiana, when her beloved Limberlost Swamp was drained for development. Seeking another quiet, natural refuge, she settled on this area, where she made an extensive garden surrounded by twenty acres of forested wilderness. (The current state historic site now contains 125 acres of land.)

When I visited the home, there weren't many visitors, but the staff was busy preparing for a benefit dinner. By the garden shed, some plants were offered for sale—descendents of the same plants Porter cultivated when she and her family lived here. Porter and her daughter are buried on the site near the writer's favorite oak tree.

Gene Stratton-Porter State Historic Site
1205 Pleasant Point, Rome City, Indiana 46784
260-854-3790
May to November

I-27 from Richmond to Uncle Tom's Refuge

▶Fountain City

In Fountain City, you'll find the Levi Coffin House. Built in 1839 and now a National Historic Landmark, this house was one of the best-known spots on the Underground Railroad. One of the thousands of slaves who traveled through the home on their way to freedom was "Eliza." Her story was told in one of the bestsellers of the nineteenth century, *Uncle Tom's Cabin* by Harriet Beecher Stowe (1811–1896). Chapter eight is entitled "Eliza's Escape." But in the previous chapter she makes her way from one ice floe to another across the Ohio River from Kentucky to Ohio, just south of this area. Eliza eventually wakes up in such a refuge:

> The next morning was a cheerful one at the Quaker house. "Mother" was up betimes, and surrounded by busy girls and boys, whom we had scarce time to introduce to our readers yesterday, and who all moved obediently to Rachel's gentle 'Thee had better,' or more gentle 'Hadn't thee better?' in the work of getting breakfast; for a breakfast in the luxurious valleys of Indiana is a thing complicated and multiform, and, like picking up the rose-leaves and trimming the bushes in Paradise, asking other hands than those of the original mother.[13]

Levi Coffin State Historic Site
P.O. Box 77, 113 US 27 N, Fountain City, Indiana 47341
765-847-2432
www.in.gov/ism/StateHistoricSites/LeviCoffinHome/index.aspx

▶Geneva
Gene Stratton-Porter

If you travel north on US 27, you come to the town of Geneva, which is best known as the site of Limberlost Cabin, the home of writer Gene Stratton-Porter. The cabin was immortalized in books such as *A Girl of the Limberlost* (which was the first American book to be translated into Arabic). Porter has another site near I-80 in the northwest part of the state. But if you are willing to go out of your way, you'll find the place where she was originally inspired to become a naturalist and nature writer. The swamp that she loved is here, and is now known as Loblolly Swamp. A group called Friends of the Limberlost holds guided tours of the cabin and special events around holidays like Halloween and Christmas. The house was built in 1895 of white cedar logs brought from Wisconsin. When the area became developed and the swamp was drained, Porter and her family moved to Rome City, where they built a new home called Wildflower Woods.

Elnora, the girl in the title of *A Girl of the Limberlost*, meets a lady called the Bird Woman, who lives in the swamp near her home. She seems to speak to Elnora in Porter's own voice:

> I have a sneaking impression that the mystery, wonder, and the urge of their pure beauty, are going to force me to picture and paint our moths and put them into a book for all the world to see and know. We Limberlost people must not be selfish with the wonders God has given to us. We must share with those poor cooped-up city people the best we can. To send them a beautiful book, that is the way, is it not, little new friend of mine?[14]

Limberlost Cabin, home of novelist and naturalist Gene Stratton-Porter

Porter wrote many "beautiful books" that celebrate the nature she discovered in the swamp and captured in photos and, later, films. A few examples are *The Song of the Cardinal*, *Music of the Wild*, and *At the Foot of the Rainbow*.

Limberlost State Historic Site
P.O. Box 356, 200 East Sixth Street, Geneva, Indiana 46740
260-368-7428
www.in.gov/ism/StateHistoricSites/Limberlost/index.aspx

▶ Highway 24: Peru and Roann

US Highway 24 is an especially scenic drive through east-central Indiana that follows the Wabash River. In Peru, you can visit the boyhood home of composer Cole Porter.

In Roann, just north of US 24, the Eel River flows south and eventually joins up with the Wabash. The Eel River is mentioned in one of the seminal Indiana books, Ross Lockridge's *Raintree County*:

> Johnny Shawnessy probably had a better guess about the river's name than anyone else as he was the only person in the County for years who made any research into the Indian culture. He finally decided that the river's name was related to the Indian word "Shakamak," meaning long fish or eel. There was a Shakamak River in southern Indiana; and in the northern part of the state, an Eel River, which in the Miami tongue had been called the Kenapocomoko, or River of Snake Fish.

The only drawback to Johnny's theory was the fact that he never found an eel in the Shamucky River.[15]

▶ Highway 41: Vincennes

Maurice Thompson

This historic town on US Highway 41 near the Illinois border dates back to a settlement by the French in 1832. From 1800 to 1813, Vincennes was the capital of the Indiana Territory, the name given to the western part of the Northwest Territory. You can still see the capital here, as well as the birthplace of author Maurice Thompson (1844–1901).

The home where Thompson was born in 1840 looks like it belongs in Vincennes, but it was actually moved here from the Thompson's original birthplace, the town of Fairfield, Indiana. Why was it moved here? In 1900, Thompson wrote a romance novel that became a best seller: *Alice of Old Vincennes*. The novel tells the story of Alice, a French orphan girl who falls in love with one of the members of the expeditionary team led by George Rogers Clark. The novel was so popular that it was turned into a Broadway play, which later toured the nation. At one time Vincennes was given the nickname "Alicetown." If you watch the local high school foot-

Indiana author Maurice Thompson

Maurice Thompson's birthplace

ball team play today, you'll see that they are called the Vincennes Alices.

Thompson wrote other books about Indiana, including *Hoosier Mosaics* (1875), a collection of stories about Indiana small town life. He never actually lived in Vincennes but spent much of his life in Crawfordsville. The house, which was moved to Vincennes in 1846, is now the gift shop for the historic site:

Territorial Capitol State Historic Site
1 West Harrison Street, Vincennes, Indiana 47591
812-882-7422
www.in.gov/ism/StateHistoricSites/CorydonCapitol/index.aspx

►Online Resources
Excellent Web site

www.bsu.edu/ourlandourlit/literature/Authors

Endnotes

1 As mentioned on the Indiana Historical Society Web site (www.indiana history.org/lhs/exhibits/golden.html).

2 Ade, George. *Single Blessedness*, pp. 172–73.

3 Ade, George. *Single Blessedness*, p. 69.

4 Gray, Ralph D. *Indiana History*, p. 196.

5 Quoted in a talk by Ray Boomhower given in 1994 (www.indianahistory.org/pop_hist/people/kv.html).

6 Dreiser, Theodore. *A Hoosier Holiday* (Indiana University Press, 1998), p. 28.

7 Thompson, Maurice. *A Banker of Bankersville* (New York: Street & Smith, 1900), p. 69.

8 Nicholson, Meredith. *A Hoosier Chronicle* (Boston and New York: Houghton Mifflin Company, 1912), p. 7.

9 Dreiser, *A Hoosier Holiday*, p. 14.

10 Dreiser, p. 300.

11 Dreiser, p. 16.

12 Dreiser, p. 311.

13 Stowe, Harriet Beecher, *Uncle Tom's Cabin, Or Life Among the Lowly* (New York: Houghton, Mifflin and Company, 1899), p. 156.

14 Porter, Gene Stratton. *A Girl of the Limberlost* (New York: Grosset & Dunlap, 1909), p. 49.

15 Lockridge, Ross. Raintree County (Boston:Houghton Mifflin, 1948), pp. 93–94.

chapter three

Iowa

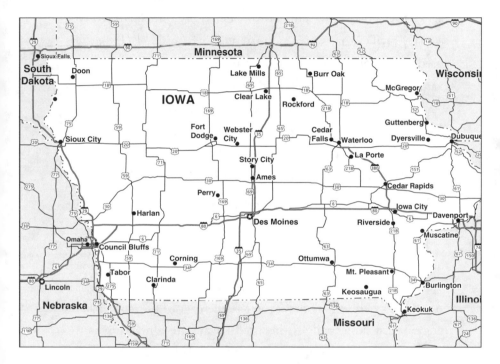

Driving Tours

1. I-80: The Writers and the Bridges
2. I-29: Siouxland and the Twin Sisters with All the Answers
3. I-20: The Field of Dreams Tour
4. Route 52: The House in the Big Woods Tour
5. The Southeast Iowa Tour

"*I*s this heaven? No, it's Iowa." That line from a 1988 film called *Field of Dreams* made the town of Dyersville, Iowa, and a ball diamond built in a cornfield, into a tourist destination (bring your own bat and mitt). On my interstate atlas of the United States, along with caves, museums, state parks, and other monuments, the "Field of Dreams Movie Site" is listed in small red type near Dyersville; that's how popular it still is. *Field of Dreams* was based on the 1982 novel *Shoeless Joe,* by W. P. Kinsella. It's only one example of a literary reference that still plays a role in the state's identity. In the book and the movie, Iowa is a symbol of American values. The landscape and people of the state are intertwined with the plot. Even the nickname of Iowa, the Hawkeye State, is taken from a literary work—it's said to come from the name of the scout, Hawkeye, in the 1826 novel *The Last of the Mohicans,* by James Fenimore Cooper.

If you want to be embraced by your literary kith and kin in Iowa, the obvious draws are university towns such as Ames, hometown of U.S. Poet Laureate Ted Kooser and birthplace of mystery writer Sara Paretsky, as well as the former residence of Pulitzer-Prize-winning novelist Jane Smiley (who used Iowa State University as the basis for her novel *Moo* and the area around Ames as the setting for her novel *A Thousand Acres);* and the world-class Writers' Workshop in Iowa City. But there are plenty of other things to do and places to go among the cows and corn.

I-80: The Writers and the Bridges

The interstate that crosses Iowa and spans the state from the Illinois border on the east to the Nebraska border on the west is a good starting point for driving tours of all sorts. I found this to be a straight, flat, and long drive; I love to break up my own trip by getting off the highway periodically and exploring the hills of the countryside. The sites on this tour are arranged from east to west.

►Muscatine

Muscatine is about fifteen miles south of I-80; take Exit 271 south on IA Highway 38. Like Mark Twain (1835–1910), who lived here with his mother at 109 Walnut in 1853, I love a good sunset. He thought the sunsets he saw during his stay here were peerless. I recommend vistas from either Weed Park or the Wildcat Den State Park.

Or you can try a Japanese garden and sculpture court on the grounds of the Muscatine Art Center. In addition to nineteenth-century American and European art, the art center's collection focuses on the Mississippi River and includes historical artifacts, toys, quilts, musical instruments, and paperweights.

Twain's brother Orion became part-owner of the local paper, the *Muscatine Journal,* in 1853. Twain not only spent quite a few summers in the town but also filed reports with the newspaper as he roamed the country—his first travel writings. Four of these letters are signed with a "W," which may be an abbreviation for one of Twain's early pen names: W. Epaminondas Adrastus Blab.[1]

The Mark Twain National Wildlife Refuge, just south of Muscatine, honors the writer's time in this part of Iowa. There's also a Mark Twain Overlook and a plaque with a quote from Twain in which he praises those aforementioned Muscatine sunsets. It's located just south of downtown at Brook and Second Streets.

Muscatine is also the birthplace of Ellis Parker Butler (1869–1937) at 607 West Third Street. Parker wrote more than thirty books and was best known as a humorist. Butler, in fact, is regarded as one of the most popular authors during the era of pulp fiction. His most successful book was called *Pigs Is Pigs* (1906). Other novels for young people such as *Jibby Jones* (1923) are set in the fictional

Ellis Parker Butler

Riverbank, Iowa, which is based on Muscatine. Although he depicts growing up in Muscatine as an idyllic, Tom Sawyer-type of experience, he still dreamed of leaving his hometown to become a writer. As he later wrote to his daughter:

> In 1896 I was pursuing my literary career, and almost catching up with it, while I sent my manuscripts to New York and sold prunes to Charley Fuller and navy beans to Otto Brothers and sardines and clothespins to Frank Witman. I happened to visit New York with a friend and I asked three editors if they thought I should come to New York. "Are you the fellow who is writing in Iowa and sending your manuscripts to New York?" they asked. "Yes, I am," I said breathlessly. "Then by all means," they said, "do come to New York and send your manuscripts to Iowa."[2]

Nearly every month, Muscatine holds a festival of some sort. If you come the last weekend in July, you can enjoy Great River Days, a three-day community celebration. Heritage Days is held the third weekend in September.

►Iowa City

In the novel *Shoeless Joe*, W. P. Kinsella (1935–) paints a picture of driving into the city from I-80. The narrator is bringing the reclusive writer J. D. Salinger and the onetime baseball player Moonlight Graham back to see the baseball field he has built:

> The deeper we penetrate Iowa, the greener it gets. It has been summer for all my odyssey, but a lean, scanty summer of thin trees and cropped yellow grass. Here, near the heart of the nation, everything is lush: The corn is waist high, the trees, fat-leaved, the grass tall, and the earth soft.
>
> I wheel off the interstate at Exit 244.

If you take this exit just south of Iowa City yourself, you'll be rewarded with lots of literary connections. The nomenclature "Athens of the Midwest" may seem a bit over the top, but it doesn't take long to get immersed in this town's love of literature . . . especially if you're joining the nation's top literary talent for a highly touted public reading. Iowa City attracts would-be writers and famous novelists alike for the Iowa Writers' Workshop, which is part of the University of Iowa.

The workshop was started in 1936 but flouished under the directorship of writer Paul Engle (1908–91), who held the position from 1941 to 1965. (Engle himself is an Iowa native, having been born in 1908 in Cedar Rapids.) It was one of the first schools to pursue the teaching of writing; before this, English teachers usually believed great writers were born, not made. Teachers at the Writers' Workshop have included Robert Frost, John Cheever, Philip Roth, Kurt Vonnegut, Jr., and Robert Penn Warren. (Vonnegut wrote his novel *Slaughterhouse Five* while teaching in the workshop.) Grant Wood, known more for his "American Gothic" painting than his writing, was also on the faculty. Graduates read like a Who's Who of twentieth-century American fiction. They include:

Paul Engle, longtime director of the Iowa Writers' Workshop

- John Irving. There are many University of Iowa references in his novel *The World According to Garp.*
- Mark Strand, former U.S. Poet Laureate
- Flannery O'Connor
- Wallace Stegner
- Jorie Graham
- W. P. Kinsella, author of *Field of Dreams.* He was born in Canada, but studied in the writing program in the late 1970s. His most famous novel, *Shoeless Joe,* was published in 1982. It's obvious the University of Iowa and Iowa City were on his mind as he was writing this book. One character, the narrator's brother, is a professor at the University of Iowa who specializes in the study of the corn weevil. The sofa in the living room of the narrator's house was "plucked from the front lawn of a house in Iowa City."

Like moths to the flame, programs also draw those specializing in international writing, play writing, and literary nonfiction. To celebrate its bookish tradition, the town features the Iowa Avenue Literary Walk, a series of forty-nine bronze panels placed into the concrete sidewalk along Iowa Avenue from Clinton Street to Gilbert Street. Each panel offers a quotation about books and writing from an author connected in some way to the town, including Flannery O'Connnor, Tennessee Williams, W. P. Kinsella, and Gail Godwin.

Other writers have either grown up in Iowa City or lived there. They include Peter Hedges (1962–   ), a playwright (*What's Eating Gilbert Grape*), who currently lives in Iowa City, and Philip Bourjaily, freelance outdoor writer, who was born there.

Most notably, Berkeley Breathed (1957–   ), author of the Pulitzer Prize-winning comic strip Bloom County (which ran from 1980 to 1989), lived in Iowa City when he began drawing the strip, and there are indications that Bloom County is actually Iowa City. One comic character said that Des Moines is just ninety-four miles from Bloom County, for instance. The Bloom Boarding House appeared as a photo within the strip occasionally; the photo is of the Linsay House, 935 East College Street. The Prairie Lights Bookstore was referred to as the Prairie Lights Newsstand. You can view the final Bloom County Strip at the Iowa City Public Library, 123 South Linn Street.

If you never get your fill of readings, check out the schedule at Prairie Lights Books. It's one of the largest independent booksellers to be found anywhere.

▶Amana Colonies

You reach the Amana Colonies by exiting I-80 at Exit 225 and heading north on US 151. In the Amana Heritage Museum, on SR 220 just east of US 151, you will find books related to the settlers of the Amana Colonies who lived communally and worked together in the seven closely united villages that were founded in the mid-1800s. But I won't tell if you only come for the food that is served family-style on steaming platters and heaping bowls, and many other notable products such as furniture, meats, woolens, and wines. Don't leave without a jar of strawberry preserves.

Prairie Lights Books in Iowa City

The Times Club, a cafe on the second floor of Prairie Lights Books

The Amana Heritage Museum

Amana Heritage Museum

4310 220th Trail. Amana, Iowa 52203
319-622-3567
www.amanaheritage.org
Monday through Friday, 9:00 a.m. to 4:00 p.m.

▶Riverside

This small town just south of Iowa City on Route 22 claims to be the home of none other than James T. Kirk, captain of the starship U.S.S. *Enterprise* on the beloved 1960s television show *Star Trek*. In his book *The Making of Star Trek*, Gene Roddenberry (1921–1991) said that Captain Kirk "was born in a small town in the state of Iowa" in the year 2228. A local fan wrote to Roddenberry, who sent a certificate confirming that Riverside was, in fact, the fictional captain's fictional birthplace.[3] Each June an event called Trek Fest is held in Riverside. Visit www.trekfest.com or call 319-648-3672 to find out more.

►Mt. Pleasant/Henry County

Mount Pleasant, which is south of Iowa City on Route 218, is the seat of Henry County. It's also the place where the amazing story of Harry Pidgeon (1869–1954) began. Many of us dream of escaping our everyday life. But when Pidgeon acted on that desire, he eventually became one of the greatest sailors of all time. Born in quiet Henry County in 1869, he was either a farmer or a ranch hand for the first twenty-seven years of his life.

But then he started to travel. Boy oh boy, did he ever travel: He took a raft down the Yukon River in Alaska. He became a photographer in the Sierra Nevada Mountains. He built his own boat, which he called the Islander, from plans he found in a book in a local library. He took a test trip to Catalina and then to Hawaii. Once there, he decided to keep going. He sailed around the world single-handed, a trip that took four years. He repeated this feat in 1932.

His adventures in the South Sea Islands were vividly recounted in his memoir *Around the World Single-Handed.*

►Des Moines

Here's an excuse to read a cute kids book. Lori Erickson based *Sweet Corn and Sushi: The Story of Iowa and Yamanashi* on a friendship between Iowa and Japan that began in 1960. An Iowan who had served in the military in Japan spearheaded a bequest of thirty-five pigs and fifteen hundred tons of corn to help Japan rebuild its agricultural industry after two devastating typhoons. As a way to say thanks, the people of Yamanashi sent to Iowa a two-thousand-pound bell that is similar to those found in Japanese temples. You can see the bell in real life at the Iowa State Capitol, East Ninth and Grand, or take a "virtual tour" at www.legis.state.ia.us/Pubinfo/Tour and click on the Capitol Grounds section.

If you didn't get enough of the Gutenberg Bible in Guttenberg (see entry later in this section), you can look at a page of the real thing at the Salisbury House. There are thirty-five hundred volumes in the library, as well as a copy of *The Kelmscot Chaucer* produced by William Morris in 1896. Charles Weeks, who was born on a farm in 1876 and made a fortune manufacturing cosmetics, was into Tudor England in a big way, as you'll be able to surmise as you enjoy the furnishings of his home and other art objects he collected.

Salisbury House
4025 Tonawanda Drive, Des Moines, Iowa 30312
515-274-1777
www.salisburyhouse.org
March 1–December 31
Tuesday through Friday and Sunday, 1:00 p.m. and 2:30 p.m.

▶The Bridges of Madison County
The Novel

If you ask someone to name a literary work involving Iowa, the first book they mention is likely to be *The Bridges of Madison County*. Written in 1992, it became a film starring Clint Eastwood and Meryl Streep in 1995. More than a decade after the movie was released, the Madison County area still lures tourists who want to visit the real-life bridges described in the story.

First, let me introduce the author: Robert James Waller was born in 1939 in Rockford, Iowa, a small town of nine hundred inhabitants on the banks of the Shellrock and Winnebago Rivers. He was educated at the University of Iowa, the University of Northern Iowa, and Indiana University. His father operated a produce business, and his mother was a housewife. He wasn't always a writer. In fact, he is a man of many talents. He was the dean of the University of Northern Iowa's College of Business from 1979 to 1986. He is also a singer, having played nightclubs and concerts for twenty years. And he is an avid photographer.

As a business school professor, Waller lectured on problem solving and other topics. Why did he became a writer? As he explained in an interview: [4]

> Though I periodically had tried writing fiction, nothing ever came of it. But after visiting the covered bridges in Madison County, Iowa, toting my cameras on a rainy summer day, something happened I cannot explain, and the story formed. Driving homeward to northern Iowa, the story took on more and more detail. I dropped my gear just inside the front door, went to my computer, and began writing the book. It was, in a phrase, given to me.

When he started writing novels in the 1990s, his life changed. He has used the state liberally as a backdrop for his novels. His book

The Bridges of Madison County has sold twelve million copies to date. It tells the story of a love affair between a wandering photographer and an Iowa housewife. In another Iowa-based novel, *Slow Waltz in Cedar Bend*, Waller describes another love affair that turns out differently than the one in *Bridges*. The protagonist, like Waller, is a professor, but the university in the book is "Cedar Bend," rather than Waller's own Cedar Falls. Today, Waller lives on a remote ranch in the high desert of Texas.

▸The Bridges

If you want to discover the bridges of Madison County for yourself, you'll be happy to know six of the original nineteen bridges still remain. All are listed on the National Register of Historic Places. The bridges were originally covered to help preserve the large timbers that pave them, which would be more expensive to replace than the roof. The following three bridges have connections to the novel:

- The Roseman Bridge, built in 1883, is the one the novel's protagonist, Robert Kincaid, is trying to find when he stops at Francesca Johnson's house for directions. She leaves a note, inviting him to dinner, at this bridge. Take Route 92 out of Winterset, heading west, to find it.
- The Holliwell Bridge, built in 1880, appears in the movie. It's just southeast of town on G50.
- The Cedar Bridge, built in 1883, is depicted on the cover of the novel. It's where Francesca goes to meet Robert Kincaid to help

Hogback Bridge

Cedar Bridge

him take photographs. You can find this bridge just north of town on G4R.

The center of the area is Winterset, which hosts a Covered Bridge Festival each October. Or you can get your scenic overlook from a limestone ridge in Pammel State Park. You'll find a map leading to the bridges and other sites related to the novel at www .madisoncounty.com/Map.html.

Getting back to civilization there's a Madison County Historical Museum (815 South Second Street) that's really more of a village, with more than a dozen nineteenth-century buildings on an eighteen-acre site.

And you won't want to miss the house at 216 South Second Street that has been restored to its appearance when John Wayne was born in it in 1907. Lots of his photographs and plenty of memorabilia from his movie career are on display, such as the eye patch from the movie *True Grit*.

John Wayne Birthplace, Winterset, Iowa

Birthplace of John Wayne
216 South Second Street, Winterset, Iowa 50273
515-462-1044
www.johnwaynebirthplace.org
Open seven days a week
10:00 a.m. to 4:30 p.m.

▶Perry

Perry is a manufacturing town in an agricultural region that's all about acknowledgment. Its Carnegie Library Museum (1123 Willis Avenue) is an homage to the public library system, a celebration of books and the places people have gathered to read them in small town America for decades. Next to the museum's store you'll find Soumas Court, an outdoor relaxation area that includes the Wall of Witnesses, which honors key citizens of Perry, such as librarian Flora Bailey. For more information on the museum, call 515-465-7713.

To get a glimpse of Perry's past, you can visit the Dallas County Forest Park Museum and Arboretum just south of SR 141 on K

Avenue. Or you can immerse yourself in history big time by going to www.hometownperryiowa.org, where the lives of Perry residents have been preserved in the form of twelve thousand photographs, five hundred interviews, decades of census data, architectural information on buildings and homes, and other text.

Perry also has a civilized place to not only get a good cup o' tea but also to reflect on the appropriateness of its name: the Thymes Remembered Tea Room and Calico Shop.

Thymes Remembered Tea Room and Calico Shop
1020 Otley Avenue, Perry, Iowa 50220
515-465-2631
www.thymesrememberedtearoom.com
January 1–May 31
10:00 a.m. to 4:00 p.m.
June 1–December 31
10:00 a.m. to 5:00 p.m.

▶ Corning

If you're a fan of late-night television, make a pilgrimage to the roots of one of the giants of the medium by taking Exit 70 off I-80 and driving south for about twenty miles on IA Highway 148. You come to the small town of Corning, which is where Johnny Carson was born on October 23, 1925. At this writing, the small house where he was born is being restored and turned into a museum. Carson hosted *The Tonight Show* for thirty years. He never wrote an autobiography, but you can read about him in books such as *Johnny Come Lately* by Fred De Cordova and *Here's Johnny! My Memories of Johnny Carson, The Tonight Show, and 46 Years of Friendship*, by Ed McMahon.

Tours of Carson's house at 500 13th Street are available by appointment only; call 641-322-5229 for more information.

▶ Harlan/Shelby County

Harlan is on US Highway 59 about ten miles north of I-80 at Exit 40. Shelby County is the birthplace of writer Paul Frederick Corey, who was born on a 160-acre farm in Shelby County in 1903. Corey's father died when he was only two, leaving his wife and children to struggle to keep the farm going. Corey began his education in a one-room schoolhouse but went on to graduate from the University of Iowa in 1925. He published novels, magazine and newspaper articles, and other writing throughout this career but was best known—and is best remembered—for the Mantz trilogy of novels about farm life: *Three Miles Square* (1939), *The Road Returns* (1940), and *County Seat* (1941). The novels follow an Iowa farm family named the Mantzes who struggle to maintain farm life amid the rapid industrialization of the early twentieth century. Corey died in 1992.

►Clarinda

If you've been driving through the Iowa countryside visiting Johnny Carson's home and other sites and you need a quick book fix, head to Clarinda. This town at the intersection of US Highway 71 and IA Highway 2 has a bookstore I highly recommend. Vaughn's Books has delighted readers of all ages on the scenic town square since 1981. Clarinda is the birthplace of Norman Maclean (1902), author of *A River Runs Through It*, and swing-era bandleader Glenn Miller. Each June the sixteen-hundred-member Glenn Miller Birthplace Society has four days of entertainment featuring musical groups from across the country.

Vaughn's Books
114 East Washington Street, Clarinda, Iowa 51632
712-542-2390

►Tabor

This town in the southwest corner of the state was a center of the abolitionist movement in the nineteenth century when John Brown kept a storehouse of weapons here. Brown met in Tabor with other abolitionists to plot his raid on Harpers Ferry.

Tabor is also the model for the town of Gilead, the setting for Marilynne Robinson's (1943–   ) 2004 novel of the same name. Gilead is portrayed as a small, secluded town, and the book tells the story of the Reverend John Ames, an elderly pastor who is dying of a heart condition. The character's grandfather is based on the real-life John Todd, who was also an abolitionist. Robinson vividly describes Iowa country life in passages such as this:

> But one afternoon a storm came up and a gust of wind hit the henhouse and lifted the roof right off, and hens came flying out, sucked after it, I suppose, and also just acting like hens.

I-35: From the Music Man to the Poet's Town

Just as I-80 crosses Iowa from east to west, I-35 transects it from north to south. Most of the sites on this tour are clustered north of Des Moines.

▸Ames

This city of about fifty-thousand residents is well known as the home of Iowa State University and the Ames Straw Poll, which plays a role in the Republican Party presidential nomination process every four years.

Ames has also been home to several notable American writers. Neal Stephenson (1959–), who grew up in the town and who is known for his works of speculative fiction such as *The System of the World* and *Quicksilver*. U.S. Poet Laureate Ted Kooser (1939–) was born in Ames and attended Iowa State University.

Ames was also the birthplace in 1947 of mystery writer Sara Paretsky, who created the V. I. Warshawski series of mysteries. She spent her childhood in Lawrence, Kansas, however, and her experiences there influenced her fourteenth novel in the series, *Bleeding Kansas*.

Jane Smiley's novel *A Thousand Acres* is set in late-1970s Iowa, on a thousand-acre farm that is part of a compound of farms. Smiley moved to Iowa in 1973. The story is based on Shakespeare's *King Lear*, and Smiley was also influenced by a book by Barry Commoner about the poisoning of groundwater. She says as she drove from Minneapolis to Ames—looking at the gloomy, flat, dark winter landscape—she decided to set the novel there. In a later interview with the BBC she recalled, "I said, oh, this is where I should set it." The fictional setting is Zebulon County, Iowa. The Iowa landscape is not only part of the story but an integral part of the characters as well. The father-farmer Laurence Cook is described as follows:

> He was never dwarfed by the landscape. The fields, the buildings, the white pine wind break were as much my father as if he had grown them and shed them like a husk. Trying to understand my father had always felt something like going to church week after week and listening to the minister. . . marshal the evidence for God's goodness or omniscience, or whatever.

▶Clear Lake

This town is probably best known as the place "Where the Music Died." February 3, 1959, a small plane crashed, killing Buddy Holly, Ritchie Valens, and J.P. "The Big Bopper" Richardson. The term "The Day the Music Died" became part of our culture after Don McLean released the song "American Pie" in 1971.

On a more positive note, Clear Lake is also the site of the Iowa Storytelling Festival each July, when yarns are spun in Clear Lake City Park.

▶Story City

I love the name of this town; you can probably figure out why. Iowa's oldest continually running theater and only operating antique carousel are located in Story City. Not only that, but each September the town puts its name to good use by hosting its own storytelling festival that continues to grow in popularity.

> Mason City
> "Trouble, oh we got trouble,
> Right here in River City!
> Trouble with a capital "T"
> That rhymes with "P"
> And that stands for pool"

That song from the musical *The Music Man* refers to a fictional Iowa town called River City. But River City is actually Mason City, the hometown of the author-composer of *The Music Man*, Meredith Willson (1902–1984). Willson was an orchestra leader who was active in radio shows in the 1940s and 1950s. He describes the trials involved in getting *The Music Man* produced in a memoir called *But He Doesn't Know the Territory.* (The title is taken from one of the songs in *The Music Man.*)

Willson, in fact, did know the territory depicted in the musical and movie. His boyhood home is at 314 South Pennsylvania Avenue (tours available). He played flute and piano in local bands, and graduated from Mason City High School in 1919. He wrote about growing up in Iowa in a memoir titled *And There I Stood with My Piccolo* (1948). The Broadway composer Frank Loesser was reportedly so amused by Willson's stories of Iowa that he suggested they be turned into a musical. Willson wasn't always sympathetic in his depiction of the community where he grew up. The song "Iowa Stubborn" was obviously not written by the tourism bureau with lines such as, "So what the heck, you're welcome, glad to have you with us, even though we may not ever mention it again."

Nevertheless, the town celebrates Willson with The Music Man Square, which features a statue of Willson dressed as a bandleader and a museum displaying memorabilia of Willson's career. The square, located at 308 S. Pennsylvania Avenue, also features performers dressed in period costumes strolling around like the characters in the movie. You can find out more at www.themusicman square .org or by calling 866-228-6262.

The town also boasts the largest concentration of Prairie School and Frank Lloyd Wright architecture outside of Wright's hometown, Oak Park, Illinois. The Park Inn Hotel and City National Bank in downtown Mason City were his work.

▶Rockford

Robert James Waller, the author of *The Bridges of Madison County*, was born here in 1939. The city is located at the confluence of the Shell Rock and Winnebago Rivers. Waller followed the Shell Rock to Cedar Falls, where he became the dean of the School of Business at the University of Northern Iowa before becoming a bestselling author. The river has been important to Waller; in 2008 he gave a talk called "What the River Has Taught Me" to Project AWARE, an environmental group dedicated to cleaning up Iowa's rivers.

▶Lake Mills

Wallace Stegner (1909–1993), called the "Dean of Western Writers," was born here, though the family moved to Montana when he was very young. Stegner won the Pulitzer Prize for his book *Angle of Repose* in 1972 and was revered as a writing teacher at Stanford University.

I-29: Siouxland and the Twin Sisters with All the Answers

This highway roughly follows the Missouri River as it traces the western border of Iowa. Here, you can learn about a number of notable American women writers, as well as the author who gave the name "Siouxland" to this area.

▶Sioux City

Esther "Eppie" Pauline Friedman Lederer (1918–2002), who wrote a syndicated advice column under the name Ann Landers, was born in Sioux City on July 4, 1918. She became a fixture in American society for decades as people wrote seeking advice for personal problems. She was known for a sharp, direct, no-nonsense style.

But that's not all. The other great advice columnist of her time, Abigail Van Buren or "Dear Abby," was born in Sioux City as Pauline "Popo" Esther Friedman on July 4, 1918. The twins not only competed against one another professionally, but also had a stormy personal relationship.

▶Doon

Frederick Manfred (1912–1994) was the pen name for Frederick Feikema, who was born in this small town in the northwest part of the state about fifty miles north of Sioux City. He is perhaps best known for coining the term "Siouxland" to describe the area around Sioux City. A prolific writer, he published many novels, some of them set in Iowa, such as *This Is the Year* (1947), a classic Midwestern farm novel.

▶Hawarden

Hawarden is the birthplace of Iowa writer Ruth Suckow (1892–1960). Suckow is one of those regional writers who are virtually forgotten by the public at large, but who are fondly remembered and celebrated by a dedicated group of literary enthusiasts in the area she wrote about. In 1992, for instance, the Ruth Suckow Memorial Association (www.ruthsuckow.org) hosted activities in seven Iowa cities to celebrate the centenary of her birth. A new play, *Just Suppose*, brought Suckow to life.

Ruth Suckow was the daughter of a Congregational minster who served towns around Iowa. Many of her books are set in Iowa, and she has been called "the Willa Cather of Iowa." Her first novel, *Country People* (1924), describes the life of German farmers. She is known for her stark and honest view of life in the Midwest. Her collection of sixteen short stories, *Iowa Interiors,* is considered one of the best books about life in Iowa. You can find out more about her at the Ruth Suckow House in Hawarden, which she affectionately called the "prairie house with the long windows." This house, originally at 1022 Central Avenue, was moved to Calliope Village in Hawarden in 2000. There is also a Ruth Suckow Park and Ruth Suckow Memorial Library located in Earlville, Iowa, where she lived from 1920 to 1926.

I-20: The Field of Dreams Tour

▶ Dyersville

Dyersville is associated with the novel *Shoeless Joe* and the 1989 film *Field of Dreams* because the movie was filmed at the century-old Lansing farm in the area. The Iowa Film Board persistently lobbied to have the movie filmed there, and the baseball diamond depicted in the movie is preserved and open to the public. Today, the adage "They Will Come" still applies; people from all over the world have migrated to the baseball field. Admission is free.

Field of Dreams Movie Site
28995 Lansing Road, Dyersville, Iowa 52040
888-875-8404
April through November
9 a.m. to 6 p.m.
www.fieldofdreamsmoviesite.com

▶ Cedar Falls

How would you like to be able to say that you sold everything you ever wrote? That's a claim that could be made by Bess Streeter Aldrich (1881–1954), who was born in Cedar Falls and created strong female characters before the advent of "Chick Lit." Among her nine novels, *Song of Years* is most closely based on the early history of Cedar Falls, which was then called Sturgis Falls. A park in Cedar Falls is named for her, and there are plenty of other things to see in this area. You can learn more about her at www.bessstreeteraldrich.org.

But Aldrich's is not the only literary legacy in town. Robert Waller, author of *Bridges of Madison County,* lived in Cedar Falls.

See the Madison County section for more about him. Cedar Falls is also the birthplace (in 1919) of writer Ronald Verlin (R. V.) Cassill. Cassill (1919–2002) is the author of many novels, including *Labors of Love* (1980) and *Clem Anderson* (1961), as well as numerous short stories. He also was an influential teacher of writing at a number of universities and through his instructional book, *Writing Fiction* (1975).

The arts are still thriving in Cedar Falls. Among half a dozen museums and several arts centers are those operated by the University of Northern Iowa.

▶ Waterloo

Mona Van Duyn (1921–2004) was born in Waterloo but grew up in the small town of Eldora, Iowa, (population thirty-two hundred) where she developed a love for reading and writing at an early age, affinities not often shared by her classmates. In a 1991 interview she recalled a typical punishment in her small Iowa grade school: "One was made to stay after school and learn a poem." She received an M.A. from the University of Iowa. In 1959, Van Duyn published her first book of poems, *Valentines to the Wide World*. She achieved fame in the literary world when she won the National Book Award for Poetry with the collection *To See, To Take*. She also received the Pulitzer Prize for Poetry in 1991 for *Near Changes*.

▶ Grundy County

The Grundy County area just south of I-20 and west of Cedar Falls was the birthplace of Iowa writer John Herbert Quick (1861–1925). To be more precise, Quick was born on a farm near the town of Steamboat Rock. He suffered from polio as a child. He worked as an editor, teacher, and school principal, and was even the mayor of Sioux Falls from 1898 to 1900.[5] His 1922 novel, *Vandemark's Folly*, is considered a classic of Iowa literature. It is set in fictional Monterey County, Iowa:

> Vandemark Township and Monterey County, as any one may see by looking at the map of Iowa, had to be reached from Wisconsin by crossing the Mississippi at Dubuque and then fetching across the prairie to the journey's end;

and in 1855 a traveler making that trip naturally fell in with a good many of his future neighbors and fellow-citizens pressing westward with him to the new lands.

Some were merely hunting country, and were ready to be whiffed off toward any neck of the woods which might be puffed up by a wayside acquaintance as ignorant about it as he. Some were headed toward what was called "the Fort Dodge country," which was anywhere west of the Des Moines River. Some had been out and made locations the year before and were coming on with their stuff; some were joining friends already on the ground; some had a list of Gardens of Eden in mind, and meant to look them over one after the other until a land was found flowing with milk and honey, and inhabited by roast pigs with forks sticking in their backs and carving knives between their teeth.[6]

▸Webster City

This is the birthplace of Benjamin McKinlay Kantor (1904–1977), who wrote under the name MacKinlay Kantor. He started out his career as a reporter after high school with the *Webster City Daily News* and later for the *Cedar Rapids Republican.* Kantor wrote in many genres: autobiography, articles, novels, and short stories. His best-known work is a Civil War novel, *Andersonville* (1955), which won the Pulitzer Prize. Many of Kantor's novels, such as *The Voice of Bugle Ann* (1935), celebrate Midwesterners living decent lives that are focused on respect for the land. In *Midnight Lace* (1948), a young woman moves from Chicago to live a simple life in rural Iowa. He turned his novel *Glory for Me* into the screenplay for the movie *The Best Years of Our Lives.*

In Burnside, a small town southwest of Webster City, the Pulitzer Prize-winning author and journalist Clark R. Moellenhoff was born in 1922. Mollenhoff also served briefly as special counsel to President Richard M. Nixon. He won the Pulitzer in 1958 for his reporting on influence peddling and wrongdoing in government. He graduated from Webster City Junior College in 1941 and one of his early jobs as a reporter was with the *Des Moines Register.*

►La Porte

This small town on Route 218 just south of Waterloo features a curiosity called the Future Farmers of America Agricultural Museum. This museum contains an amazing book among its carriages, hay forks, and other antique farm implements. It's a haberdashery catalog found in the walls of a local home while it was being renovated. The book was transformed by a local woman into a striking work of art: she pasted postcards and illustrations from magazines into the book's pages.

Future Farmers of America Agricultural Museum
416 Main Street, La Porte City, Iowa 50651
319-342-3619
Saturdays and Sundays
1:00 to 4:00 p.m. or by appointment

►Fort Dodge

Thomas Heggen was born here in 1918. His story eerily parallels that of Ross Lockeridge, the author of the novel *Raintree County* (see the Indiana chapter), a parallel explored in John Leggett's 1974 dual biography titled *Ross and Tom*. Both achieved success around the same time, and both died too young.

Heggen served in the U.S. Navy during World War II, and he turned his experiences into short stories that were woven into a novel titled *Mister Roberts*, which quickly became popular. The novel was adapted for the stage, where it became an even bigger hit and won a Tony Award in 1948. Although Heggen achieved great success with the Broadway play, he found himself unable to follow up with a second novel, and under the pressure, he became addicted to barbiturates and alcohol. He was found dead in his bathtub in 1949; his death was ruled a probable suicide. In 1955, *Mister Roberts* became a hit movie starring Henry Fonda, James Cagney, and Jack Lemmon.

Route 52: The House in the Big Woods Tour

This scenic tour takes you to sites in the northeast part of the state, just south of Minnesota and west of Illinois.

▶Guttenberg

After enjoying the scenery of the rolling countryside on US 52 (otherwise known as the Great River Road), you'll find yourself nestled between high bluffs and the Mississippi River and know you've arrived in Guttenberg. You can impress your fishing friends by visiting the Fishery Management Station, Fish Hatchery, and Aquarium (five blocks east of US 52 on River Park Drive) that features thirty-five species of fish native to the Mississippi River basin, as well as a freshwater mussel display.

But to wow the book lovers among you, I suggest a visit to the local library (603 South Second Street) to sneak a peak at a Gutenberg Bible facsimile. (The town of Guttenberg was originally named after Johann Gutenberg, the inventor of movable type. However, in 1848, an error in the spelling was made on the second plat of the city, and, for whatever reason, the town's name was left as Guttenberg—with two ts.) Printed in 1913–1914, this Bible facsimile was purchased from the Johannes Gutenberg Print Shop in Mainz, Germany, after World War II. This two-volume set of an edition of 310 facsimile sets was reproduced using modern printing methods. This facsimile set was on display in the Gutenberg Print Shop in

The Guttenberg library's Gutenberg Bible facsimile

Mainz, Germany, during an air attack on August 12, 1942, and as a result, the covers and some pages were damaged by fire and water. However, it was decided not to rebind the set or trim the burned portions because the fact that the set survived the bombing was an important part of its history.

Guttenberg Public Library
603 South Second Street, Guttenberg, Iowa 52082
563-252-3108

▶ McGregor

If you are driving on US Highway 52, this town with a population of less than one thousand is definitely worth a stop. Paper Moon Books & Beyond is a bookstore operated by Jennifer and Louise White, a mother/daughter team, with the assistance of resident cats.

Beyond the bookstore, McGregor still has always had something for everybody. French explorers Marquette and Joliet stopped by in 1673 and Zebulon Pike visited in 1805. In the state park named for the later explorer (Pikes Peak State Park), you can see fossils in sandstone and limestone walls and American Indian effigy mounds. You can no longer attend a penny circus held by the five young Ringlings in their backyard, but you can board an electrically powered boat for a guided tour of the underground river cavern in Spook Cave. The River Junction Trade Company offers remnants of Hollywood movie sets and reproductions of nineteenth-century dry goods. The Twisted Chicken Restaurant is run by Kim Hayes, a former sound recording artist who made documentaries. The White Springs Night Club is a 1950s road house.

Paper Moon Books and Beyond
206 A Street, McGregor, Iowa 52157
563-873-3357

▶ Dubuque

David Rabe, playwright and screenwriter, was born here in 1940. He graduated from Loras College, a small Catholic college in Dubuque, and went on to study theater at Villanova University. He wrote the play and screenplay for *Hurlyburly*, and the film version of John Grisham's novel *The Firm*.

If you pass through Dubuque in mid-June, you can enjoy the three-day America's River Festival on the banks of the Mississippi. If you're interested in calligraphy, fine paper, letterpress, and other aspects of "slow printing," take a class at Dubuque Book Arts (www.exquisiteletterpress.com).

▶ Burr Oak

Laura Ingalls Wilder and her family lived and worked in a local hotel for only a part of a year (1876–1877), but that's enough for you to join the stream of travelers who have spent at least a night in Burr Oak. Conveyances of your predecessors were likely to have been less comfortable than your car, as Burr Oak was founded in 1851 on the stagecoach line and the covered wagon trail going north and south across Iowa.

The Ingalls family, saddened by the loss of their son, moved on to Burr Oak, where Pa's friend Mr. Steadman had purchased a hotel. The family lived in the hotel (called the Masters Hotel), and Ma and Pa helped the Steadmans manage it. They did not like the work, and moved first to some rented rooms over a grocery, and then to a little brick house outside of town. The family's last child, Grace, was born in Burr Oak on May 23, 1877. The family was homesick for their friends in Walnut Grove, so they returned in the summer of 1877.

If you're a *Little House on the Prairie* fan, you'll love looking at the author's personal belongings and be very impressed that the restored eleven-room Masters Hotel building, now a museum, is believed to be her only childhood home that remains on its original site. Be sure to visit the cemetery on the hill, where Laura and her friend Alice Ward often walked to escape from the busy town. A guide will point out the significance of other period furnishings, and after your tour you can picnic on the grounds. Hours vary depending on the season, but it's open all year.

Laura Ingalls Wilder Park and Museum
3603 236th Avenue (US 52), Burr Oak, Iowa 52101
563-735-5916
www.lauraingallswilder.us

The Southeast Iowa Tour

Rivers not only mark the physical landscape of the southeast corner of Iowa, but they strongly affected the lives of the writers who lived there. The most illustrious literary figure by far was Mark Twain.

▶ Burlington

Naturalist Aldo Leopold (1886–1948) was born on Clay Street in Burlington. You can find out more about him in the Wisconsin chapter.

Louella Parsons (1881–1972), inventor of the gossip column, lived on North Hill in Burlington after she was married at age seventeen to real estate agent John Parsons. She hated small town life, which might have played a role in the marriage's demise in 1914. Parsons, who was born Louella Rose Oettinger, left Burlington and moved to Chicago, where she began writing the first gossip column about the film industry.

▶ Keokuk

Looking for a side trip to cure cabin fever? Winter is the best time to watch bald eagles that perch in trees along the Mississippi River and pluck fish from the currents. And in December, festive displays and one-hundred thousand lights transform Rand Park into the "City of Christmas." The downside is that the George M. Verity Riverboat Museum, housed in a steamboat built in 1927, closes for the season. When rivers were the main means of transportation, Keokuk was called the "gate city," not only for Iowa, but also for the North and West, due to its location at the foot of the Des Moines rapids, which prevented steamboats from moving farther up the river. Passengers and goods had to be unloaded and either go by barge over the rapids or on land.

But any time is a good time to visit the Mark Twain Center housed in the Keokuk Public Library. Mark Twain lived here from 1854 to 1856 with his mother, just before he left home to work on the Mississippi riverboats. He wrote some comic letters for the *Keokuk Saturday Post* under the name Thomas Jefferson Snodgrass. He worked in Keokuk in a print shop when a young man. He gave his first after-dinner speech at the Hawkeye Hotel at Second and Main.

Many of Twain's possessions and a collection of his works are proudly displayed in the public library. While working in the printing shop of his brother Orion, he set most of the type for the city's first directory. In it, he listed himself as an antiquarian, explaining that every town should have one and nobody else had applied for the post.

After visiting the center, walk a few blocks northeast to the home of Samuel Freeman Miller, Iowa's first U.S. Supreme Court Justice, which is maintained as a museum. If you don't mind hoofing it a little more, there's a self-guided walking tour of some thirty other houses that were built at the turn of the last century.

Keokuk was important during the Civil War because there were several hospitals that cared for the wounded transported via the Mississippi River from southern battlefields. If you're lucky, you'll be here when a Civil War reenactment of the Battle of Pea Ridge is being staged.

▶Keosauqua

The name Keosauqua means "great bend," a reference to the loop the Des Moines River takes around the town. Before there were bridges, it was an important place to cross the river. The Mormons did just that on their westward trek in the 1840s, and Keosauqua was also an important stop on the Underground Railroad. There's nothing left of a prehistoric American Indian village that was located here, but there are many noteworthy Georgian and Greek Revival structures left to admire. A hotel built by Edwin Manning at 100 Van Buren Street to overlook the river is a noteworthy example of Steamboat Gothic architecture. T. S. Eliot signed the hotel register on September 13, 1919.

Keosauqua is the birthplace of Phil Stong (1899–1957), the prolific author of more than forty books, the best known of which is *State Fair*, a 1932 novel that was turned into no less than three musicals. The most famous version was the 1945 Rodgers and Hammerstein musical that included songs such as "It Might as Well Be Spring."

This story about the Frake Family is set at the Iowa State Fair in the late 1920s. Stong himself grew up on a farm here that had been in his family for nearly a century.

▶Ottumwa

Northwest on the Des Moines River from Keosauqua, in Ottumwa, you'll find one of the longest-running independent bookstores in the state. Kevin and Gina Throckmorton provide refreshments as well as books at Chapters Books & Coffee. You'll also enjoy visiting a nearby indie bookstore, Riddles Books & Coffee.

Chapters Books & Coffee
1141 North Quincy Avenue, Ottumwa, Iowa 52501
641-682-1330

Riddles Books & Coffee
2110 North Court Street, Ottumwa, Iowa 52501
641-682-3060

Ottumwa also is known for being the fictional hometown of Corporal Radar O'Reilly on the classic TV show M*A*S*H, based on the 1968 book by Richard Hooker (1924–1997), the pseudonym of writer H. Richard Hornberger.

Endnotes

1   "Mark Twain's contributions to the *Muscatine Journal*," www .twainquotes.com/Muscatine/muscatine.html.

2   Chapin, Henry B. "Lighting Out for the Territory Back East: Ellis Parker Butler, American Humorist," Books at Iowa 37: November 1982.

3   Coffey, Dan, Eric Jones, Berit Thorkelson. *Iowa Curiosities* (Morris Book Publishing, 2005), 99.

4   Reading Group Guides. *A Thousand Country Roads*. www.reading groupguides.com/guides3/thousand_country_roads2.asp.

5   *Dictionary of Midwestern Literature*, p. 424.

6   Quick, Herbert. *Vandemark's Folly* (Indianapolis: The Bobbs-Merrill Company, 1922), 114.

chapter five

Michigan

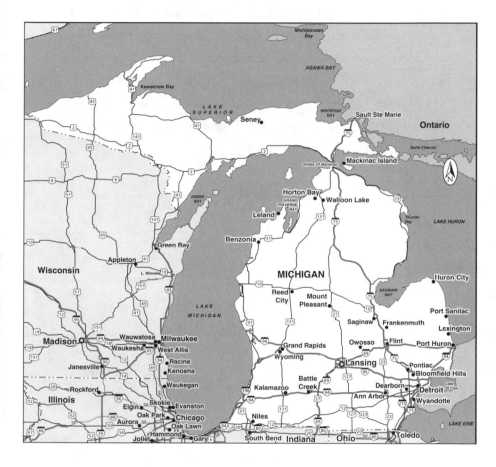

Driving Tours

1. I-94: From the Motor City to Ring's City
2. I-75 North to Bay City: Greaseballs and Greenhouses
3. I-96 Around the Lake: Wineries, Wooden Shoes, and Writers
4. I-69/75 North to Mackinac Island: As Good as It Gets!

Michigan **137**

Ready for fun in the sun? Pack up snacks, a floppy hat, and the latest page turner and head for the sandy beaches that line the Great Lakes. They provide the climate and access to world markets that have made Michigan significant in agriculture and industry. But what about the arts? Your lazy days along Michigan's waterways will more than likely turn into activity that is creative as well as recreational. Some of the names that put Michigan on the literary map are Ernest Hemingway, Bruce Catton, Elmore Leonard, Robert Traver, Theodore Roethke, Marge Piercy, and Joyce Carol Oates. The scenic view you'll get from your site of literary significance is a special bonus.

I-94: From the Motor City to Ring's City

I-94 can speed you from one shore to the other in less than five hours. But what's your big hurry? Because I'm a member of a Buddhist group headquartered in Ann Arbor, I've gone this route more times than I'd care to count. Yet each time I arrive home far later than I'd expected, usually having purchased an antique, book, or non-franchise meal.

▶ Detroit

> The grayness and the grit
> the dirty, funny, hard-hearing city,
> home of grease-caked hands
> and the baddest right hook you've ever seen.

—B. P. Flanigan, "Freeway Series"

Less a big city than a federation of ethnic villages bound together by auto plants, a place with more basements and bowling alleys than any other metropolis in the country.

▶ Ze'ev Chafets, *Devil's Night, and Other True Tales of Detroit*

These excerpts promote the traditional image of Detroit as a gritty, working-class city. But there's more to the Motor City than, um, motors. For a more bucolic view of the area, look to the poetry of Judith Minty (1937–). She was born in Detroit and spent summers there. Her poem "A Sense of Place" from the 1975 collection *Lakesongs and Other Fears* is very evocative of Michigan—the changes of the seasons and the spirit of Native Americans.

Judith Guest was born in Detroit in 1936 and graduated from the University of Michigan, after which she taught school in the Detroit suburbs. Her best known novel, *Ordinary People,* is set in the Chicago suburbs, however. It was made into a movie directed by Robert Redford that starred Mary Tyler Moore. Another novel, *Second Heaven,* focuses on adults who choose to live in Detroit, and how living there affects their behaviors and daily events.

Nelson Algren is another author with Detroit roots who became more famous as a Chicago writer. Although he was born in Detroit in 1909, his family moved to Chicago when he was three years old. It was in Chicago that he gathered material for books like *The Man with the Golden Arm* and gained his claim to fame.

Nelson Algren

The Heidelberg Project was created in 1986 by artist Tyree Guyton (1955–) and his grandfather, Sam Mackey, who died in 1992, as an outdoor art environment on Detroit's East Side, a neighborhood referred to as "Black Bottom." You can see results of attempts to turn Detroit into an indoor and outdoor museum, such as an artist colony, creative art center, community garden, and amphitheater, as well as the development of Heidelberg Street. There have also been books released, such as a children's book by Linda McLean and a coffee table book entitled *Connecting the Dots: Tyree Guyton's Heidelberg Project.*

Heidelberg Project
3360 Charlevoix Street, Detroit, Michigan 48207
313-267-1622
www.heidelberg.org

There are newspaper clippings, along with many other forms of memorabilia, at the Motown Historical Museum (2628 West Grand Boulevard). It's only a modest, two-story house, but the sounds and careers that were made at this headquarters of Motown Records in the '60s and '70s were huge.

Motown Historical Museum
2648 West Grand Boulevard
Detroit, Michigan 48208
313-875-2264

A poet, novelist, and social activist, Marge Piercy (1936–) has created work that tends to be highly personal. *Braided Lives* (1997), for example, gives different perspectives of growing up in her hometown of Detroit through the eyes of two cousins. *The Crooked Inheritance Poems* (2006) is, in effect, a study of her upbringing in the not-so-trendy parts of Detroit.

Wayne State University in Detroit hosts an annual "Made in Michigan Writers Series" that celebrates poetry, short fiction, and essays by Michigan writers. The goal of the series is to promote recognition of the state's artistic and cultural heritage. Typically, ten new books are featured with approximately four of the authors on hand for readings and book signings.

Charles Fisher Home
Wayne State University
Contact: Maureen Leonard
313-377-5608
moleonard@wayne.edu

►Dearborn

Between the Henry Ford Museum and Greenfield Village, it's hard to know which item to mention first. Okay, I'll start with the desk of Edgar Allen Poe (1809–1849). How, you ask, did Poe's portable writing table make its way to the Detroit suburbs? It's one of the vast collections of objects—often morbid, sometimes strange—assembled by the founder of the Ford Motor Company, Henry Ford (1863–1947). Along with the surface on which "The Raven" was possibly written is a test tube containing Thomas Edison's last breath, the chair in which President Abraham Lincoln was sitting when he was

Henry Ford, founder of the Ford Motor Company

fatally shot, and the limousine in which President John F. Kennedy was riding when he was fatally shot. The chair and car are roped off, but you can sit in the seat that Rosa Parks refused to give up on the Montgomery City bus on December 1, 1955.

Did I mention that there are eighty vintage buildings—Thomas Edison's laboratory and the Wright brothers' bicycle shop, to mention only two. You'll also find more than one hundred historic cars and landmarks of motoring, such as a 1946 diner and a 1940s Texaco filling station. Those were the days.

Inventor Thomas A. Edison

Henry Ford Museum and Greenfield Village
20900 Oakwood Boulevard
Dearborn, Michigan 48121
800-835-5237
www.hfmgv.org

▶Ann Arbor

When the street signs change color to maize and blue, you'll know you're in Ann Arbor. Football aside, it's a cosmopolitan community with plenty of musty antique bookstores competing with classy galleries for your attention. An antiquarian book fair is held in mid-May.

Edison's Menlo Park glass house at Greenfield Village

Playwright Arthur Miller fell under the spell of the University of Michigan, agreeing before his death at age eighty-nine in Connecticut to allow his alma mater to name a new theater in his honor. It wasn't yet open when this was written, but before long, you'll be able to watch a show at the Charles R. Walgreen, Jr., Drama Center and Arthur Miller Theatre on the North Campus.

The original Borders bookstore is located in Ann Arbor as well as the company that has overseen the proliferation of this chain, the Borders Group. Actually, store number one is no longer in its original location on State Street. It moved to 330 East Liberty Street awhile back.

Just down the street from the original Borders is a used and rare bookstore, the Dawn Treader Book Shop, which is a personal favorite of mine. The store isn't as small as it looks at first. The aisles seem to wind on and on with more than seventy thousand titles to tempt you. I love wandering the narrow aisles and looking at the memorabilia in glass cases, including letters Robert Frost (1874–1963) wrote when he was visiting the University of Michigan.

Dawn Treader Book Shop
514 East Liberty Street, Ann Arbor, Michigan 48104

734-995-1008
www.dawntreaderbooks.com

If you are a fan of mystery and crime books, wend your way to Aunt Agatha's New & Used Mysteries, Detection & True Crime Books. There's a bumper sticker on the door announcing that "The Game Is Afoot," and that says it all. You'll find special sections devoted to kid's mysteries and Michigan mysteries.

Aunt Agatha's New & Used Mysteries, Detection & True Crime Books
213 South Fourth Avenue, Ann Arbor, Michigan 48104
734-769-1114
www.auntagathas.com

If you're looking for spiritual and personal development books, as well as a great cup of tea, head to Crazy Wisdom Bookstore & Tea Room. This peaceful oasis specializes in books about psychology, integrative and holistic medicine, and spirituality. Every weekend, live music performances take place in the upstairs tea room.

Crazy Wisdom Bookstore & Tea Room
114 South Main Street, Ann Arbor, Michigan 48104
734-665-2757
www.crazywisdom.net

Nicola's Books is located in a shopping center, but it has a good selection of books as well as magazines. Authors frequently visit to read from their works.

Nicola's Books
Westgate Shopping Center
2513 Jackson Avenue, Ann Arbor, Michigan 48103
734-662-0600

Laura Kasischke (1961–), a professor at the University of Michigan, is a poet and novelist. Her novels include *Suspicious River* (1996) and *White Bird in a Blizzard* (1999). After spending time at the well-known writers' colony Yaddo, her goal became to find a way to communicate with the natural world before motors and machines interrupted it. She writes: "Even in the smallest things like midgets and darters, the small things that grow in a pond just after it has opened up, give you a sense of place."

▶ Battle Creek

Kimball House Museum is a beautiful fourteen-room mansion on Maple Street in Battle Creek, home of cereal and healthy living. But it's more than a run-of-the-mill museum: They publish a journal; their pictorial history is entitled "Gold-in-Flakes"; their mission since 1916 has been to promote education. They are the Historical Society of Battle Creek and, besides Tony the Tiger, they have many prominent citizens to feature.

One room in the Kimball House Museum is devoted to Sojourner Truth (1797–1883), the famous ex-slave and abolition leader of the nineteenth century. She gained fame from her memoir *The Narrative of Sojourner Truth: A Northern Slave*, published in 1850. When Truth visited in 1856 she was so impressed with the tolerance and openness of the citizens of Battle Creek that she took up residence the next year. A former slave, she was illiterate, but the written words she inspired as she spent the next twenty-seven years traveling the country agitating for human rights still have an impact today. She and several members of her family are buried in Oak Hill Cemetery on the east side of town. Monument Park includes a twelve-foot figure of her likeness. The Sojourner Truth Institute of Battle Creek, as well as the Heritage Battle Creek Research Center, house her archives and continue to carry on her life's work.

On a less serious note, if you visit Battle Creek in mid-June you and your family can enjoy the Battle Creek Cereal Festival, which features the world's longest breakfast table. Find out more at www .bcfestivals.com.

Kimball House Museum
165 North Washington Street, Battle Creek, Michigan 49017
616-965-6513
www.heritagebattlecreek.org/kimball.htm

▶ Kalamazoo

When I-96 was a plank road heading from Grand River Trail to Kalamazoo, Mark Twain commented that the ride would have been enjoyable had not "some unconscionable scoundrel now and then dropped a plank across the road." The home of Western Michigan University, Kalamazoo boasts several respected private schools, including the academically renowned Kalamazoo College. The

I Sell the Shadow to Support the Substance.

SOJOURNER TRUTH.

Former slave Sojourner Truth

Gwen Frostic Reading Series at Western Michigan's Little Theater brings poets and writers from the area to an appreciative audience.

Literary types will want to visit the Michigan News Agency. It dates back to 1947, and its friendly and knowledgeable owners encourage extended browsing of the up to six thousand magazines and books by local writers.

Michigan News Agency
308 West Michigan Avenue, Kalamazoo, Michigan 49007
269-343-5958
www.michigannews.biz
6:00 a.m. to 8:00 p.m.

▶Niles

Niles is the birthplace of one of the greatest American short story writers and sportswriters, Ringgold "Ring" Lardner (1885–1933). One of his best-known books was also his first: *You Know Me Al*, a collection of stories published in 1916. When it was first published, a writer for the *Wall Street Journal* called this book one of the best pieces of American humor writing ever. While with the *Chicago Tribune*, Lardner originated the syndicated sports column "In the Wake of the News," which continues to this day.

One of Lardner's most frequently anthologized stories, "Haircut," draws on the pranks and the atmosphere of small-town life in Michigan around the turn of the twentieth century.

If you visit the pleasant, scenic town of Niles, you'll find the Ring Lardner Middle School at 801 North 17th Street. To learn more about the writer, visit the Fort St. Joseph Museum, which holds a collection of clippings, photos, and items related to the Lardner family's time in the town. In Trinity Church, Lardner reportedly carved his initials in the wall behind the organ and on the back of a choir seat. The family home, now a state landmark, is at 519 Bond Street. It's now a private residence, but there's an historical marker across the street with information about Lardner.

▶Royal Oak

Royal Oak, a town near Niles, is home to one of the state's best-known independent bookstores, Classic Book Shop, managed by David Oyerly.

Classic Book Shop
32336 Woodward Avenue, Royal Oak, MI 48073
248-549-0220

I-75 North to Bay City: Greaseballs and Greenhouses

The Michigan Tourism Bureau would order me a special set of cement overshoes if I didn't mention Frankenmuth. Don't eat breakfast before you take Exit 144 off I-75 because you'll want room for plenty of Frankenmuth fare. Some is produced by the Frankenmuth Pretzel Company and the Frankenmuth Brewery. Some have Bavarian roots, such as bratwurst, weisswurst, roasted almonds, and rosettes. But make sure you get a world-famous,

Ring Lardner

family-style chicken dinner. Frankenmuth is also famous for its festivals, but every day is a holiday at Bronner's Christmas Wonderland, the world's largest Christmas store. Okay, but now back to things literary . . .

▶Wyandotte

Novelist and screenwriter Thomas McGuane was born in Wyandotte, Michigan, in 1939. He attended the exclusive Cranbrook-Kingswood School, but was far more influenced by his time hunting, fishing, and working in Wyoming and Montana. He met his friend and fellow Michigan writer, Jim Harrison (1937–), at Michigan State University, where he graduated with honors in 1962 with a B.A. in Humanities.

McGuane's novels vividly portray colorful characters living on an emotional or psychological knife-edge. The novels include *The Sporting Club* (1968), *The Bushwacked Piano* (1971), and *Ninety-Two in the Shade* (1973), which was a finalist for the National Book Award. In *The Bushwhacked Piano*, the protagonist, Nicholas Payne, moves, like the author himself, from Michigan to Montana to Florida. His screenplays include *Rancho Deluxe* (1973) and *The Missouri Breaks* (1976).

►Flint

Rivethead: Tales from the Assembly Line is a collection of Ben Hamper's columns for the *Michigan Voice*, which topped the New York Times Best Seller list for weeks in 1991. Hamper is still writing; you can find out more about him at www.michaelmoore.com/hamper.

Ted Weesner grew up in Flint, Michigan. He left school at age sixteen, spent three years in the army, and later attended Michigan State University and the University of Iowa. He received his B.A. in English from MSU in 1962. His first novel, *The Car Thief* (1972), won the Great Lakes Writers Prize, and a later novel, *The True Detective* (1987), was cited by the American Library Association as one of the notable books of 1987. *The Car Thief* opens with a vivid description of the snow:

> as wet as a blanket soaked in water, as gray and full in the sky as smoke from the city's concentrations of automobile factories.

Flint's blue-collar image was portrayed by Michael Moore (1954–) in the documentary *Roger and Me*, which elaborated on the love/hate relationships between the city and GM. But there is also a rich cultural heritage. Buckham Gallery, 134 West Second, for example, features performance art and poetry readings.

►Bloomfield Hills

The former home of George Booth (1864–1949), who founded the *Detroit News*, can be found on the campus of the Cranbrook Academy of Art. The campus has a beautiful garden that I highly recommend you walk through. The school was created through a collaboration between Booth and artist Eliel Saarinen. They were noted proponents of the arts and crafts movement that unified life and art.

Cranbrook Academy of Art
39221 Woodward Avenue, Bloomfield Hills, Michigan 48304
248-645-3300
www.cranbrook.edu

▶ Saginaw

Saginaw is the hometown of the poet Theodore Roethke (1908–1963). His work with his father in the family floral company as a child influenced many of his later poems. The greenhouses once stood on the land behind the family home. He attended elementary school at John Moore School and Arthur Hill High School. He later became a brilliant teacher who wrote lovely poems, including those about the aforementioned greenhouses.

The town celebrated his centennial in 2008 and has preserved his boyhood home at 1805 Gratiot Avenue. The home was actually a refuge of sorts, as Roethke suffered from bipolar disorder and alcoholism and came back to this house to recuperate from various breakdowns until his death at age fifty-five. He won two National Book Awards and a Pulitzer Prize for his work.

George Booth home

Theodore Roethke Home Museum

Saginaw is home to the annual Michigan Bean Festival held Labor Day weekend, and to the annual Riverside Saginaw Film Festival, usually held in late summer. Find out more at www .michiganbeanfestival.org and www.riversidesaginawfilmfestival.org, respectively.

Theodore Roethke Home Museum
1805 Gratiot Avenue, Saginaw, Michigan 48602
989-928-0430
www.roethkehomemuseum.org

I-96 Around the Lake: Wineries, Wooden Shoes, and Writers

It was the misfortune of Ogden Nash to be from the East. If he had been from this part of Michigan, he never would have written: "I think that I shall never see a billboard lovely as a tree. Indeed, unless the billboard falls, I'll never see a tree at all." Here you will see plenty of trees without roadside obstructions. And you may be inspired to write a poem of your own by the many visual and literary forms created by the artists who've made their home in this area.

▶Benzonia

An illness as an infant left Gwen Frostic (1906–2001) with a limp and slurred speech. But her parents never assumed Gwen could not or should not do anything, especially when it came to interacting with nature. She became one of Michigan's most noted poets and publishers. Several of my friends are fascinated with her wood block-print designs that perfectly capture the beauty of Michigan flowers, leaves, and trees.

You can visit the gallery, library, and walking trails on her 285-acre wildlife sanctuary. The facility includes one of the most complete nature libraries in Michigan. You can also view fifteen original Heidelberg presses churning out products that feature designs carved by Frostic. I guarantee that you will be inspired.

Gwen Frostic Prints
Route 608, 5140 River Road, Benzonia, Michigan 49616
231-882-5505
www.gwenfrostic.com

▶Grand Rapids

Lovers of great writing will enjoy reading the quotations posted throughout the Frederik Meijer Gardens and Sculpture Park by Michigan poets, such as Theodore Roethke and Jim Harrison, connecting people to the plants. The gardens are magnificent and a theme of natural tranquility and artistic beauty pervades the park.

The area around Grand Rapids is heavily Dutch. The town of Holland is proud of its windmill and its Dutch Village, and you can buy wooden shoes at gift stores in the area. One of Grand Rapids' writers came to this town from the Netherlands when he was a boy, David DeJong (1901–1967). His first novel, *Belly Fulla Straw*, appeared in 1934. Many of his books are set in Michigan, and they illuminate the difficulties facing poor Dutch immigrants attempting to settle into a new life in a new country. His brother Meindert DeJong (1906–1991) wrote award-winning children's books.

Frederik Meijer Gardens and Sculpture Park
1000 East Beltline NE, Grand Rapids, Michigan 49525
616-957-1580
www.meijergardens.org

▶Fremont

This town about thirty miles north of Grand Rapids is the birth-place of Dan Gerber (1940–   ). He was born into the family that created the successful line of Gerber baby foods and was expected to take over management of the company one day, but he decided to be a writer and race car driver instead. When he suffered a near-fatal crash, he focused on the former activity. Gerber continued to live in Fremont to raise his children and, although he no longer calls Michigan home, fictionalized towns based on his hometown play an important part in his writing. The residents of such a town find their voice in the stories in *Grass Fires* (1987).

►Leelanau Peninsula

In addition to wineries and eateries, the Leelanau Peninsula has been home to many writers, including Jim Harrison, Kathleen Stickney, and William H. Mulligan. Mulligan is the author of non-fiction books about Michigan, such as *Irish Immigrants in Michigan's Copper Country*.

Leelanau Books is located in a lovely little white frame house in Leland. It's a terrific place to find books about the local region and other aspects of Michigan life, such as those many wineries.

Leelanau Books
109 North Main, Leland, Michigan 49654
888-257-0133
www.leelanaubooks.com

I-69/75 North to Mackinac Island: As Good as It Gets!

You, dear reader, will pick your own favorites out of this book, and I wouldn't want to prejudice you in advance. But this section is pretty hard to beat. It's a two-for-one deal: you get a fabulous place to take a vacation and you get to trace the youthful haunts of Ernest Hemingway and several other writers that are among America's greatest. Go for it!

►Lansing

The Michigan Historical Museum (717 West Allegan Street) not only houses state archives and a state library, but is also a pilgrimage for genealogists from around the country. The building was designed by Detroit architect William Kessler, who relied heavily on native construction materials.

Lansing writer Andrea King Collier is the author of *The Black Woman's Guide to Black Men's Health* (2007) and *Still With Me* (2003), a memoir.

A good number of the writers in this chapter attended and/or taught at Michigan State University, located in Lansing. The Michigan State University Writing Center is a place for writers to meet and discuss their work. Actually coming to Spartan Country is optional; you can visit the center online at writing.msu.edu. You can even order products from the locally beloved Dairy Store at shop.msu.edu. But the writers I describe below no doubt savored their ice cream on the premises, which I totally recommend.

I also suggest the Lansing Jazz Fest, a free two-day music festival held each August (www.jazzlansing.com).

Michigan State University Writing Center
300 Bessey Hall, Lansing, Michigan 48824
http://writing.msu.edu

▶East Lansing

Lev Raphael has described himself as an "escaped academic" who became a successful writer. Although he apparently escaped from Michigan State, where he obtained a Ph.D. in American Studies, he did later teach creative writing and other courses.

Raphael was born and raised in New York City, the son of Holocaust survivors. He is the author of a series of academic murder mysteries following protagonist Nick Hoffman. *Let's Get Criminal, The Edith Wharton Murders,* and *The Death of a Constant Lover* are all set at the fictional "State University of Michigan."

Diane Wakoski (1937–) has published more than forty books of poetry and is a creative writing teacher at Michigan State. Her poetry has appeared in literally hundreds of broadsides, limited special editions, anthologies, and journals. Wakoski was honored with the William Carlos Williams Prize for *Emerald Ice: Selected Poems, 1962–87,* in addition to numerous other awards that include a Guggenheim Foundation grant, a National Endowment for the Arts grant, and a Fulbright grant. In 2003, Wakoski received the thirteenth annual Michigan Author Award, which honors a Michigan writer for contributions to literature. This award is sponsored jointly by the Michigan Center for the Book and the Michigan Library Association.

Each May, the two-day East Lansing Art Festival attracts artists from all over Michigan (www.elartfest.com).

▶Owosso

What would you do if you found yourself staring at a grizzly you'd wounded and now had you trapped on a narrow mountain ledge? James Oliver Curwood (1878–1927) lived to tell the tale in his best-selling novel *The Grizzly King* (1916), after he had packed away his gun and sworn off hunting for sport forever. Born in Owosso in 1878, Curwood attended the University of Michigan for two years and then worked on a newspaper in Detroit. But income from royalties and movie deals on his thirty-three novels made him a millionaire. You'll be jealous when you visit Curwood Castle along the banks of the Shiawasse River. You'll be even more jealous when you realize the imposing structure was solely his writing studio, with a space for guests on the first floor and a work area upstairs. Among the memorabilia is his original writing desk. His 1908 novel *The Courage of Captain Plum* was set on Beaver Island in Michigan.

Owosso is one of several Midwestern towns that have adopted a famous writer as their own. Every year a Curwood Festival is held in Owosso. Events include a RiverDaze Raft Race, a carnival, volleyball tournament, and much more.

Curwood Festival Office
308 West Main Street, Suite III, Owosso, Michigan 48867
989-723-2161
www.curwoodfestival.com

▶Mount Pleasant

Central Michigan University's Clarke Historical Library has been chosen as the Michigan Hemingway Society's official institutional home. More than five hundred items include books by and about Hemingway (including rare first and signed editions), periodicals, movies and movie memorabilia, a draft of one of his first short stories, and two original letters written by Ernest Hemingway. A Hemingway Endowment supports the acquisition of additional materials and/or activities that increase awareness of Hemingway and his Michigan connections.

Clarke Historical Library
250 Preston Street, Mount Pleasant, Michigan 48859
989-774-3352
clarke.cmich.edu

▶Reed City

Although Guggenheim fellowship recipient Jim Harrison was born in the Michigan town of Grayling in 1937, Reed City is one of the towns in which he grew up. His children's book, *The Boy Who Ran to the Woods* (2000), is a semi-autobiographical account of his childhood in northern Michigan. His father was a county agent who moved his family to the East Lansing area so his children could attend Michigan State University. That plan worked, as Harrison received B.A. and M.A. degrees in English and Comparative Literature from Michigan State University in 1960 and 1966 respectively. He has a lifelong interest in nature and agriculture that is an integral part of his writing, and he and his family live on Lake Leelanau today. His work as a poet, novelist, essayist, and screenwriter enjoys a substantial world-wide following among critics and general readers alike. His novels and novellas include *Wolf* (1971), *A Good Day to Die* (1973), *Farmer* (1976), *The Road Home* (1999); and his volumes of poetry include *Plain Song* (1965), *Locations* (1968), *Letters to Yesenin* (1970), *The Theory and Practice of Rivers* (1989), *After Ikkyu* (1996), and *The Shape of the Journey* (1998).

▶Horton Bay

It's hard to pick my favorite single site associated with Ernest Hemingway (1899–1961) in Michigan because there are so many. Hemingway wrote about a number of areas in and around Horton Bay, Walloon Lake, Petoskey, and Harbor Springs.

Carlos Baker's (1909–1987) great biography of Hemingway begins with these words: "As soon as it was safe for the boy to travel, they bore him away to the northern woods. It was a long and complicated journey for a child only seven weeks old." He then describes the trip from Hemingway's birthplace in the Chicago suburb of Oak Park: "They took the train to Chicago, a horse cab to the Pier on Lake Michigan, the steamer *Manitou* to Harbor Springs on Little Traverse Bay, the curving tracks of the small railroad to the depot in

Petoskey, an even smaller branch line to the foot of Bear Lake, and at last a rowboat to the shore-front property that Dr. Ed Hemingway had bought from Henry Bacon the summer before."

Hemingway's love of nature grew at Bear Lake. He took his first walk by himself there when he was only one year old. He and his sister played naked in the sand and rowed in the family rowboat. He went fishing with his father there when he was three. His boyhood experiences were recounted mostly in the Nick Adams stories but in other stories too.

In his story "Up in Michigan," Hemingway calls the town "Hortons Bay." He uses the name of his real-life boyhood friend Wesley Dillworth: "Hortons Bay, the town, was only five houses on the main road between Boyne City and Charlevoix. There was the general store and post office with a high false front and maybe a wagon hitched out in front, Smith's house, Stroud's house, Dillworth's house, Horton's house and Van Hoosen's house. The houses were in a big grove of elm trees and the road was very sandy. There was farming country and timber each way up the road."

The Horton Bay General Store on the Charlevoix-Boyne City Road in the village of Horton Bay, which was established in 1876 and remains the center of village business and social life, was frequented by Hemingway and now displays photos and memorabilia. Next door the Red Fox Inn is now a bookstore that specializes in Hemingway titles. (The onetime owner, Vollie Fox, taught young Ernest to fish.)

Near the Red Fox Inn, you'll find Dillworth's Pinehurst cottage, where Ernest and his first wife, Hadley, spent their wedding night. The Little Traverse Historical Museum off Lake Street near the Municipal Marina now houses a permanent exhibit and other materials related not only to Ernest Hemingway but also to Bruce Catton. The building was the main area station of the Pere Marquette Railroad, which Hemingway refers to in several stories.

In the story "Indian Camp," his alter ego Nick Adams takes a trip with his physician father to treat an Indian woman who is sick. Indians, in fact, lived near the Hemingway cabin when he was growing up on Bear Lake, which is now called Walloon Lake.

The Perry Hotel at the corner of Bay and Lewis Streets has been the headquarters for the annual Hemingway weekend since 1990. Ernest Hemingway stayed here in 1916 after a hiking and camping trip in northwest lower Michigan with his friend Lewis Clarahan. In 2007, the weekend included an exhibit titled "Up North with the Hemingways" cosponsored by the Clarke Historical Library and the Michigan Hemingway Society. Held in Petoskey's Crooked Tree Arts Center, it featured rare photos and other items from the archives telling the story of the family's summers in northern Michigan between 1898 and 1921.

If you visit the area, you can see sites such as:

- Windemere Cottage, the home of the Hemingway family, and still owned by family members. (It is closed to the public, but you can read a description by Bob Orlin, who visited the site, at www.lostgeneration.com/article3.htm).

- Hirsch's Rooming House, 602 State Street (corner of State and Woodland) in Petoskey, where Hemingway stayed in 1919. There is a reference to it in his famous story "The Killers": "'He lives up at Hirsch's rooming house,' George said to Nick." He stayed in a room on the second floor. There is a plaque on the house stating that it is on the National Register of Historic Places.

- If you are able to get a tour of the Little Travis Historical Museum, you'll find signed editions of Hemingway books as well as postcards he sent to area residents, as well as furniture from Windemere Cottage.

In September, a conference features speakers from the executive board of the Ernest Hemingway Foundation and tours of Hemingway sites. Another weekend of film viewing discusses how well Hemingway's written word was translated to the screen. Other topics have been the Hemingway women, Hemingway on the road, Hemingway and fishing, Hemingway and the Native Americans. To subscribe to the Michigan Hemingway Society's e-mail list, send a message to majordomo@mtu.edu (with the message "subscribe heming-1") Mail can be sent to the Michigan Hemingway Society at P.O. Box 922, Petoskey, Michigan 49770.

Petoskey is also the birthplace of American historian Bruce Catton (1899–1978), author of *A Stillness at Appomattox*, for which he won the Pulitzer Prize in History in 1954. He wrote a number of other Civil War books and was regarded as the leading writer of popular histories in his day. But he also wrote lyrically about growing up in Michigan in *Waiting for the Morning Train: An American Boyhood* (1972). In it, he describes taking the train to Petoskey:

> What we could see out of the windows took on a monotonous sameness: acres and acres of stumps, low hills covered with uneven second-growth, usually aspens packed so tightly together that you could not imagine playing Indian among them, and weedy farms with tired-looking houses that had lost all their paint and most of their prospects. It was nice to go through a town, because we could see people hanging about and we could reflect in a superior way that we were traveling while they were mere stay-at-homes, but most of these places were dying lumber towns and they were depressing to look at. It was always a relief when we finally reached Petoskey and took the carriage up the hill to Grandfather's house.

►Seney

Hemingway described this peaceful village in his story "Big Two-Hearted River." Seney is famous for fishing, and Hemingway wrote about his experience fishing the Fox River near Seney. The fishing trip he described in that story is commemorated in a display in the Seney Historical Museum. The museum is in the old Seney train depot. But the depot is no longer located where Nick Adams, Hemingway's alter ego, got off the train and started walking. It has since been moved from its original location.

►Walloon Lake

The Walloon Writers' Retreat is held on Walloon Lake every fall. Workshops, readings, and panel discussions are some of the events.

The public access boat launch on Sumner Road provides a great view of Walloon Lake. Nick Adams, in Hemingway's story "Wedding Day," rowed his new bride Helen across the lake from this spot to the cottage where they stayed on their honeymoon. So did Hemingway and his real-life wife Hadley.

The Bacon Farm, a plot of land bounded by Resort Pike Road on the east and Lake Grove Road on the south, was acquired by the Hemingway family. The writer used the farm in his stories "Ten Indians," "Fathers and Sons," and "The Indians Moved Away."

▶Mackinac Island

Gloria Whelan (1923–) is a poet, novelist, and children's book writer. She won the National Book Award for her novel *Homeless Bird* (2000) but is, perhaps, better known for her books for young readers. Among her many books is a trilogy set on Mackinac Island: *Once on This Island* (1995), *Farewell to the Island* (1998), and *Return to the Island* (2000). Whelan graduated from the University of Michigan and lived with her husband, Joseph, in the woods on Oxbow Lake in northern Michigan for many years, but after Joseph's death she moved to the Detroit area, where her children and her grandchildren live.

As you look out on the lake to the ships that are continually moving freight through the Great Lakes, you might look up the work of Michigan writer Mary Frances Doner (1893–1985). She was born in Port Huron, and her father was the captain of a Lake Michigan freighter. She sometimes accompanied her father on voyages. One of her novels, *Glass Mountain* (1942), tells the story of a reckless ship captain. Others describe the life of miners in Michigan's Upper Peninsula.

Ronald J. Lewis, a professor and author of mysteries such as *Terror at the Soo Locks*, also wrote a murder mystery set on Mackinac Island.

Kathy-jo Wargin is the author of a children's book entitled *The Legend of Mackinac Island*.

Island Bookstore is, as you would expect, a great place to find books about the island itself. It's been on the island for thirty years and is open from May to October.

Island Bookstore, Mackinac Island
Main Street Centre inside the Lilac Tree Inn, Mackinac Island, Michigan 49757
906-847-6202
www.islandbookstore.com

Route 25: Thumbs Up for the Thumb

I wouldn't want to imply that you'll get a watery view every time you turn a bend while driving this state road. But I suggest that you do it in the daytime, because there are enough panoramas of Lake Huron and shoreline parks to make your traveling companions shriek "Wait! Stop here!!" on a regular basis, especially if they are camera bugs.

►Huron City

You can make a detour around Lake Huron to the east to visit many of the scenic lake towns. House of Seven Gables (517-478-4123) was the summer residence of William Lyon Phelps (1865–1943) an author, critic, and scholar. He was a wildly popular Yale English teacher who was dubbed America's favorite college professor by *Life* magazine during the 1930s. In 1987, the house was turned into an informal museum, and you can see the books still piled on tables as if waiting for the family to return from getting a snack.

►Port Huron

Thomas Edison Park includes a restored 1858 Grand Trunk Depot. Edison (1847–1931) rode the train every day, selling magazines and newspapers. The proceeds were used to buy books, as well chemicals for a laboratory he had set up in the train's baggage car. Some of his inventions were designed to provide a means of hearing for the deaf. He was almost completely deaf because he was late for the train one morning and someone pulled him aboard by his ears.

►Port Sanilac

Until the mid 1850s, this town was known as Bark Shanty Point. The Sanilac County Historical Museum and Village includes issues of the "Times," which was produced by placing a sheet of newsprint on the counter of the local store for anyone to write on. If you have a camera handy, it's hard to get a bad shot of the Port Sanilac Lighthouse, located on Lake Street, one block east of M 25.

►Lexington

Four of the beautiful old homes that line the streets of Lexington are on the National Register of Historic Places. There's one in particular that provides a perfect place to curl up with a good book. The Charles H. Moore Public Library at Main and Huron Streets was originally a law office, but now it offers twelve thousand books . . . just in case you didn't bring plenty of your own.

chapter five

Minnesota

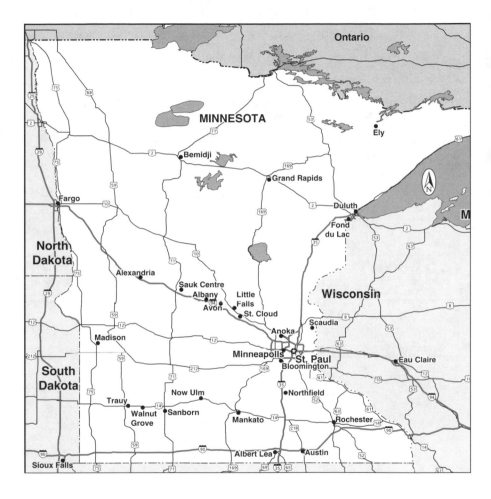

Driving Tours

1. I-90 Across the State: From Spamtown to Plum Creek
2. I-35: Bank Robbers, Ballplayers, and Bookstores
3. I-94: From Lake Wobegon to the Words Written in Stone
4. Lutefisk Capital USA

*I*f you were to write a poem about Minnesota, you might have a hard time clearing your mind of slogans: "Land of 10,000 Lakes"; "Land of Sky-Blue Waters"; "Star of the North." Maybe it's those long, cold winters that lead to the need for spinning yarns. From ethnic folktales to the tall tales of Paul Bunyan to the satirical novels of Sinclair Lewis that earned America its first Nobel Prize for Literature to the saga of Garrison Keillor's Lake Wobegon, literature is an integral part of the culture of Minnesota. And Charlie Brown was conceived here as well.

I-90 Across the State: From Spamtown to Plum Creek

Except for one jog, I-90 will take you from east to west and back again, pretty much like the crow flies. But that doesn't mean that those of us of literary ilk can't create our own zigs and zags. Here are some ideas for worthwhile detours.

▶Austin

Austin is the birthplace (in 1946) of novelist Tim O'Brien. He served in the Vietnam War from 1968–1970 and drew upon that experience in the acclaimed novel *Going After Cacciato* (1978) and in the equally acclaimed collection of short stories titled *The Things They Carried* (1990). Some stories in that collection also use Minnesota locations, especially the area around Worthington, where his family moved when he was young. His 1975 novel, *Northern Lights*, was set in the northern Minnesota countryside. He won the O. Henry Award in 1976 and 1978 and the National Book Award for Fiction in 1979.

Austin, however, is known for one even more famous product. On the town's Web site, it proudly proclaims itself Spamtown USA. Austin is home to the Hormel Foods Corporation, which makes the SPAM family of products. If you are in the area, the SPAM Museum is a must-see. Take Exit 178-B off of I-90 to get to canned meat heaven.

There is a literary connection to SPAM, which is not surprising, since it's such an integral part of American culture. It's called SPAM-ku, short for SPAM Haiku—a collection of short poems about SPAM. While you're driving across I-90, you might entertain yourself by reciting (or composing) poems on the SPAM Haiku archive (http://mit.edu/jync/www/spam/).

SPAM Museum
1101 North Main Street, Austin, Minnesota 55912
507-437-5100

▶Albert Lea

If the name Kirsten Larson rings a bell, you probably have a daughter or niece who knows about Minnesota because she reads American Girl literature. You'll find Kirsten as well as other dolls of literary note—some dating back to the nineteenth century—in the Story Lady Doll & Toy Museum. When you've had your fill of

Cinderella, Pooh Bear, and Madeline, head for a library focusing on local history and genealogy. It's housed in the Freeborn County Museum and Historical Village.

Story Lady Doll & Toy Museum
131 North Broadway Avenue, Albert Lea, Minnesota 56007
507-377-1820
www.storyladymuseum.com
Tuesday through Saturday, noon to 4:00 p.m.

Freeborn County Historical Museum
1031 Bridge Street, Albert Lea, Minnesota 56007
507-373-8003
www.smig.net/fchm
Tuesday through Friday, 10:00 a.m. to 5:00 p.m.

▶ Mankato

Every writer dreads a typo. Mahkata means "Blue Earth" in the Dakota Indian language which refers to the clay that lines the riverbanks. But however it's spelled, the town is located on a great bend in the Minnesota River where it joins the Blue Earth River. The Blue Earth County Heritage Center Museum at 415 East Cherry Street features an audioplay about Maud Hart Lovelace, author of the ten-book Betsy and Tacy series, which was immensely popular with young girls and is still beloved by its ardent fans. Lovelace (1892–1980) was inspired to write these books by the family stories she told to her daughter at bedtime. They still have a devoted following today, as you will learn on the Betsy-Tacy Society Web site (www.betsy-tacysociety.org).

To many Betsy-Tacy book fans, Mankato is actually Deep Valley, the setting for the books following the two friends Betsy and Tacy. Lovelace also wrote a three-book Deep Valley series in which Betsy and Tacy play minor roles. Hill Street, another important location in the stories, is actually Center Street in real life, and on Center Street you can find a stone bench bearing a bronze plaque that reads:

> To honor Maud Hart Lovelace, who here began the childhood daydreams that one day would be our window to the past.

The Web site also includes a detailed, self-guided tour that will lead you to more than fifty sites featured in the thirteen books. For example, Betsy's fictional home was Lovelace's real-life home, and the Carnegie Library mentioned frequently in the books is now the Carnegie Art Center.

Blue Earth County Heritage Center Museum
415 East Cherry Street, Mankato, Minnesota 56001
507-345-5566

Tacy's House and Gift Shop
333 Center Street, Mankato, Minnesota 56001
507-345-9777
Saturday, 1:00 p.m. to 3:00 p.m.

▶New Ulm
Author and illustrator Wanda Gag was born in New Ulm in 1893. She became famous for a highly successful children's book called *Millions of Cats*. Although it might not make it into the millions category, her work is displayed in quite a few libraries and museums around town plus in the Wanda Gag House, which the author referred to as a "children's paradise."

But even if there wasn't a literary connection, this town that has a distinctly European (German not Scandinavian, for a change) essence is well worth a visit. There's a glockenspiel with animated figurines that depict the history of New Ulm when the bells ring. There are a lot of museums, monuments, and a restored general store. And, dear reader, which would you rather visit: a brewery or a shrine called "Way of the Cross"? I'm not revealing my answer, but I must mention that there is a tasting session after the brewery tour.

Each year in mid-July, New Ulm celebrates its German heritage with Bavarian Blast, with plenty of "oompah" bands, crafts, and a parade.

Wanda Gag House
226 North Washington Street, New Ulm, Minnesota 56073
507-359-2632
www.wandagaghouse.org
Open May through October
Saturday, 10:00 a.m. to 4:00 p.m.
Sunday, 11:00 a.m. to 2:00 p.m.

▶Sanborn

You'll feel like you're driving into the past as you head down the gravel road to 12598 Magnolia Avenue in the town of Sanborn. That's the location of an old sod house that has been preserved from pioneer days and that recalls the house described in Minnesota novelist Ole Rölvaag's *Giants in the Earth*:

> On the side of a hill, which sloped gently away toward the southeast and followed with many windings a creek that wormed its way across the prairie, stood Hans Olsa, laying turf. He was building a sod house. The walls had now risen breast-high; in its half-finished condition, the structure resembled more a bulwark against some enemy than anything intended to be a human habitation. And the great heaps of cut sod, piled up in each corner, might well have been the stores of ammunition for defense of the stronghold.

You can not only see the sod house, but stay in it for the night: it's a comfortable bed and breakfast as well. Compare its virtues to those of a "dugout" that is also on the site. Laura Ingalls Wilder lived nearby.

But that's not all: the address is also home to Autumn Sparrow Press, which published the book *Butterscotch Sundaes: My Mom's Story of Alzheimer's*, by Virginia McCone.

Sod House on the Prairie Bed and Breakfast
12598 Magnolia Avenue, Sanborn, Minnesota 56083
507-723-5138
www.sodhouse.org

▶Tracy

Yep, if it's a Midwestern state it's likely to have a Laura Ingalls Wilder connection. And it's probably going to tout that connection. Tracy gets in the act with the annual Laura Ingalls Wilder Pageant. Their claim to fame is based on an account in *By the Shores of Silver Lake* of Laura's first train ride from the depot in Walnut Grove to Tracy. At this point, the Ingalls family was on the edge of the prairie.

> They were still licking their fingers when the engine whistled long and loud. Then the car went more slowly, and slowly the backs of shanties went backward outside it. All the people began to gather their things together and put on their hats, and then there was an awful jolting crash, and the train stopped. It was noon, and they had reached Tracy.

►Walnut Grove

Eight miles from Tracy is a town that was one of Laura's homes and the site of *On the Banks of Plum Creek*. Several of Laura Ingalls Wilder's books, as well as the popular television series *Little House on the Prairie*, are set in the town of Walnut Grove, which has become a popular pilgrimage site for Little House fans. The required Laura Ingalls Wilder Museum is off U.S. 14 at 330 Eighth Street. In this case it is not only a museum, but an entire site that is comprised of a chapel, schoolhouse, onion-domed house, covered wagon display, early settler's house, and old-fashioned depot. An extensive doll collection is on view, along with memorabilia from the stars of the television series who have visited the museum.

Walnut Grove does its best to keep Wilder's legacy alive, and visitors can enjoy attractions such as:

- The Ingalls Dugout Site, 1.5 miles north of Walnut Grove on County Road 5. The remains of the family's dugout home are surrounded by thirty acres of restored native grasses.
- The Laura Ingalls Wilder Historic Monument, which commemorates early settlers such as the Ingalls, 1.6 miles north of Walnut Grove on County Road 5
- The Masters Home, where Laura worked, is at the corner of Eighth Street and County Road 20. It's a private home.
- Pa's Bell is located in the belfry of the English Lutheran Church, 450 Walnut Grove

Each July the town's citizens come together—appropriately enough, on the banks of Plum Creek—to produce "Fragments of a Dream," an outdoor pageant based on *On the Banks of Plum Creek*. In the amphitheater, one can see a live performance of the Ingalls's family life in Walnut Grove, narrated by the character of Laura. Also on the site is the 1890s Grandma's House, featuring some three hundred dolls.

Laura Ingalls Wilder Museum
330 Eighth Street, Walnut Grove, Minnesota 56180
www.walnutgrove.org
lauramuseum@walnutgrove.org
800-528-7280
Open April through October; hours vary by month

I-35: Bank Robbers, Ballplayers, and Bookstores

This part of the book doesn't cover that many miles, all told. But in literary terms, when you're in the land of the twins, you're in the land of the giants. There is a lot to see and do, and be sure to pack light. You'll need all the space you can get for the new books you're bound to buy.

▶ Northfield

On your way to the Twin Cities, pull off I-35 at Exit 69 and head to Northfield, the site of the last bank Jesse James attempted to rob. The failed robbery attempt was immortalized in the 1972 film *The Great Northfield Minnesota Raid*. It's also commemorated in a number of books, including *The Story of Cole Younger*, an autobiography that recently has been reprinted; *Jesse James Northfield Raid*, by John Koblas; and *Robber and Hero: The Story of the Northfield Bank Raid*, by George Huntington. The local museum has plenty of information related to the event, and reportedly, in the basement, the skeleton of one of the supposed robbers.

Jesse James attempted to rob the Northfield Bank.

Northfield Historical Society Museum
408 Division Street South, Northfield, Minnesota 55057
507-645-9268
www.northfieldhistory.org
Seasonal hours

▸Minneapolis/St. Paul

The vibrant literary cultures of Minnesota and St. Paul have been virtually overlooked by travel writers. Yet, the area is full of active readers and writers, many of whom make pilgrimages to two theaters in the Twin Cities to watch the broadcast of Garrison Keillor's successful radio show, *A Prairie Home Companion*. And you can trace the early years of one of the country's greatest writers, F. Scott Fitzgerald, who grew up in St. Paul.

The classic 1956 novel *Bang the Drum Slowly*, by writer Mark Harris (1922–2007), who was living in the state at the time while earning a PhD in American Studies at the University of Minnesota, opens in snow-covered Minneapolis. Baseball player Henry Wiggen is driving to Rochester to pick up his sick teammate, Bruce, at the Mayo Clinic. When the two drive south out of town, Bruce tells Wiggen to follow the river.

> Moving south he noticed cows out of doors. "We are moving south all right," he said, "because they keep their cows out of doors down here." He knew what kind they were, milk or meat, and what was probably planted in the fields, corn or wheat or what, and if birds were winter birds or the first birds of spring coming home. He knew we were south by the way they done chicken. "We ain't real south," he said, "but we are getting there. I can taste it."

Bang the Drum Slowly was made into a TV drama later that year starring Paul Newman, and in 1973 was produced as a movie starring Michael Morarity as Henry and Robert De Niro as Bruce.

Robert M. Pirsig, author of the classic 1974 book *Zen and the Art of Motorcycle Maintenance*, was born in Minneapolis in 1928. His father was a professor at the University of Minnesota. The book tells the story of the author's motorcycle trip across the country with his son Chris. Pirsig studied biochemistry at the University of Minnesota, but he was expelled after two years for trouble with his grades and lack of attention to his studies. He later studied at Benares University in India as well as the University of Chicago.

Another Minneapolis native (born here in 1922) is Charles M. Schulz, the creator of the beloved *Peanuts* comic strip. He grew up in St. Paul, where he attended Richard Gordon Elementary School and Central High School. His first cartoon, *Li'l Folks*, appeared from 1947 to 1950 in the St. Paul Pioneer Press. One of the characters was given the name Charlie Brown. The name reportedly came from a coworker at a Minneapolis company where Shulz worked as a teacher, Art Instruction, Inc. The "Little Red-Haired Girl" that Charlie Brown had a crush on was also based on an employee at Art Instruction with whom Schulz was in love. Many of the other characters in Peanuts (which began appearing in syndication in 1950) were based on relatives and people Shulz knew in Minnesota.

The fifty-three-foot waterfall in Minnehaha Park, at Minnehaha Parkway and Hiawatha Avenue on the banks of the Mississippi, was made famous by Henry Wadsworth Longfellow's epic poem "The Son of Hiawatha." Minnehaha Falls purports to be the "laughing water" to which Hiawatha journeyed. A statue of Hiawatha and Minnehaha stands on the island immediately above the falls. The site has attracted a number of visitors, including Henry David Thoreau. Today visitors flock to an interpretive information center that was styled after Longfellow's home in Massachusetts. Robert Johnson, who ran a fish market in downtown Minneapolis (his nickname was "Fish"), woke up one fine day and decided to build not only this house, but also a zoo. Not to be entirely grandiose, the house is only a two-thirds scale replica of the original in Cambridge.

Poet, novelist and critically acclaimed science fiction and horror writer Thomas M. Disch (1940–2008) was born in Iowa in 1940 but grew up in Minneapolis, where he attended a military school and a public high school. Though highly regarded as a serious literary writer, he also enjoyed publishing in the popular genres, including a series of horror novels in the 1980s and 1990s that are set in Minneapolis.

F. Scott Fitzgerald

▶ *F. Scott Fitzgerald*

In St. Paul, devotees of F. Scott Fitzgerald can see the neighborhood in St. Paul where he lived. He was born on September 24, 1896, in a house at 481 Laurel Avenue. Actually, there are two houses on the site; Fitzgerald was born in the one on the left.

His family lived at several houses in town, moving on the periphery of its finest residential areas and on the fringe of moneyed society: 294 Laurel, 514 Holly, 499 Holly, 509 Holly, 593 Summit, and finally a fine house at 599 Summit Avenue on St. Paul's "show street."

Fitzgerald described his family's status and wealth in his first novel, *This Side of Paradise*, which he wrote in his third-floor room at 599 Summit. At the time, at 516 Summit Avenue, lived another soon-to-be-famous novelist named Sinclair Lewis. (You'll read more about Lewis in the section on Sauk Centre.) Early in the novel, Amory

Blaine visits a young woman who lives in a fine house, the door of which is opened by one of the three butlers in Minneapolis.

Fitzgerald ran up and down the middle of Summit Avenue when he received the news that his novel had been accepted for publication by Scribner's; he stopped drivers at random to tell them of his success.

Fitzgerald and his wife, Zelda, lived in St. Paul for a year, from late summer 1921 to October 1922. During this time, Zelda was pregnant and Fitzgerald completed his second novel, *The Beautiful and Damned*.

Although Summit Avenue is said to have the longest stretch of Victorian homes in the nation, reviews have been mixed. Frank Lloyd Wright declared it the worst collection of architecture in the world, and Fitzgerald called it a mausoleum of American architectural monstrosities. So there.

In *This Side of Paradise*, Fitzgerald's hero, Amory Blaine, visits the Minnehaha Club, the exclusive country club in Minneapolis. He and a friend are said to be weekly visitors to the Stock Company: "Afterward they would stroll home in the balmy air of August night, dreaming along Hennepin and Nocollet Avenues, through the gay crowd."

Don't miss the former St. Paul Academy building at 25 North Dale Street, where Fitzgerald began to keep a diary at age fourteen and where his grades were so poor that his parents sent him to a Catholic prep school in New Jersey. The building has a new statue of Fitzgerald outside of it. It's also fun to walk by the St. Paul YMCA, where his play *Coward* was staged in 1913; it's hard to believe that although tickets were twenty-five cents apiece, the event was sold out and raised $250 for charity.

When you're in downtown St. Paul, you can visit a few other sites that played their roles in the life of this great American writer:

- The Commodore Hotel, where Scott and Zelda Fitzgerald lived after their baby, Scottie, was born.
- The W.A. Frost building, which has a restaurant with an old tin ceiling that was once a neighborhood drugstore. You can easily imagine the young writer having ice cream sodas here.
- The Fitzgerald Theater, 10 East Exchange Street, home of the long-running radio show *A Prairie Home Companion*. This is St. Paul's oldest theater, built in 1910 as the Sam Shubert Theater. It's home not only to the radio show but to a variety of films, plays, and concerts.

▶ A *Prairie Home Companion*

This radio show, created in 1974 by writer and novelist Garrison Keillor, has done much for celebrating and promoting books, writers, and the love of literature. Part of every show includes an original story told by Keillor in monologue as "The News from Lake Wobegon." This fictional town has roots in Keillor's own Minnesota childhood (see the section "Avon and Stearns County: Searching for Lake Wobegon" later in this chapter). Keillor has been tracing the adventures of his characters in these monologues every week for years, and in books such as *Lake Wobegon Days*.

Keillor also produces "The Writer's Almanac" (http://writers almanac.publicradio.org), a short daily radio feature in which he reads a poem and describes significant events that occurred that day in literary history.

Garrison Keillor

St. Paul was also the birthplace of African American photographer and novelist Gordon Parks (1912–2006), who writes (in his *A Choice of Weapons* memoir) of getting a job as a piano player for eighteen dollars a week at the Stumble Inn in Bemidji. He had a rough upbringing in the Twin Cities, where he had been sent to live with his sister after his mother died. He was thrown out of the house and later dropped out of high school. He went on to take photos for the covers of such magazines as *Life* and *Vogue*, and author eight books. An alternative learning center at 1212 University Avenue West was recently named in his honor.

You can also walk by the simple frame house at 130 Colorado Street. This is the setting where the character Lev Simon was said to have eked out a living as a bootlegger during Prohibition to pay for his sick child's medicine in Norman Katkov's 1949 novel *A Little Sleep, A Little Slumber*.

But if you're tired of traveling, you can enjoy coffee or cocoa and hear some poetry by local artists at any number of coffee shops in the Twin Cities. Dunn Bros looks like a classic 1960s-era coffee house and frequently features live music. And the shop roasts its own beans. It's popular with students from Macalester College. In Minneapolis, Urban Bean Coffee Shop features a drink called the Furley Freak, named after a Don Knotts TV character.

Dunn Bros
1569 Grand Avenue, St. Paul, Minnesota 55015
651-698-0618

Urban Bean Coffee Shop
3255 Bryant Avenue South, Minneapolis, Minnesota 55408
612-824-6611

Budding writers can take classes and find support at the Loft Literary Center, one of the country's largest and most active writers' centers. There's an espresso machine to help with inspiration, as well as a wide open space. You can take courses in poetry and fiction writing, and listen to others read their work. It's also a popular location for book release parties.

Loft Literary Center
1011 Washington Avenue South, Suite 200, Minneapolis, Minnesota 55415
612-379-8999
www.loft.org

The Twin Cities, as you might expect, are rife with bookstores. The legendary Hungry Mind/Ruminator Books in St. Paul closed in 2004, but at Friends of Minneapolis Public Library Bookshop, 300 Nicollet Mall, Minneapolis, you'll find inexpensive castoffs from library shelves. Uncle Hugo's Science Fiction Bookstore specializes in mysteries; in the back, you'll find both new and used books at Uncle Edgar's. Both are at 2864 Chicago Avenue, Minneapolis (612-824-9984). Another store specializing in mysteries is Once Upon a Crime, 604 West 26th Street, Minneapolis (612-870-3785), which is known for inviting famous writers for book signings.

Query Booksellers, 520 East Hennipin Avenue, Minneapolis (612-331-7701) specializes in gay literature, while leftists flock to Arise! Bookstore & Resource, 2441 Lyndale Avenue South, Minneapolis (612-871-7119). Two other well-known bookstores are Magers & Quinn Booksellers, 608 Second Avenue South, Suite 19, Minneapolis (612-371-2002) and Micawber's Books, 2238 Carter Avenue, St. Paul (651-646-5506). The Amazon Bookstore Cooperative, 4755 Chicago Avenue, Minneapolis (612-821-9630) is the oldest feminist bookstore in the country. And BirchBark Books and Native Arts, 2115 West 21st Street, Minneapolis (612-374-4023) is owned by Minnesota author Louise Erdrich.

In St. Paul, kids will love the Red Balloon Bookshop, 891 Grand Avenue (651-224-8320), where books are arranged both by age and category. Those interested in local-interest titles should go to the Minnesota History Center, 345 Kellogg Boulevard West, St. Paul (651-296-6126).

▸Stillwater

If you brake for a bookstore, you're going to need to visit your mechanic after a visit to Stillwater, which calls itself "North

Loome Booksellers

America's First Booktown." Whether your passion is antique, first edition, or hardcover fresh from the bestseller list, you're likely to find it here. Visit www.booktown.com to whet your appetite. It's a particularly good place for rare and out-of-print books, which you'll find at St. Croix Antiquarian Booksellers, 232 S. Main Street (651-430-0732) and Loome Booksellers, 320 North Fourth Street (651-430-1092). The latter store has particularly good collections in religious books.

▶ Scandia

Swedish Vilhelm Moberg (1898–1973), who was first published at age thirteen, described this region—one he had never seen—in a series of four novels, collectively called *The Emigrants*. In volume two, *Unto a Good Land*, he wrote:

> The St. Croix River, separating the new state of Wisconsin from the Minnesota Territory, made a large end as it flowed by Stillwater. Right here near the town the current was slow, almost imperceptible, and the river expanded into a small lake, on which all the timber floated down from above had been gathered; here on the west bank it would be hauled up and milled. A little farther to the west the ground rose in high hills, and the town of Stillwater had been built between these hills and the river.

Several of Moberg's relatives emigrated to Minnesota, but he remained in Sweden. He did take a research trip through the United States in 1948, but fired off letters to relatives asking for descriptions of thunderstorms, the price of postage stamps, and other details that he brought to life in his novels. Although he lost his struggle with depression, his suicide note was very precise: "The time is twenty past seven; I go to search in the lake for eternal sleep." Scandia loves to boast that the first (but by no means the last) Swedes in Minnesota chose to settle here. There are plenty of monuments and museums (not to mention shops, restaurants, and festivals) that tout the virtues of their pioneer ancestors. But their association with Moberg seems to still be lost in the bottom of the lake.

▶Fond du Lac

The Fond du Lac Follies written by syndicated columnist Jim Northrup (1943–   ), appears in several Native American publications, and his *Walking the Rez Road* (1995), a collection of stories and poems, won a Minnesota Book Award. You can visit the Fond du Lac Cultural Center and Museum, where you can research documents, photos, and artifacts related to Native Americans, and the Lindolm Service Station at the intersection of state highways 33 and 45 in Cloquet is the only gas station designed by Frank Lloyd Wright.

Fond du Lac Cultural Center and Museum
1720 Big Lake Road, Cloquet, Minnesota 55720
218-878-7582
www.fdlrez.com/Museum/index.htm
Monday through Friday, 9:00 a.m. to noon and 1:00 p.m. to 4:00 p.m.

▶Duluth

"The coldest winter I ever spent was a summer in Duluth." That quip has been attributed to Mark Twain, although it's unclear who uttered it first. Lovers of manuscripts won't care if it's cloudy or sunny when they get to the local branch of the Karpeles Manuscript Library. It claims to be the world's largest private holding of important original manuscripts and documents, and displays are rotated on a regular basis. The Duluth location is only one of several Karpeles libraries around the country. You'll find manuscripts of Benjamin Franklin, Clara Barton, Florence Nightingale, and much more. The Carlson Book & Record is gone but not forgotten. But if you want to pretend your visit to the Fitgers Brewery Complex is highbrow, you can visit the museum and bookstore.

Karpeles Manuscript Library
902 East First Street, Duluth, Minnesota 55805
218-728-0630
www.rain.org/~karpeles/dulfrm.html
Open every day, noon to 4:00 p.m.

Fitger's Brewhouse Brewery and Grille
600 East Superior Street, Duluth, Minnesota 55802
218-279-2739
www.brewhouse.net

Monday through Friday, 11:00 a.m. to 10:00 p.m.
Saturday and Sunday, 11:00 a.m. to 11:00 p.m.

▶Grand Rapids

Before tourists invaded Grand Rapids to enjoy its forests and fish-ing lakes, woodsmen invaded by the thousands to be outfitted and fed in the 1800s. Learn more at the Forest History Center, which includes a replica of a late nineteenth-century logging camp. What does this have to do with literature? Think about it. If there had been no paper, Frank Baum wouldn't have been able to write *The Wizard of Oz*. Without *The Wizard of Oz*, Judy Garland might have remained Frances Ethel Gumm. That was her name when she lived on South Pokegama Avenue. The house is now restored to its 1925 appearance and called the July Garland Museum. There's a yellow brick road leading to the Itasca County Historical Society Museum in a restored 1895 Richardsonian Romanesque-style school build-ing. And if your kids weren't thrilled enough by the outhouse in the Forest History Center, take them to the Children's Discovery Museum where they can dig for dinosaur fossils and talk to a tree. Nothing will please them like a festival? The Judy Garland Festival is the fourth weekend in June and the Tall Timber Days Festival is the first weekend in August.

Forest History Center
2609 County Road 76, Grand Rapids, Minnesota 55744
218-327-4482
www.mnhs.org/places/sites/fhc
Seasonal hours, but open year-round

Judy Garland Museum
2727 US Highway 169 South, Grand Rapids, Minnesota 55744
800-664-JUDY
www.judygarlandmuseum.com
Seasonal hours, but open year-round

▶Ely

How many times have you heard someone say about a poem: you either love it or you hate it. Ely, which is the gateway to the Boundary Waters Canoe Area Wilderness, seems to spark that same reaction. In naming it his number one vacation spot, Charles Kuralt rhapsodized: "On the map, Ely appears to be at the end of the road. For people who love wilderness and beauty and solitude, on the contrary it's at the center of the world." But in 1900 Billy Sunday made this pronouncement: "The only difference between Ely and Hell is that Ely has a railroad into it." That railroad was a result of a rumor of a gold strike. The gold turned out to be iron, but Ely lends its name to a rare local rock formation that formed 2.7 billion years ago when lava flows solidified underwater. You can see an outcropping of Ely greenstone, known as Pillow Rocks, at 12th and Main Streets. If you have one kid who loves bears and another who fancies wolves, you can make them both happy here. The North American Bear Center at 2032 Sheridan Street features life-size, stuffed bears and an interactive board with eight natural bear sounds. The International Wolf Center at 1396 SR 169 isn't content to stop with its award-winning exhibits, but also takes you into the forest to howl at wild wolves and join dog sledding excursions. Other museums include the fine Ely/Winton History Museum (1900 East Camp Street) and the Dorothy Molter Museum (2002 East Sheridan Street).

Of all the characters described in this book, I definitely wish I could have met Dorothy Molter. Not only was she a free spirit after my own heart, but she also gave out free samples of her homemade

The Dorothy Molter Museum

root beer to passing canoeists and visitors from around the world. I love root beer. I love free stuff. You'll find the Dorothy Molter Museum just east of Ely, on the south side of MN Highway 169. It's open daily from Memorial Day to Labor Day. And, because I also love books, I'm finally getting around to telling you another amazing Ely story with a literary hook that could have been featured on another one of my favorite things: *Antiques Roadshow*. There was a painting inconspicuously hanging for more than fifty years in the library that in 1988 was discovered to be "Breakfast in the Garden," a long-lost masterpiece by Frederick Frieseke. A New York collector bought it for $500,000, and the city used the proceeds to create the Donald G. Gardner Trust. Besides funding the library, the money goes to the Northern Lakes Arts Association to sponsor theater, dance, music, literary, and visual arts events.

There are also a number of good bookstores in town, such as Lisa's Second Floor Bookstore, 105 North Central Avenue; Piragis Northwoods Company, 105 North Central Avenue, and Chapman Street Books & Prairie Fire Tobacco, 139 East Chapman Street.

▸ Bemidji

I couldn't begin the section about Bemidji with anything other than Paul Bunyan. James MacGillivray (1856–1938), who was an itinerant newspaper reporter but was associated with the *Detroit News*, wrote the first published Paul Bunyan article in 1906. Further versions appeared in the July 24, 1910, printing of *The Round River Drive*. Four years later illustrated pamphlets written by a Minneapolis ad man, William B. Laughead (1897-1958), put other characters into the national spotlight, including the beloved Babe the Blue Ox and Johnny Inkslinger (my personal favorite). It's only fair to mention that Paul and William were on the same payroll—that of the Red River Lumber Company. The great lumberjack's presence continues today in such Bemidji institutions as the Paul Bunyan Telephone Cooperative, Paul Bunyan Mall, Paul Bunyan Television (PBTV), the Paul Bunyan Sub Shop, and Paul Bunyan Mini Storage. A Paul Bunyan Playhouse puts on summer repertory at 314 Beltrami Avenue North West. And of course, there are two statues of Paul and Babe standing on the shores of Lake Bemidji.

But a significant community of real writers are now actually living amidst the lakes and pines of northern Minnesota. Fiction

An early entrepreneur capitalizing on Paul Bunyan

writer Will Weaver (1950–   ), a creative writing teacher at Bemidji State University, says his own writing is heavily influenced by the landscape in which he lives. His literary works, from his debut novel, *Red Earth, White Earth*, to his series of books for young adults, reflect the wide open spaces of the northern prairies and the forests of the northwoods.

Fiction writer Kevin McColley lives twenty-two miles northwest of Bemidji in a one-hundred-year-old farmhouse, which he says is haunted by a fiddle-playing ghost. In addition to having a neighbor named Ole, he has an affection for sled dogs. It's probably not a coincidence that he just finished a novel about a man who moves to rural northern Minnesota and raises sled dogs. McColley's work includes six novels, most notably, *Praying to a Laughing God* and a Civil War novel, *The Other Side*. McColley tried living the urban lifestyle, but he says it suffocated his writing. Believe it or not, he says he feels less isolated in the northwoods than anywhere else he's lived.

Although poet and author Susan Hauser concedes that nature feeds her creativity and her soul, she claims that her poetry and prose would be the same if she lived in a city. "I think the mistake comes when people think that art is created in the external setting," Hauser says. "And people frequently say to me, 'Oh, you live out in the country, you must go sit out under a tree and write.' No. Writing does not take place in the landscape you see outside your eyes. It takes place in the landscape inside your head."

Kent Nerburn writes mostly nonfiction that often focuses on the spiritual nature of people and places. He finds a strong emotional presence in the northern Minnesota landscape that is a sensory feast for the wordsmith. "I think that there is great nourishment for the writer here, because your imagination is projected long distances," he says. "It isn't stopped by walls, it isn't stopped by issues of the domestic, it isn't stopped by sounds that are close, it isn't bouncing off an urban environment. There are large echoes out there, and I think that's a good space in which a writer can work."

I-94: From Lake Wobegon to the Words Written in Stone

This is not scenery that you can gaze at idly from afar. You'll be immersed in the starkly beautiful landscape and captivated by the sky. Don't get me started on the rivers and lakes. And then there's that snow. Keep on reading to get a sense of how nature can nurture creativity.

▶ Avon and Stearns County: Searching for Lake Wobegon

If my editor didn't have such sharp scissors, a more substantial portion of this book would be devoted to the success of Garrison Keillor (1942–   ) and his Lake Wobegon writings, which continue to be tremendously popular. Fans of the fictional world can visit many real-life locales that are the inspiration for Keillor's writings, including:

- The Lake Wobegon Trail, a twenty-eight-mile bike trail that runs from Avon to Sauk Centre, Minnesota (Sauk Centre contains the home of novelist Sinclair Lewis, which is open to tourists).
- Stearns County, where Keillor lived thirty years ago when he began his writing career. He tells people that the "real" Lake Wobegon can be found here, near Albany and Avon, beyond the hellish shopping strip, Division Street in St. Cloud. "Holdingford, pop. 628, is the town that looks most Wobegonian to

me," he commented in a recent *National Geographic* article on the Lake Wobegon area.

- River Falls, Wisconsin, where Keillor lives when he is not in New York City.
- The Guthrie Theater in Minneapolis and the Fitzgerald Theater in St. Paul, where the *Prairie Home Companion* radio shows are frequently staged (see the section on Minneapolis and St. Paul).

J. F. Powers's (1917–1999) novel *Morte D'Urban*, which won the National Book Award in 1963, tells the story of Father Urban, a priest in Stearns County. The priest takes a train to Minneapolis:

> The country beyond Minneapolis seemed awfully empty to him, flat and treeless, Illinois without people. It didn't attract, it didn't repel. He saw more streams than he'd see in Illinois, but they weren't working. November was winter here. Too many white frame farmhouses, not new and not old, not at all what Father Urban would care to come home to for Thanksgiving or Christmas. Rusty implements. Brown dirt. Gray skies. Ice. No snow. A great deal of talk about this on the train. Father Urban dropped entirely out of it after an hour or so.

Powers was known for his studies of Catholic priests, and frequently took inspiration for his stories and novels from the Catholic Church.

Little Falls native and writer Charles Lindbergh

▶ Little Falls

Little Falls is the birthplace (in 1954) of the celebrated Native American author Louise Erdrich. She won the National Book Critics Circle Award for her 1984 novel *Love Medicine*. Today, she owns BirchBark Books in Minneapolis.

I'm counting Charles A. Lindbergh as a literary figure because he never forgot Little Falls, where he was born in 1902, and always wrote lovingly of it. Plus I'm a big fan of the work of his wife, Anne Morrow Lindbergh, the author of the wonderful meditative book *Gift from the Sea*, and continue to be fascinated by the writing that's still being generated by the kidnapping of their baby. The restored boyhood home of Lucky Lindy at 1620 Lindberg Drive includes lots of airplane stuff. But while enjoying the family possessions and furnishings, I was interested to learn that Charles A. Lindbergh Senior (1859–1924) was a progressive Republican Congressman with anti-war views that cost him later elections. In fact, his book, *Why Is Your Country at War*, was burned and the plates were destroyed. It's ironic that both the nearby Minnesota Military Museum and the Charles A. Weyerhaeuser Memorial Museum are focused on Camp Ripley. Maybe the conservationist spirits of the Lindberghs rest easier in the Minnesota Fishing Museum or the Pine Grove Park and Zoo, which preserves a rare tract of virgin white pine.

▶ Sauk Centre

Sinclair Lewis was born in Sauk Centre on February 7, 1885. You can learn about him in one of two ways (or both): at the Interpretive Center by the highway, or in town by visiting his boyhood home and other sites.

First, the Interpretive Center. If you need a break from driving and would rather see a videotape about Lewis than see the town he immortalized in the novel *Main Street*, visit the Sinclair Lewis Interpretive Center. It's at a rest stop at the northwest quadrant of I-94 and U.S. 71. It's home to a great deal of material that reveals how Lewis crafted his novels.

Lewis (1885–1951) was very methodical in the creation of his characters. He often chose real names from tombstones and telephone books, and then created characters to accompany the names. In a similar way, he invented place names and created fictional cities, often based upon his own experience. For example, the town of Gopher Prairie, Minnesota, the backdrop for Lewis's 1920 classic *Main Street*, is based heavily on Sauk Centre itself. The interpretive Lewis display in the Interpretive Center, "The Birth of a Novel," explains his methods. Much Sinclair Lewis memorabilia resides at this museum.

Sinclair Lewis

The center is also home to Lewis's writing desk, old photographs, and historical background of Sauk Centre, Lewis's diplomas, and other personal items belonging to Lewis.

Sinclair Lewis Interpretive Center
I-94 and US Highway 71, Sauk Centre, Minnesota 56378
320-352-5201
www.saukherald.com/ftp/lewis/center.html
Memorial Day to Labor Day
Monday through Friday, 8:30 a.m. to 5:00 p.m.
Saturday and Sunday, 9:00 a.m. to 5:00 p.m.

Given the scathing satire of small-town life in Main Street, plenty of Sauk Centre's citizens still harbor resentment toward him. He both shocked and immortalized the town by describing the narrow-mindedness of its inhabitants. He wasn't really popular when he worked as a substitute night clerk at the Palmer House Hotel either. In fact, he was fired for reading and sleeping on the job. The hotel still stands.

The town's Bryant Library contains a collection of all Lewis's works, many photographs, plus Lewis's death certificate, and the urn that carried his ashes from Rome, where he died, to Sauk Centre.

Lewis's house still contains much family memorabilia. His father was a doctor, and the house often served as the local emergency room. Lewis's boyhood observations provided a great deal of material for his book *Arrowsmith*, which features an idealistic doctor. The book won a 1926 Pulitzer Prize, which Lewis rejected. The house

Sinclair Lewis's home in Sauk Centre. Photo courtesy of Joyce Lyng.

is 3.5 blocks west of (what else?) Main Street on (what else?) West Sinclair Lewis Avenue.

Lewis was the first American to win the Nobel Prize in Literature. In accepting the 1930 award, Lewis commented, "in America most of us—not readers alone, but even writers—are still afraid of any literature which is not a glorification of everything American, a glorification of our faults as well as our virtues," In fact, a number of Lewis's books (e.g., *Elmer Gantry, Babbitt, Kingsblood Royal, Cass Timberlane*) were banned because of his views, which were seen as controversial.

If you love to roam a cemetery, Lewis's ashes are buried in the family plot in Greenwood Cemetery. Okay, this time you won't have to roam because I'm going to tell you that from the main entrance, you just have to go three rows and eight monuments to the left. And if you travel between Sauk Centre and Saint Joseph, you can buy a meal or stay overnight and they'll be glad for the business. Or you can pitch your tent at the Sinclair Lewis Campground and then embark on the Lake Wobegon Bike Trail, which runs for twenty-eight miles.

Each year in July, Sauk Centre hosts Sinclair Lewis Days, a week-long celebration that includes tours, parades, a Miss Sauke Centre pageant, and music.

Sinclair Lewis Boyhood Home
810 Sinclair Lewis Avenue, Sauk Centre, Minnesota 56378
www.saukherald.com/ftp/lewis/home.html
320-352-5201

▶Alexandria

If you're stuck in traffic as you read this, compare your commute to the tragic journal of a band of Vikings as told on the Kensington Runestone. The date has been verified to be 1362. No, that's not a typo. Scholars have confirmed the stone's authenticity, but nobody is sure how it ended up on the farm of Olaf Ohman, where it was discovered in 1898. Maybe you'll figure it out when you see it at the Runestone Museum (206 Broadway). In addition to other Viking and Native American exhibits, there's a replica of the 1862 stockade built to protect settlers. Nearby is the Historic Knute Nelson House (1219 Nokomis Street). He was governor from 1892 to 1895 and, in addition to boasting original furnishings, the Douglas County Historical Society maintains a family research facility there.

▶Anoka

When my computer crashes and loses the last draft of my priceless work in progress, I'm tempted to go back to the stone and chisel. Father Hennepin and Jonathan Emerson left their mark in just that way. You can still see the name of the Franciscan explorer and the date 1680 on a stone near the mouth of the Rum River. On a monument in the city cemetery, Jonathan Emerson was more garrulous. The old settler inscribed 2,500 words from the Bible and then went on to record bits of his personal philosophy. We can only hope he was satisfied with his work when he died a year later. Oh yes, I need to mention that Anoka also has a more traditional historical center, the Anoka County History Center and Library.

Anoka County History Center and Library
2135 Third Avenue North, Anoka, Minnesota 55303
763-421-0600
www.ac-hs.org
Tuesday, 10:00 a.m. to 8:00 p.m.
Wednesday through Friday, 10:00 a.m. to 5:00 p.m.
Saturday, 10:00 a.m. to 4:00 p.m.

Lutefisk Capital USA

►Madison

Madison, which calls itself "Lutefisk Capital USA," is also the birth-place (in 1926) of poet and philosopher Robert Bly. Bly's books of poetry include *The Light Around the Body*, for which he received the National Book Award for poetry in 1968. He attended St. Olaf College (1946-1947), but obtained his B.A. from Harvard University in 1950. He edited the collection *Iron John: A Book about Men*, which graces my bookshelf and was helpful to me at a certain point in my life. You can see Bly's writing studio at J. F. Jacobson Park—along with a monument to lutefisk, the dried cod prepared with lye by Scandinavians, which is definitely an acquired taste.

chapter six

Missouri

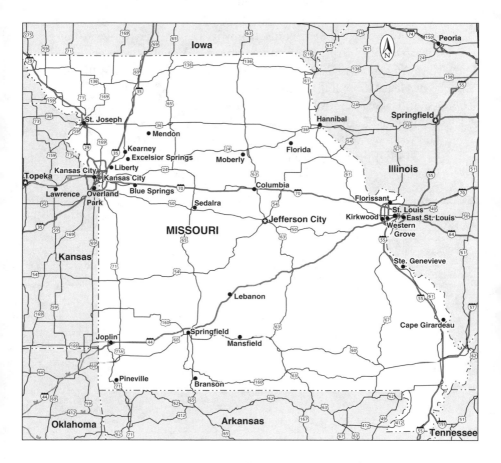

Driving Tours

1. I-55 South from St. Louis to Arkansas
2. I-44 to Joplin
3. I-70: Goin' West to Kansas City
4. I-35: Goin' South to Kansas City
5. The Great River Road: Mark Twain Country

"*I* was born here because Missouri was an unknown new state and needed an attraction."

—*Mark Twain*

Mark Twain dominates the Show-Me state's literary history, but a truly impressive number of illustrious literary figures hail from here—and many of them come from St. Louis. They range from showy stars like T. S. Eliot and Tennessee Williams to poets like Maya Angelou and Sara Teasdale. More recent writers like William Least Heat-Moon and novelists Speer Morgan and William Peden live and work here today. The Ozark Mountain country and its tradition of bawdy folktales were celebrated by Vance Randolph in such volumes as *Ozark Superstitions*, *We Always Lie to Strangers*, and the wonderfully titled *Pissing in the Snow and other Ozark Folktales*.

I-55 South from St. Louis to Arkansas

▶St. Louis

The poet Walt Whitman wrote admiringly of St. Louis, which he visited in 1879. He stayed here with relatives for three months. In his book *Specimen Days in America*, he writes:

> The points of St. Louis are its position, its absolute wealth (the long accumulations of time and trade, solid riches, probably a higher average thereof than any city), the unrivall'd amplitude of its well-laid out environage of broad plateaus, for future expansion—and the great state of which it is the head. It fuses northern and southern qualities, perhaps native and foreign ones, to perfection, rendezvous the whole stretch of the Mississippi and Missouri rivers, and its American electricity goes well with its German phlegm.

Maybe it's something in the water, and maybe it's the German phlegm of which Whitman speaks. But St. Louis has more than its share of famous people, and especially literary figures. The St. Louis Walk of Fame is one hundred stars and plaques embedded in the sidewalk honoring famous St. Louisians. Anyone can be nominated, but those inducted must have either been born here or spent part of their artistic life here, and must have had an impact on the city's cultural heritage. Plaques list their many achievements, providing a stroll that is pleasant as well as educational. Here are the locations of some of St. Louis's famous writers:

Maya Angelou	6337 Delmar
William Burroughs	6362 Delmar
Kate Chopin	6310 Delmar
T. S. Eliot	6625 Delmar
Stanley Elkin	6275 Delmar
Eugene Field	6315 Delmar
William Gass	6632 Delmar
William Inge	6624 Delmar
Marianne Moore	6625 Delmar
Irma Rombauer	6636 Delmar
Sara Teasdale	6603 Delmar
Tennessee Williams	6500 Delmar

6504 Delmar Boulevard
St. Louis, Missouri 63130
314-727-7827
www.stlouiswalkoffame.org

There are many authors who left their mark on St. Louis and vice versa. You could spend an entire day driving from one of their birthplaces or childhood homes to another—if many of them had not been torn down years ago. But you can still visit the neighborhoods where they grew up and get a flavor (however diluted) for what inspired them. I'll describe them in alphabetical order.

▶ Maya Angelou

Poet Maya Angelou (1928–   ) was born Marguerite Johnson in St. Louis in 1928. Her parents were divorced when she was three, and she was sent to Stamps, Arkansas, where she was raised by her grandmother. She was sexually assaulted as a child; her relatives beat the assailant to death, and she became mute, feeling her words had caused someone's death. A friend of her grandmother's helped her regain her voice. She was sent to San Francisco when she was twelve, where she lived with her mother (and where she became the first black streetcar conductor in that city).

Angelou has been a successful actress, a professional dancer, and writer. She was nominated for a Tony Award for her performance in *Look Away* and an Emmy Award for her performance in *Roots*. She became the first black woman to have her screenplay produced as a film with *Georgia, Georgia*. She has written several volumes of her autobiography beginning with her most famous work, *I Know Why the Caged Bird Sings*, which was nominated for a National Book Award. Her book, *Just Give Me a Cool Drink of Water 'Fore I Diiie* was nominated for a Pulitzer Prize. Angelou is currently the Reynolds Professor of American Studies at Wake Forest University in Winston-Salem, North Carolina.

▶ William S. Burroughs

William Seward Burroughs (1914–1997) was born at 4664 Pershing Avenue to a well-to-do family in St. Louis in 1914. His grandfather founded the Burroughs Adding Machine Company. William attended elementary and high school in St. Louis, and, during summers attending Harvard University, he worked as a reporter for the *St. Louis Post-Dispatch*. Shortly before the stock market crash of 1929 his parents sold their stock in the company, which enabled them to give William a two-hundred-dollar monthly allowance. This served him for the next two decades.

Burroughs is best known as one of the Beat Generation writers. His 1959 book *Naked Lunch* is considered a classic of the era. His writing is often stark, uncompromising, difficult; he used his writing to exorcise many demons, including his drug addictions, and the death of his common-law wife Joan Vollmer, which occurred during a tragic, drunken game of "William Tell." A Unitarian minister in New Hampshire writes a fascinating essay that shows the attraction of Burroughs and the Beats on generations of readers; he made a pilgrimage to Burroughs' home just to take a photo of it (www.uunashua.org/sermons/burroughs.shtml). Although Burroughs lived many places in his life, he came home at the end; he is buried in Bellefontaine Cemetery in St. Louis, located at 4947 West Florissant Avenue.

▶ *Kate Chopin*

Novelist Kate Chopin (1850–1904) was born Katherine O'Flaherty into one of the city's oldest families. Many of her stories and novels are set in the Creole culture of New Orleans, where her husband, Oscar, was from. She held a literary salon in her home at 3317 Morgan Street. She is best known for her 1899 novel *The Awakening*, which drew criticism for its frank portrayal of a young woman's sexual and artistic development. Today, Chopin is admired as a precursor of the feminist writers of the twentieth century.

Chopin and her husband met while attending a ball at the historic Oakland house, which you can still visit today. She died after suffering a brain hemorrhage while visiting the St. Louis World's Fair in 1904.

Chopin was a member of the Equal Suffrage League, an early twentieth-century women's rights group that met in the Syndicate Building in the 900 block of Locust. T. S. Eliot's mother, Charlotte, was also a member.[1]

Historic Oakland House
7823 Genesta, St. Louis, Missouri 63123
314-495-0465

▶ T. S. Eliot

St. Louis was the birthplace of many writers you might never associate with the city, and Thomas Stearns Eliot (1888–1965) is one of them. One of the greatest poets of the twentieth century, Eliot is often considered a British poet, but he was born on September 26, 1888, in a house at 2635 Locust Street. Unfortunately, that house has been demolished, and the site where the house stood is now a parking lot.

Today, Eliot may be remembered for one of his most trivial works, *Old Possum's Book of Practical Cats*. Its characters—including Shimbleshanks, Mungojerrie, Rumpleteazer, and Old Deuteronomy—were the basis for one of the most successful and popular musicals of all time: *Cats*. Eliot's most lasting influence is from his great poems, such as "The Waste Land."

St. Louis and the Mississippi River definitely influenced Eliot's poetry. He once commented that the title of one of his most famous poems, "The Love Song of J. Alfred Prufrock," was from a sign he had seen for a local manufacturer, the William Prufrock Furniture Company.[2] (The company was located at 1104 Locust; it, too, is now a parking lot.) And the "Great Brown God" mentioned in one of his "Four Quartets" is probably the Mississippi. In a 1930 letter to the *St. Louis Post-Dispatch*, he wrote about the river:

> There is something in having passed one's childhood beside the big river which is incommunicable to those who have not.[3]

▶ Stanley Elkin (1930–)

The author lived in an apartment at 469 Leland, which he described in detail in a 1965 story "The Guest." Elkin taught creative writing at Washington University for thirty years. He won the National Book Critics Circle Award for *George Mills*; his other novels include *The Dick Gibson Show*, *The Magic Kingdom*, and *Van Gogh's Room at Arles*.

▶ Eugene Field

Eugene Field (1850–1895), commonly known as the "Children's Poet," often wrote about toys. He spent the first six years of his life in a rowhouse at 634 Broadway that is now operated as the Eugene Field House and St. Louis Toy Museum. It's amazing that the house still stands; it's one of the few structures in an area dominated by parking lots for the nearby St. Louis Cardinals baseball park.

The house was preserved by the Eugene Field House Foundation, which was established in 1936 by the Board of Education of the City of St. Louis. Rotating exhibits of their extensive collection of antique dolls, toys, and other objects ensure a steady stream of happy children. Here's an excerpt from a Field poem, "Jest 'Fore Christmas," that mentions both toys and kids:

> For Christmas, with its lots an' lots of candies, cakes, an' toys,
> Was made, they say, for proper kids an' not for naughty boys;
> So wash yer face an' bresh yer hair, an' mind yer p's and q's,
> An' don't bust out yer pantaloons, and don't wear out yer shoes;
> Say "Yessum" to the ladies, and "Yessur" to the men,
> An' when they's company, don't pass yer plate for pie again;
> But, thinkin' of the things yer'd like to see upon that tree,
> Jest 'fore Christmas be as good as yer kin be!

But some visitors may be just as eager to learn more about his father, Roswell Martin Field, who initiated the 1853 lawsuit that led to the Dred Scot Decision, helping to foment the Civil War. This was, after all, the house that Daddy built, and it was designated a National Historic Landmark in 2007.

Eugene Field House and St. Louis Toy Museum
634 South Broadway, St. Louis, Missouri 63102
314-421-4689

▶ William Gass

Novelist William Gass (1924–) joined the faculty of Washington University in St. Louis in 1969 and has been associated with that institution, and the city, ever since. He is the author, among other books, of the novel *Omensetter's Luck* (which is mentioned in the chapter on Ohio, where Gass grew up), and the short story collection *In the Heart of the Heart of the Country*. Gass is the co-author, with Lorin Cuoco, of *Literary St. Louis*, a book that explores the many writers associated with the city.

▶ William Inge (1913–1973)

Born in Kansas, Inge came to St. Louis in 1943 to take a job as the drama critic for one of the local papers, the *Star-Times*. He met and was encouraged by Tennessee Williams, and wrote *Come Back, Little Sheba* while teaching at Washington University in the late 1940s. He became (along with Williams) one of the most prominent playwrights of the 1950s for such plays as *Picnic* (1953), for which he won the Pulitzer Prize, and *Bus Stop* (1955). He also wrote the screenplay for the movie *Splendor in the Grass* in 1962.

William Inge

▶ *Howard Nemerov*

Nemerov (1920–1991) won the National Book Award and Pulitzer Prize for Poetry, and was twice named Poet Laureate Consultant in Poetry to the Library of Congress. Born in New York, he taught for many years at Washington University in St. Louis. One of his poems, titled, "Found Poem" was based on information published in the *St. Louis Post-Dispatch*.

Joseph Pulitzer

▶ Joseph Pulitzer

Publisher Joseph Pulitzer (1847–1911) was born in Hungary, but emigrated to the U.S. and served in the Civil War. After the war he moved to St. Louis, where he began his career as the publisher of a German-language newspaper and later the *St. Louis Post-Dispatch*. He was known as the champion of the working class "common man." As publisher of the *New York World*, he recruited the journalist Nellie Bly. At Pulitzer's death, he left two million dollars to Columbia University, which led to the creation of the Columbia University School of Journalism and the Pulitzer Prizes.

▶ Irma Rombauer

Imagine being invited to dinner at Irma Rombauer's St. Louis home in the 1920s. You are certain to have had a good meal. Rombauer (1877–1962) was known as one of the city's most prominent hostesses when she conceived the idea to create a cookbook. She had to risk her own money to get her book *The Joy of Cooking* self-published in 1931. The timing was perfect, as cash-strapped Americans were seeking to cook meals for themselves during the Depression. The book was self-published by Rombauer's family until it was picked up by the Bobbs-Merrill Company in 1936. Today, the book remains one of the most-published cookbooks ever and has become a must-have in nearly every American kitchen.

▶ Sara Teasdale

Poet Sara Teasdale (1884–1933) was not only born here in 1884 but is now buried in Bellefontaine Cemetery, located at 4947 West Florissant Avenue.

She lived on both Lindell Boulevard and Kingsbury Place when growing up. She attended Mary Institute and Hosmer Hall, where she began writing poems. In 1918, she won the Columbia University Poetry Society Prize, the precursor to the Pulitzer Prize for Poetry, for her collection *Love Songs*. In her poem "Sunset: Saint Louis" she describes the city while crossing the Eads Bridge:

> Hushed in the smoky haze of summer sunset,
>
> When I came home again from far-off places,
> How many times I saw my western city
> Dream by her river.
>
> Then for an hour the water wore a mantle
> Of tawny gold and mauve and misted turquoise
> Under the tall and darkened arches bearing
> Gray, high-flung bridges.
>
> Against the sunset, water-towers and steeples
> Flickered with fire up the slope to westward,
> And old warehouses poured their purple shadows
> Across the levee.
>
> High over them the black train swept with thunder,
> Cleaving the city, leaving far beneath it
> Wharf-boats moored beside the old side-wheelers
> Resting in twilight.

▶ Tennessee Williams (1911–1983)

Playwright Tennessee Williams, who was born here, set *The Glass Menagerie* in the seedy neighborhood where he lived on Westminster Place. Thomas Lanier Williams, better known as Tennessee Williams, grew up in the late 1920s and early 30s in the family

Tennessee Williams (right) with Andy Warhol (left)

home at 6254 Enright. He reportedly modeled his landmark play *The Glass Menagerie* on this tenement, but there is a difference of opinion about the roots of this great American play. It's not surprising when you consider that Williams reportedly lived at as many as twenty-nine different places in the city when he was growing up.[4] Another boyhood home is said to be at 4633 Westminster Place, a building that still stands and that was sometimes referred to as the "Menagerie Apartments."

"The apartment faces an alley," he explains in the introductory instructions for the play, "and is entered by a fire escape, a structure whose name is a touch of accidental poetic truth, for all of these huge buildings are always burning with slow and implacable fires of human desperation."

The Glass Menagerie contains multiple St. Louis references: from Tom's job at Continental Shoemakers, modeled after the writer's own job at the International Shoe Factory (now the City Museum); to Tom visiting the movie houses on Grand; to Laura's playing hooky in Forest Park.

In a literary coincidence, Williams attended an elementary school named after another St. Louis-born writer, Eugene Field. He graduated from University City High School. He attended Washington University in St. Louis, which is a fact he would probably not like to have mentioned: after finishing fourth in a playwriting contest on campus he stormed angrily into his professor's office and complained. He later left the university and had the name of the school removed from his 1975 Memoirs.[5] He and writer A. E. Hotchner were both on the staff of the *Eliot Review*, the campus literary magazine.

In his memoirs, he writes:

> The last time I was in St. Louis, for a visit at Christmas, I had my brother Dakin drive me about all the old places where we had lived in my childhood. It was a melancholy tour. Westminster Place and Forest Park Boulevard have lost all semblance of their charm in the twenties. The big old residences had been converted into sleazy rooming-houses or torn down for nondescript duplexes and small apartment buildings.[6]

▶Calvary Cemetery

This cemetery north of St. Louis was created as a result of the cholera epidemic early in the twentieth century. Writers buried here include Kate Chopin and Tennessee Williams. The former slave Dred Scott and the missionary Thomas Dooley also have their final resting places here.

▶Eads Bridge

The Eads Bridge, which connects St. Louis and East St. Louis, was completed in 1874 and has long been associated with the city. Walt Whitman does not mention the Eads Bridge by name in *Specimen Days in America*, but he is doubtless speaking of it when he writes:

> I have haunted the river every night lately, where I could get a look at the bridge by moonlight. It is indeed a structure of perfection and beauty unsurpassable, and I never tire of it.[7]

▶St. Louis Dickens Festival

Every year, the Gateway Christian Church, located at 1951 Des Peres Road, hosts a St. Louis Dickens Festival in December, during the holiday season. Live music, crafts, games, and refreshments are held in an English village of the Dickens era, which is supposed to be the writer's home town of Chatham.

Dickens himself visited St. Louis on his tour of the states. He attended a soiree and ball given in his honor in 1842. In his book *American Notes*, he wrote:

> I think [St. Louis] must rather dispose to fever ... Just adding, that it is very hot, lies among great rivers, and has vast tracts of undrained swampy land around it. I leave it to the reader to form his own opinion.

Dickens traveled to St. Louis from Cairo, Illinois, on the steamboat *Fulton*. This vessel would become the model for the Eden described in the novel *Martin Chuzzlewit*.

Charles Dickens traveled to St. Louis by steamboat.

▶Ste. Genevieve

If you're reading this book because you're a research scholar or genealogist, the town of Ste. Genevieve, located one hour south of St. Louis, is probably already on your itinerary. The records at the library, courthouse, and churches are the oldest in the West. Ste. Genevieve itself was the topic of many early records. As the first permanent settlement in Missouri, the political and social events held here were attended by the movers and shakers long before the Louisiana Purchase. French traditions are still evident in festivals and architecture, and many of the buildings are open to the public and well worth a visit. I'm a passionate bird watcher, but I'll resist the temptation to digress into a tribute to the greatness of the publications of John James Audubon (1785–1851). But I can't help but mention that the Ste. Genevieve Museum (at Merchant and Third Streets) has a collection of rare documents and birds he mounted during his residence in Ste. Genevieve. If you want to do yourself a favor, read a book by Richard Rhodes (1937–), another Missouri native: *John James Audubon: The Making of an American*.

If you love a good mystery story, consider staying at the Steiger Haus Murder Mystery Bed & Breakfast. This is not a single building but a historic settlement. You can stay in one of five different places, all constructed between 1811 and 1910. While staying there, you have the chance to solve a murder mystery.

Steiger Haus Murder Mystery Bed & Breakfast
242 Merchant Street, Sainte Genevieve, Missouri 63670
573-883-3600

▶Cape Girardeau

Whether you love him or love to hate him, Rush Limbaugh (1951–) is a force of nature. He was born in this city and served as its city attorney for a while. You can pick up directions for a tour of all things Rush at 1707 Mount Auburn. But wait, there's another tour in town: The Great Murals Tour. The really awesome collection of murals began at the newspaper building of the *Southeast Missourian* in 1947 with "The Art of Printing" and "The Art of Making a Newspaper." A good starting point is the Mississippi River Tales Mural on the downtown floodwall. Most of the murals are located in the historic Old Town neighborhood, near the river.

I-44 to Joplin

▶ Mansfield

I know what you're thinking: enough already about Laura Ingalls Wilder (1867–1957). The writer left her mark on several Midwestern states, including Missouri. But as the father of two wonderful girls, I'm turning the spotlight to Wilder's daughter, and nobody is going to stop me. Not only is Rose Wilder Lane (1886–1968) a notable author in her own right (write?), but she was the one who encouraged Mom to write in the first place. That was when they lived here, having moved from the prairies of the Dakota Territory in 1894. Mother and daughter are buried in the Mansfield Cemetery, and Rose gets equal billing in the house that looks just like it did when she grew up here.

Actually, Mansfield is an especially significant stop for book lovers who are tracing Wilder's life. That's because she wrote all nine of the books in her Little House series while living here, publishing the first in 1932.

Visitors to the Wilder home today can see the study where she worked, which looks exactly as she left it. There's also a guest room where sister Carrie stayed. The museum presents artifacts pertaining to pioneer history and four handwritten manuscripts. And you'll find exhibits about the lives of Laura and her daughter Rose. An annual festival showcases 1800s history, local crafts, folk music, and a parade.

Laura Ingalls Wilder/Rose Wilder Lane Home and Museum
3068 Highway A, Mansfield, Missouri 65704
www.lauraingallswilderhome.com
417-924-3626

▶ Lebanon

Lebanon is one of several small Missouri towns where playwright Lanford Wilson (1937–) spent his boyhood. He was born in Lebanon, lived with his mother in Springfield until age five, and then moved to a farm in Ozark. He received the Pulitzer Prize in 1980 and was named to the Theater Hall of Fame in 2001. He is considered one of the founders of the Off-Off-Broadway theater movement. His plays include *Balm in Gilead* (1965), *The Hot L*

Baltimore (1973), and *Talley's Folly* (1979). *The Mound Builders* (1975) focuses on a Mississippian archeological excavation to explore a university scientist's past and present.

While in Lebanon, be sure to visit the independent bookseller Lebanon Books at 1116 North Lynn Street.

▶ Branson

Only in America would millions of people each year flock to a town with a population of less than ten thousand that is served by no major highway, never mind any other convenient means of transportation. Strangely enough, it is the fact that it is hidden in the Ozark Mountains that gives this community its character. A large part of the credit (or blame) can be attributed to a minister-author. If you're a fan of the novel *The Shepherd of the Hills*, which was first published in 1907, you know where to find the landmarks better than I do. Written by Harold Bell Wright (1872–1944), the novel is set in Branson and was a huge bestseller. If you're not, you probably prefer that I discuss other topics or direct you to the Ozark National Scenic Riverways that were immortalized for their exceptional beauty by Wright.

Wright is said to have been the first American writer to make one million dollars from his writing, and the first to sell a million copies of a novel. Over twenty-one movies were made from screenplays based on his novels, including *The Winning of Barbara Worth* (1926) with Gary Cooper, and the John Wayne film *The Shepherd of the Hills* (1941).

If you haven't made up your mind yet, take a Jeep-driven guided tour to the Shepherd of the Hills Homestead (5586 SR 76W). The farm has been preserved exactly as it is described in the novel. Or see the story of *The Shepherd of the Hills* dramatized in the nearby outdoor amphitheater each evening throughout spring, summer, and early fall. This love story features more than eighty cast members, a burning cabin, and a real flock of sheep.

I find it really interesting that Wright's spiritual message was based on a life lived in simplicity, that he got a lot of grief from critics, and that he kept sticking to his story that he wasn't trying to create great literature but to speak to the common citizen. Yet, his was the first American novel to sell a million copies, not to

Harold Bell Wright, who helped make Branson what it is today

mention spawn four different movies (one starring John Wayne that has dynamite Technicolor) . . . and launch Branson into the stratosphere.

Shepard of the Hills Homestead and Outdoor Theater
5586 West MO Highway 76, Branson, Missouri 65616
www.theshepherdofthehills.com
800-653-6288

▶ Pineville

This Missouri Ozark town was where Vance Randolph (1892–1980) settled in the 1920s. Although he was born in Kansas to a well-to-do family, he dropped out of high school and later became famous as a chronicler of the ways of the Ozark mountain people of Missouri and Arkansas. His books include *Ozark Folksongs, Ozark Superstitions*, and *The Talking Turtle: and Other Ozark Folk Tales. His Pissing in the Snow and Other Ozark Folktales* was a bestseller.

▶ Joplin

Joplin was the birthplace in 1902 of poet Langston Hughes. He didn't live here very long; he grew up in Kansas, Illinois, and Ohio, and is described in more detail in the Ohio chapter. In 2002, a St. Louis-based African-American cultural organization called Divinity Inc. celebrated the writer's one-hundredth birthday with a week-long festival to honor him and to celebrate poetry. It was called "Dream Explosion: The Langston Hughes Black Poetry Festival."

Also in Joplin you'll find The Book Barn, an independent bookstore, which specializes in quality used books.

The Book Barn
3128 South Main, Joplin, Missouri 64804

I-70: Goin' West to Kansas City

▶ Webster Groves

Phyllis Diller (1917–)

This illustrious comedienne is not known for literary work, but I couldn't resist mentioning her memoir because of its great title: *Like a Lampshade in a Whorehouse.* You'll read about the home where she grew up just west of St. Louis, at 30 Mason Avenue in Webster Groves. Her husband painted the house pink.

Webster Groves is also home to Pudd'nhead Books, an independent seller of fiction and nonfiction books for children and adults, as well as coffee. Several book clubs are held at the store.

Pudd'nhead Books
37 South Old Orchard Avenue, Webster Groves, Missouri 63119
www.puddnheadbooks.com

▶ Kirkwood

This town just south of exit 78 on I-70 is the birthplace of poet Marianne Moore (1887–1972). She was born ten months before

T. S. Eliot. Her father was the pastor of the Presbyterian church, but by the time Marianne was born, her father had been committed to a mental hospital after he tried and failed to invent a smokeless furnace. She lived in Kirkwood until she was seven. Many of her poems exhibit precise descriptions of animals, such as fish. She was known for eccentric dress, occasionally wearing a tricorn hat and cape.

Poet and Kirkwood native Marianne Moore

►Sedalia

It might not be worth a special trip unless it's time for the annual Scott Joplin Festival, but if you're in the neighborhood be sure to stop in at Sedalia Book and Toy. The famous composer Scott Joplin (1867–1917) lived here in the late 1890s when he wrote the "Maple Leaf Rag" and other famous compositions. You can see a mural of the composer on the wall of the Wilken Music Co. at 207 South Ohio Street. The Ragtime Store at 321 South Ohio contains a collection of ragtime music and other merchandise. The short story writer and mystery novelist Joel Townsley Rogers (1896–1984) was born here.

Sedalia Book & Toy
3127 Broadway Boulevard, Sedalia, Missouri 65301
660-827-0940
www.bookandtoy.net

I-35: Goin' South to Kansas City

►Kansas City

This is the birthplace of William Least Heat-Moon, born William Lewis Trogdon in 1939. He attended the University of Missouri-Columbia, and taught at Stephens College. When he was laid off in 1978 and separated from his wife, he went on an epic, fourteen-thousand-mile journey "Ghost Dancing" across America, prowling the backroads and gathering stories of American towns and people. His description of that journey, *Blue Highways*, was rejected by several publishers until he changed his name to "Least Heat-Moon" to honor his family's Osage ancestors. The book turned out to be a bestseller. He currently teaches at the University of Missouri-Columbia.

Kansas City is also the birthplace of Calvin Trillin (1935–), the urbane, Yale-educated writer for the New Yorker and many other publications. Trillin spoke in a Salon.com interview about growing up in the Jewish community of Kansas City:

> It's true that when you talk about being from Kansas City—and I've been reluctant to give up being from Kansas City—people assume that you're a Methodist. But you're not necessarily a Methodist.[8]

Richard Rhodes, the journalist and historian, was born in Kansas City, Kansas, but was raised in and around Kansas City, Missouri. Rhodes had a horrible childhood suffering abuse at the hands of his stepmother in Kansas City, Missouri, an episode described in his memoir titled *A Hole in the World*. He was saved by the Andrew Drumm Institute, an institution for boys that still exists in Independence, Missouri. Rhodes has authored more than twenty books; his best-known work, 1986's *The Making of the Atomic Bomb*, won him the Pulitzer Prize.

The Black Archives of Mid-America includes documents that explore lives of African American writers in Kansas City.

For details, visit www.blackarchives.org.

The Writers Place is a gathering place for writers and readers. It holds writing workshops, readings, and other events related to literary pursuits.

The Writers Place
3607 Pennsylvania, Kansas City, Missouri 64111
816-753-1090
www.writersplace.org

The Writers Place, a literary community center in Kansas City

In September 2007, Prospero's Books made a dramatic gesture to protest the decline of reading in America: it burned many of its twenty thousand books. The store is dedicated to literature and to supporting the arts community in Kansas City. You'll find rare books upstairs, children's books downstairs, and everything else in between.

Prospero's Books
1800 West 39th Street, Kansas City, Missouri 64111
816-531-WORD
www.prosperosbookstore.com

▶ Excelsior Springs

This town is spa central, but you can visit the woolen mill historic site when you decide to put your clothes back on. Elms Resort &Spa is still operating. That's where the photo was taken of Harry S. Truman (1884–1972) gleefully holding an early copy of the *Chicago Daily Tribune* with the headline reading "Dewey Defeats Truman." A former speakeasy once frequented by Al Capone (1899–1947), the Elms is said to be haunted as well.

Elms Resort & Spa
401 Regent Street, Excelsior Springs, Missouri 64024
816-630-5500
www.elmsresort.com

▶ Kearney

This town is famous for being the birthplace of the outlaw Jesse James (1947–1882), who was made famous as much by dime novels glorifying the Old West as by his actual exploits, making him as much a literary figure as an historical one. A festival is held every September in his honor. At the Jesse James Farm Historic Site there are books for sale in the gift shop, as well as crafts and memorabilia. A play is staged in August and September.

▶ Liberty

The William Jewell College Library contains original illustrations by children's author Lois Lenski (1893–1974). She was an illustrator of children's books for more than fifty years. She also wrote a series of novels about girls growing up in different regions of the country. One of these books, *Strawberry Girl*, set in Florida, won the Newberry Medal.

►Mendon

This hilly farming area in Missouri was the location for much of the filming of the 1936 movie *The Voice of Bugle Ann*. Based on the 1935 novel by MacKinley Kantor, it tells the story of hound dog Bugle Ann and her owner, Spring Davis. It vividly depicts the fox-hunting culture in this part of the state.

The Great River Road: Mark Twain Country

►Hannibal

I'm sure I don't need to tell you that Hannibal is the river town immortalized in Mark Twain's *The Adventures of Tom Sawyer* and *The Adventures of Huckleberry Finn*. Although it was the boyhood town of Samuel Clemens, if you ask any of the 350,000 visitors who tour

Hannibal's most famous resident, Mark Twain

the restored site each year whose house they are visiting, they are more likely to answer "Tom Sawyer." This is the most developed and tourist-oriented of all literary places in the Midwest with a wax museum, riverboat, and theater, in addition to many other beautifully restored literary sites.

I must confess that I've been known to fall under the tourist spell myself. During the National Tom Sawyer Days in early July there is a National Fence Painting Championship and a Frog Jumping Contest, among many other activities. My parents took a photo of my brother and me pretending to paint the famous fence when we were kids, and I insisted that my daughters reenact the scene when they were about the same age.

The author and his daughters in front of Tom Sawyer's Fence in Hannibal

And yet it's not all hoopla. The bookshop occupying the main floor of the Becky Thatcher Home features the largest selection of books by or about Mark Twain to be found. You might be able to score a first edition or one that is out of print. Children's classics, regional interest, and discount books are also offered. And if you must have a T-shirt or other such souvenir, the selection is better and more affordably priced here. You can also visit Judge Clemens' Law Office and the Grant Drug Store where the family lived when they were in financial straits.

Two miles south of Hannibal on Route 79, be sure to visit the Mark Twain Cave immortalized in *Tom Sawyer* (where it is called McDougal's Cave). According to Twain, the original owner of the cave, an eccentric doctor named E. D. McDowell, turned the cave into a mausoleum for his daughter, who died at age fourteen. "The body of this poor child was put in a copper cylinder filled with alcohol, and this was suspended in one of the dismal avenues of the cave."

Huckleberry Finn as depicted in the book's first edition

It's a shame Samuel Clemens never met Margaret Tobin Brown, now better known as "The Unsinkable Molly Brown," heroine of the *Titanic* and immortalized in the Broadway musical and subsequent Hollywood film. She was on her way back to her hometown of Hannibal when the boat went down. Her original Irish immigrant's cottage where she was born is restored to its 1860s condition, and there are plenty of photos to document her rise from rags in Hannibal to the riches of high society in Denver.

Mark Twain Boyhood Home and Museum
Hannibal Convention and Visitors Bureau
505 North Third Street, Hannibal, Missouri 63401
www.marktwainmuseum.org

►Florida

"Recently someone in Missouri has sent me a picture of the home I was born in. Heretofore I always stated that it was a palace but I shall be more guarded now." This remark from Mark Twain was probably made before the birthplace of Samuel Langhorne Clemens became a National Memorial Shrine and was preserved within a steel, glass, and stone building.

Twain would have probably been highly amused at the way his birthplace has been preserved. The tiny cabin was moved from its original site about one quarter of a mile from where it stands today and is now part of an indoor exhibit at the site. The exhibit includes a handwritten manuscript of *The Adventures of Tom Sawyer*, items from the author's home in Hartford, Connecticut, a reading room, and first editions of his books. In case you're wondering where the cabin originally stood, look for the granite monument in the 2,775-acre Mark Twain State Park, located in Stoutsville.

Mark Twain Birthplace State Historic Site and Mark Twain State Park
37352 Shrine Road, Florida, Missouri 65283
573-565-3449
www.mostateparks.com/twainsite.htm

►Fleming Park/Lake Jacomo

At the Burroughs Audubon Society Library you can learn about birds, take a hike, browse through books, and discover how to turn your backyard into a wildlife sanctuary.

Burroughs Audubon Nature Center and Bird Sanctuary
7300 SW West Park Road, Blue Springs, Missouri 64015
816-795-8177
www.burroughs.org

►Moberly

This is the birthplace of novelist Jack Conroy (1898–1990), who grew up in a coal mining camp with the colorful name of Monkey Nest. The difficult life of the miners left a strong impression on Conroy: his father, brother, and two uncles all died in mining accidents. His best-known novel, *The Disinherited* (1933), depicts the life of working-class people struggling to make a living between the two world wars.

Endnotes

1   Vega, Elizabeth. "Wrecking Brawl," St. Louis News, www.river
    fronttimes.com/2001-06-13/news/wrecking-brawl.

2   "Poetic Injustice—Need for a Memorial to T.S. Eliot in St. Louis,
    Missouri," http://findarticles.com/p/articles/mi_m1282/is_n10_
    v47/ai_16936611.

3   Hall, Elizabeth Armstrong. "Map Quest," St. Louis Magazine, www
    .stlmag.com/media/St-Louis-Magazine/June-2007/Map-Quest.

4   "Tennessee Williams Genealogy," www.usgennet.org/usa/mo/
    county/stlouis/williams/gen.htm.

5   "Previously unknown Tennessee Williams poem found in the bud-
    ding playwright's 1937 Greek exam," Washington University in St.
    Louis Web site, http://news-info.wustl.edu/tips/page/normal/5005
    .html.

6   Williams, Tennesee and John Waters. *Memoirs* (New York: New
    Directions Publishing, 2006), 16.

7   Whitman, Walt. *Specimen Days in America* (New York: W. Scott,
    1887), 240–41.

8   Salon: Calvin Trillin interview, www.salon.com/weekly/interview
    960624.html.

chapter seven

Ohio

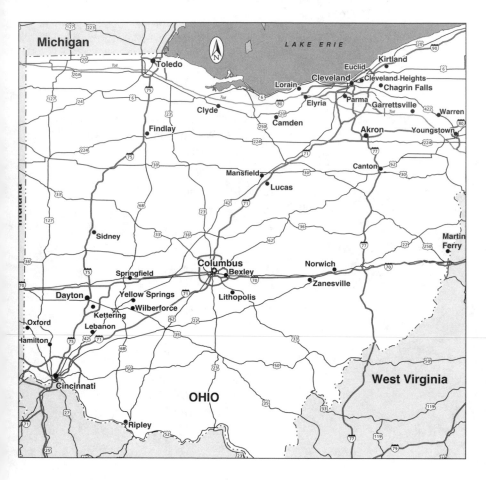

Driving Tours

1. I-70: From the "Little White Town" to the "Cool River"
2. I-80/90: From the 1,000-Foot Tree to Winesburg, Ohio
3. I-71: From "Uncle Tom's" Creator to Shawshank Prison
4. I-75: From the Old Mill Stream to the Elizabethan Poet
5. I-77: From the Canterbury Tales to the Signal House

$\mathcal{A}$s demonstrated by its crucial role in the Underground Railroad saga, Ohio is a welcoming and inclusive place. The birthplace of many notable African-American writers whose parents found the state to be a good place to raise a family, Ohio's industries and opportunities have also attracted other older, already established black authors. From Charles W. Chesnutt to Nikki Giovanni, many African Americans from Ohio celebrate their heritage in their writing. Nobel laureate Toni Morrison was born in the steel mill town of Lorain, and Langston Hughes was named class poet of his Ohio high school.

Art is another subset of Ohio's claims to fame. Comic strip characters Calvin and Hobbes were born here, and the humorist James Thurber's first drawings were done here. You'll find a museum dedicated solely to children's book art, and a quirky wax museum depicting scenes from the Bible. Certain writers also found inspiration in the state's natural surroundings. Novelist Louis Bromfield created an extensive farm where he could implement his new planting techniques, and where he entertained other writers and Hollywood celebrities. Writer Zane Grey learned to fish in the Muskingum River that flows through his hometown of Zanesville, and he pursued this interest throughout his life. Ohio continues to provide a fertile working environment and inspiration for successful writers like mystery novelist Les Roberts.

I-70: From the "Little White Town" to the "Cool River"

▶Camden

Just south of I-70 near the Indiana state line you travel a few miles to Camden, where the writer Sherwood Anderson was born to a poor family on September 13, 1876. Anderson lived here only a year. His father, Irwin, ran a harness shop in a two-story wooden building at 25 Main Street, just north of Central Street. The family rented four rooms in a one-story house at what is now 142 South Lafayette Street. In his autobiographical work *Tar: A Midwest Childhood*, Anderson described Camden as "a little white town in a valley with hills on each side." He spent many of his formative years in the town of Clyde, which he used as a model for Winesburg in his classic collection of stories titled *Winesburg, Ohio*. (See listing for Clyde later in this chapter.)

▶Columbus

Author James Thurber (1894–1961) said the following about his birthplace: "Columbus is a town in which almost anything is likely to happen and in which almost everything has." Thurber's play *The Male Animal* (co-written with Elliott Nugent) is set at a large Midwestern university that resembles the Ohio State University as it was when he was a student there. His student "pad," where he lived with his family from 1913 to 1917, is now a beautifully restored nineteenth-century house furnished in period style. Now a venue for special readings and programs, the house serves as a literary center that awards an annual Thurber Prize for American Humor.

If you get tired of looking at memorabilia and drawings while you're at the house, you can compose a literary gem of your own on the very typewriter Thurber used while at the *New Yorker* magazine. But don't be surprised if a ghost is looking over your shoulder. One page on the Thurber House Web site (www.thurberhouse.org/house/ghosts.html) is devoted to descriptions of ghostly encounters. Thurber himself wrote about one scary episode in his story "The Night the Ghost Got In." The spirits are believed to be victims of a fire that destroyed a nearby lunatic asylum.

Columbus has plenty of festivals, many of which are literary. The Ohioana Book Festival (www.ohioanabookfestival.org) honors the state's writers each May. The Ohioana Library Association hosts a "Books and All that Jazz" gala in October (www.ohioana.org). And Thurber House hosts a series of literary picnics.

Thurber House
77 Jefferson Avenue, Columbus, Ohio 43215
614-464-1032
www.thurberhouse.org

►Bexley

A suburb just east of Columbus, Bexley is the birthplace of one of the most prolific and successful writers in America—Robert Lawrence Stine, better known as R. L. Stine (1943-   ). More than three hundred million copies of his Goosebumps books have sold since the series began in the early 1990s.

Stine describes his childhood in an autobiographical book, also for kids, called *It Came from Ohio!* (1997). Most of us can relate to his fear of jumping in the water during summer camp and his embarrassment at having to wear a duck costume instead of a more suitably scary outfit at Halloween. But he was precocious, starting to write at age nine when he found a typewriter in his attic. Known as "Jovial Bob" Stine at Ohio State University, he edited the school's humor magazine, the *Sundial*, before graduating in 1965.

Paul Laurence Dunbar State Memorial

▶Dayton

When I pulled up in front of the Paul Laurence Dunbar State Memorial, the friendly staff greeted me and asked if my car was locked. I said that it was. The staff is just as attentive to tour groups. The restored former home contains many items from the later nineteenth- and early-twentieth centuries. Although this was Dunbar's final residence when he died at age thirty-four in 1906, his mother lived there until 1934. Thanks to her care in preserving his belongings, many are on display here. I was surprised to learn that Dunbar was a friend of the Wright brothers, whose own homes and workshop are just a few blocks away.

Dunbar was the first African American student to attend Dayton's Central High School, where he edited the school newspaper. He went on to be one of the first notable African American poets, influencing many other literary greats such as Langston Hughes.

Dayton hosts a weekend Cityfolk Festival each July that includes fellowships for Ohio artists (www.cityfolk.org)

Paul Laurence Dunbar State Memorial
219 North Paul Laurence Dunbar Street, Dayton, Ohio 45402
937-224-7061
www.aviationheritagearea.org/paulLaurence.htm

▶Yellow Springs

Antioch College has fallen on hard times, but the reputation of one of its most illustrious students, the television writer and dramatist Rod Serling (1924–1975), still flourishes. He began writing stories here in 1946 and found work as a writer for the Cincinnati radio station WLW while he was still in college. He moved to Cincinnati with his wife after graduation and continued to work at WLW, churning out public service announcements and commercials. Serling's first big break came in 1951 when he sold a group of scripts to WKRC-TV in Cincinnati. Later, he created television dramas like *Requiem for a Heavyweight* that are now considered classics. Serling's first nationally known script, *Patterns*, told the story of an ambitious executive named Fred Staples, who was lured from Cincinnati to New York. Eventually, Serling created the series *The Twilight Zone*, which attracted a large audience in the 1960s and is an iconic show in American television. At the height of his fame in 1962, he returned to Antioch College to teach dramatic writing for a year.

An October getaway for women held at Yellow Springs includes a literary tea (www.getawaysforwomen.com).

▶ Lithopolis

In this little town you'll find a memorial consisting of a museum, library, and foundation dedicated to Adam Willis Wagnalls, cofounder of the Funk & Wagnalls publishing house, and to his wife, Anna. Adam Willis Wagnalls (1843–1924) was born in Lithopolis. He and Isaac Kaufman Funk partnered in 1877 and their company became best known as a publisher of encyclopedias and reference works such as the *Literary Digest*. The museum contains original letters from writer O. Henry and paintings by John Ward Dunsmore and others that were used for *Literary Digest* covers. But literary associations aside, the iconic jokes using "Funk & Wagnalls" as a play on words are hard to forget, especially when the answers to questions posed to Johnny Carson's character Carnac the Magnificent were "kept in a mayonnaise jar outside Funk & Wagnalls's porch since noon today."

Each September a Honeyfest is held on the grounds of the Wagnalls Memorial (www.lithopolishoneyfest.com).

Wagnalls Memorial
150 East Columbus Street, Lithopolis, Ohio 43136
614-837-4765, ext. 104
www.wagnalls.org

▶ Martins Ferry

This town was the birthplace, on March 1, 1837, of William Dean Howells, a notable literary figure of the nineteenth century. If you like Mark Twain, Emily Dickinson, and Henry James, you have Howells to thank, at least in part. As the influential editor of the *Atlantic Monthly* magazine, he published all of these writers, and became friends with Twain and James. His own writing is almost forgotten, in part because much of it appeared only in the magazine and not in hardcover books. His best-known work is the novel *The Rise of Silas Lapham* (1885). He wrote about Ohio in his novel *The Kentons* and in his autobiographical work *A Boy's Town*. The latter work contains the following passage:

It seems to me that my Boy's Town was a town peculiarly adapted for a boy to be a boy in. It had a river, the great Miami River, which was as blue as the sky when it was not as yellow as gold; and it had another river, called the Old River, which was the Miami's former channel . . . All these streams and courses had fish in them at all seasons, and all summer long they had boys in them, and now and then a boy in winter when the thick ice of the mild Southern Ohio winter let him through with his skates.

►Norwich

This is a perfect place to pull off I-70 and take a break as you drive across Ohio. At Norwich Exit 164, the old National Road, U.S. Route 40, is very close to the new interstate. If you're curious about roads that helped settlers move west through the country long before the highway system was created, drive north just a minute or two to the National Road/Zane Grey Museum.

The two subjects of the museum are connected. Zane Gray, who lived in nearby Zanesville, had an illustrious ancestor. Colonel Ebenezer Zane was commissioned by the Continental Congress to develop a road through what was at that time the western wilderness—Pennsylvania and Ohio. The road he constructed eventually became the National Road, the only significant road linking the East Coast and western frontier in the early nineteenth century. Objects belonging to Western novelist Zane Grey and copies of his manuscripts are displayed.

National Road-Zane Grey Museum
8850 East Pike, Norwich, Ohio 43767
Wednesday though Saturday, 9:30 a.m. to 5 p.m.
Sunday, noon to 5 p.m.
Closed holidays and during fall and winter months
740-872-3143, 800-752-2602
http://ohsweb.ohiohistory.org/places/se07/index.shtml

►Zanesville

This town on the Licking and Muskingum Rivers has a lot going for it. You can check out the factory outlet of Zanesville Pottery on the National Road at 7395 East Pike. And don't miss a chance to cross the Y-Bridge. This amazing architectural wonder is positioned at the point where the two aforementioned rivers meet. The bridge over the river(s) gets halfway across, at which point it splits in two separate directions, thus forming the shape of a perfect capital letter Y. It's worth driving over the bridge just for the experience, as long as you don't get confused and turn the wrong way.

Zanesville is also the birthplace of two novelists: Charles D. Stewart (1868–1960) and Zane Grey (1872–1939). Stewart only lived in Zanesville as a boy, after which his family moved to Wisconsin. He wrote humorous sketches for *Peck's Sun* and a regular column in *The Century* magazine. His book titles include *The Fugitive Blacksmith* and *Finerty of the Sand-House*.

The much more famous of the two Zanesville authors is Zane Grey. No, Zanesville was not named for him; it was named for his maternal great-grandfather, Ebenezer (see the listing for the National Road-Zane Grey museum earlier in this chapter). And his name wasn't Zane Grey, either: he was born Pearl Zane Gray (with an *a*) and used Zane Grey (with an *e*) as his pen name. Confusing? One thing that's not a mystery is that he was born at 705 Converse Avenue in Zanesville on January 31, 1875.

As a boy, Gray (or Grey) fished in the Muskingum and Licking Rivers. He later wrote about a character named Muddy Miser who taught him the joy of fishing and encouraged him to "one day fish the seven seas," a suggestion that Grey pursued seriously in later life when he grew rich from his Western novels and sailed the waters of the world on his 140-foot schooner. A present-day bar named Muddy Miser's Cool River Café is named for this character, a reclusive old man who lived in an abandoned pottery house. The owner of the café displays letters and other objects related to Zane Grey. It's located on the banks of the Muskingum River near the Y-Bridge, in fact. Grey wrote about his early years in a book called *The Living Post*:

> Whatever I have achieved and whatever the future may hold for me in the world of letters, I owe much to my early home training, to my school teachers, to the boys I played and fought with, to the girls who cared for me in spite of my unworthiness, to all that pertains to the old Zanesville. Perhaps some day I shall embody in my best story something of this truth. When I roamed through Brush's Woods and along Joe's Run, and fished with my beloved old friend, Muddy

Miser, the hermit of Dillon's Falls, I may have been living the free, wild life of an unrestrained youngster, but also I was storing up a treasure-mine of memories and ideals that were some day to make me a writer.

Grey turned those memories into books such as *Riders of the Purple Sage*, *Desert Gold*, and *Heritage of the Desert*. When he returned to Zanesville on a visit in 1921, he was greeted by three thousand schoolchildren and honored at a banquet at the Masonic Temple.

Muddy Miser's Cool River Café
112 Muskingum Avenue, Zanesville, Ohio 43701
740-588-9210
www.muddymisers.com

I-80/90: From the 1,000-FootTree to Winesburg, Ohio

▶Youngstown
The beautiful Arms Family Museum of Local History doesn't have a literary connection per se, but its associated archival library is a great resource for anyone who wants to do research on the Mahoning Valley of Ohio or the families who have lived there. If you're working on the genealogy of one of those families, be sure to take advantage of the archival holdings, which include diaries, Bibles, photographs, deeds, wills, and other ephemera.

The Arms Family Museum of Local History
648 Wick Avenue, Youngstown, Ohio 44502
(573) 221-9010
Tuesday through Sunday, 1 to 5 p.m.
xwww.mahoninghistory.org/armhome.htm

▶Warren
William H. Gass's (1924–   )1966 novel *Omensetter's Luck* was influenced by growing up in the small town of Warren. In a recurring image, a boy speaks of living in a tree a thousand feet tall that "goes way up into the air and you can see clean to Columbus." Although Gass was born in Fargo, North Dakota, his family soon moved to Warren, which he once described as "a dismal, industrial town." His

father taught mechanical drawing at a high school in Warren and played minor league baseball. Both parents suffered from illness—his father from debilitating arthritis and his mother from alcoholism—and he has described writing as a way to "get even" for an unhappy childhood. He attended Kenyon College in Gambier, Ohio, before receiving his bachelor's degree in philosophy from Cornell University. When Gass was a student at Kenyon College, it was known as a center for a literary school of thought called the New Criticism, which influenced his work and attitudes. He won the National Book Critics Circle Award three times and taught for many years at Washington University in St. Louis.

In 2009, Warren was chosen as one of the five sites of the Ohio Chautauqua tour, a traveling series of living history, music, education, theater, and more.

▶ Garrettsville

This bucolic little town just west of Warren and near Exit 193 on I-80 is the birthplace of poet Harold Hart Crane (1899–1932), who used the name Hart Crane. Crane's boyhood home is near the bridge over the river, at 10688 Freedom Street. It's worth stopping to read the historical marker in front of the house. It's a private home, so try not to disturb the current residents. You might be forgiven, though, for letting out a little whoop of excitement when you learn that Crane's father struck it rich in the candy business . . . and invented Life Savers! C. A. Crane ran the largest maple syrup business in the world from a brown-tiled building at Franklin and South Pine. The tower room in the home was a favorite retreat for Crane: in fact, he is said to have cranked up the volume of the Victrola in this room so he would not hear his parents arguing beneath him. Evidently his father was sweet only in regard to his business.

Crane read widely in his youth and dreamed of being a writer, which led to his own set of arguments with his father. He and his father had the classic stereotypical conflict about his future. Dad wanted Hart to settle down to a respectable business life, and son wanted to be a poet. Crane moved to New York (Life Savers notwithstanding) and followed his dream.

Few traces of his youth in Garretsburg and Warren, Ohio, find their way into the poetry of Hart Crane. Referring to his occasional work as a laborer in his father's factory, he wrote:

Behind
My father's cannery works I used to see
Rail-squatters ranged in nomad raillery

Much of Crane's work is rich, beautiful, and not particularly accessible. You have to work to fully appreciate it, but, like many difficult things, it's worth the effort. Crane is one of those poets you study in college English class and are in danger of forgetting about afterwards. That would be a shame. Crane is, unfortunately, remembered for his poetic death at a young age: he jumped from a boat named the S. S. Orizaba off the Florida coast and was never seen again.

If you walk to 8115 High Street, you can visit the James A. Garfield Historical Society and see artifacts owned by another area native, the twentieth president of the United States.

▶Chagrin Falls

One of my daughters' favorite comic strips when they were growing up was Calvin and Hobbes. The creator of this witty strip, Bill Watterson (1958–   ), was born in Washington, D.C., but moved to Chagrin Falls with his family when he was six. He began drawing comic strips for the local high school's newspaper when he was a student there. Like the writer William H. Gass, he attended Kenyon College, where he drew for the school newspaper The Kenyon Collegian.

He retired in 1995 and currently lives a secluded life in Chagrin Falls. The town is famous (or infamous) for its annual "pumpkin roll," in which high school juniors and seniors slide down a local hill after covering it with "pumpkin goo."

▶Cleveland Heights

Les Roberts (1937–   ) is a Cleveland Heights–based writer best known for his detective novels, which feature protagonist Milan Jacovich. The novels are particularly fun for Clevelanders because of the liberal sprinkling of references to Cleveland and the surrounding area. In his memoir We'll Always Have Cleveland (2006), Roberts speaks lovingly of his adopted home:

> Since I moved to northeast Ohio, Greater Cleveland has
> inspired and nurtured and fostered me—and on more than
> one occasion pissed me off—clearly stamping my writing style
> and greatly influencing the person I have become.

Roberts was born in Chicago. "I've lived in Cleveland for nineteen years," he told me. "I had never even set foot in Cleveland until 1987 when I was here for three months producing a local TV show. I fell in love with the place, went back to Los Angeles (where I lived) to create my Cleveland private eye series, and eventually moved here for good in 1990."

I asked Roberts if he visits coffee shops or cafes to write. "I guess I'm too old these days to 'hang out' anywhere," he joked. Because he's a local celebrity, he says, it's impossible to work in public anyway. "Someone will inevitably come up to me and derail my train of thought when I'm writing."

When it comes to local haunts, Roberts favors a place that appears in many of his mystery novels: *Nighttown, in Cleveland Heights*. It's located a few blocks from detective Milan Jacovich's apartment. "It's the kind of place where everyone who's at the bar is eager to talk with anyone else, even if they're a stranger. It's one of the best jazz clubs in America, and it's also a very good restaurant. I'm proud to tell you that they've actually named a sandwich after Milan Jacovich."

Roberts loves to use real Cleveland locations in his stories. One of Jacovich's favorite restaurants, for instance, is the Sun Luck Garden on Taylor Road. The restaurant's owner made an enlargement of the cover of *We'll Always Have Cleveland* and the paragraph that describes her restaurant (with high accolades for the signature spicy mussels). You can't miss it because it's posted on the front door of the restaurant.

▶ Cleveland

Surveyor Moses Cleaveland picked his town site on Lake Erie in 1796. However, the editor of the *Cleveland Gazette and Commercial Register* had to drop a letter from his masthead for it to fit across the page. He chose the first "a" in "Cleaveland" to be expendable. So Cleveland was influenced by writers and editors right from its beginning.

You may never have heard of Charles Waddell Chesnutt (1858–1932), but he was an early advocate of equal rights for African Americans. Before Zora Neale Hurston and Langston Hughes, Charles W. Chesnutt was writing about racial issues and African American folklore. Chesnutt's parents were freed slaves, but his grandfather was a slaveholder. Although he had a very light complexion, Chesnutt never attempted to pass for a white man. He wrote stories about such complex subjects as miscegenation and racial identity, including "passing." He also wrote a biography of the abolitionist Frederick Douglass.

Although Chesnutt was born in Cleveland, he grew up in Fayetteville, North Carolina. He moved back to Cleveland in 1904 after his marriage, and lived at 9719 Lamont Avenue. He was never terribly successful as a writer in terms of gaining a large readership, and the full measure of his work was recognized only after he died in Cleveland in 1932.

The great African American poet Langston Hughes (1902–1967) was born in Joplin, Missouri, but moved to Lincoln, Illinois, and later to Cleveland when his mother found work in the area's steel mills. Hughes thrived in Cleveland; when his mother and stepfather moved to Chicago, he decided to stay to finish high school. He found many mentors in the city. A white couple, Russell and Rowena Jelliffe, hired him as a teacher at a community center called "Playground House," where he gave art lessons to children. An English teacher at the school introduced him to poets such as Carl Sandburg and Walt Whitman. By his senior year at Central High School he was writing poems that were gaining attention, and he was named "class poet." His poems were published in the school magazine, the *Central High Monthly*; he graduated in 1920.

Hughes claimed another African American writer from Ohio, Paul Laurence Dunbar (1872–1906), as one of his major influences. He is remembered today with the Langston Hughes branch of the Cleveland Public Library, which is located at 10200 Superior Avenue in the Cleveland housing development area. He had a forty-year association with Karamu House, the country's oldest African American cultural arts institution. He produced many plays with Karamu house at a time when other theaters were segregated. Every year at holiday time, Karamu House stages Hughes's play "Black Nativity."

note

Karamu House,
2355 East 89th Street, still produces plays by African Americans and holds a variety of classes in the performing arts. Find out more by calling 216-795-7070 or at www.karamu.com.

Langston Hughes

►Elyria
Sherwood Anderson

A momentous event in the history of American literature took place in Elyria on November 28, 1912. That was the day Sherwood Anderson (1876–1941) left town, becoming the archetype of the American businessman caught between the ideal of business success and respectability and the dream of creative fulfillment in the arts. Anderson was president of his own company—the Anderson Manufacturing Co. (Home of "Roof-Fix Cure for Roof Troubles")—and was known around town as the "Roof-Fix Man." He belonged to the Chamber of Commerce and attended charity balls with his wife, Cornelia. In his spare time, he wrote novels and short stories. He apparently became disenchanted with the cheating and dishonesty that was part of the business life, and his desire to become a writer grew.

He later wrote, in *A Story Teller's Story*, "One morning my mind became a blank and I ran away from Elyria." He literally walked out of his office and out of town, abandoning not only his business, but his wife and three small children. In an "amnesia letter" he later wrote to his wife, he said he apparently wandered on foot the twenty-five miles to Cleveland, occasionally sleeping in the open. He went into a drugstore, where the pharmacist called a friend mentioned in a notebook Anderson was carrying. He was sent to a hospital, where he was found to be suffering from nervous exhaustion caused by overwork. (I learned much about Anderson's life from a fascinating biography titled *Sherwood Anderson: A Writer in America*, by Rideout and Modlin, University of Wisconsin Press.)

Anderson lived in Elyria from 1906 to 1913. The town was undergoing rapid industrialization and expansion during this time, and Anderson incorporated some of the details of the town's growth into his novel *Poor White*. A group of Elyria citizens once attempted to create a Sherwood Anderson Literary Center. They placed a marker about Anderson in his hometown of Clyde, but their leader, William Schuck, moved away and the effort was abandoned. The Lorain County Historical Society has created a Sherwood Anderson Day to educate townspeople about the writer's presence in their town. The group's desire to embrace Anderson is in stark contrast to his rejection of the type of life the town supported and celebrated.

▶Lorain

The first African American woman to win the Nobel Prize for Literature (in 1993) was born in this working-class steel-mill town in 1931 and given the name Chloe Anthony Wofford. Her father, a welder, and her religious mother had moved to Ohio from the south to escape segregation and to obtain a better education for their children. Chloe graduated from Lorain High School in 1949. She took the name Toni (which is adapted from her middle name, Anthony) while a student at Howard University. Although Toni Morrison's writing is not autobiographical, she fondly alludes to her past, stating:

> I am from the Midwest so I have a special affection for it. My beginnings are always there. . . . No matter what I write, I begin there . . . It's the matrix for me . . . Ohio also offers an escape from stereotyped black settings. It is neither plantation nor ghetto.

In fact, she was surrounded by white people in Lorain, and she says that black culture was something she discovered through inquiry. She went on to write seven moving novels about growing up and living black in America, many set in Ohio. Her themes, however, are universal—ones to which all Americas can relate. Morrison has received many honors and awards in addition to the aforementioned Nobel Prize. She is currently at Princeton University as a professor and the founder/sponsor of the Princeton Atelier student arts workshop.

▶ Clyde

You can tell how Sherwood Anderson felt about his hometown just south of I-80/90 by reading the stories in *Winesburg, Ohio*, which is one of my personal favorites. Anderson vividly described noble, courageous people who lived lonely lives confined by the strict morals of the time and the narrow minds of their fellow townspeople.

Anderson may have gained fame for his depiction of small-town Ohio life in *Winesburg, Ohio*, but the citizens of Clyde, Ohio, where the writer grew up, originally reviled him and called his work a "dirty book" because it supposedly depicted the townspeople in a bad light. The local librarian burned the book when it first came out.

These days, things have changed. When you leave I-90 and head into Clyde, you pass the Winesburg Hotel. Downtown, near the train tracks, you find a historical marker describing Anderson's connections to the town. Anderson wrote about his childhood in Clyde in autobiographical works *A Story Teller's Story* and *Tar: A Midwest Childhood*. The family lived at 120 Spring Avenue and at 214 Race Street; both houses are now private residences.

If you find the picturesque Clyde Public Library, an original Carnegie Library at 222 West Buckeye Street, you'll also be in the Clyde Museum. The museum, which is in the basement, includes a modest tribute to Anderson in the form of an exhibit.

But if you ask nicely, the reference librarian might be able to provide a map showing sites around town that are associated with *Winesburg, Ohio*. They include a pond in Community Park that was called Waterworks Pond in the book. In the story "The Strength of God," for example, the Reverend Curtis Hartman shows tenderness for his wife when they are out riding by the pond. The Presbyterian Church, at 133 West Forest, also plays an important role in the story. It's where the reverend stood and looked across the street at the house where the schoolteacher Kate Swift lived:

214 Race Street, one of Anderson's homes in Clyde

The Presbyterian Church which appears in *Winesburg, Ohio*

An old postcard depicting Main Street in Clyde, Ohio, around the time Sherwood Anderson lived there.

Three times during the early fall and winter of that year Curtis Hartman crept out of his house to the room in the bell tower to sit in the darkness looking at the figure of Kate Swift lying in her bed and later went to walk and pray in the streets. He could not understand himself. For weeks he would go along scarcely thinking of the school teacher and telling himself that he had conquered the carnal desire to look at her body.

You can still find many of the streets named in *Winesburg, Ohio's* stories—Elm, Duane, Buckeye, and Main. The Methodist Church that the characters Alice Hartman and Will Hurley belong to in the story "Adventure" is at Maple and Race Streets.

I-71: From "Uncle Tom's" Creator to Shawshank Prison

▶ Cincinnati

The Harriet Beecher Stowe House commemorates Harriet Beecher Stowe (1811–1896), who began writing while teaching at the Hartford Female Seminary. Stowe and her father, the Reverend Lyman Beecher, lived in Cincinnati from 1832 to the early 1850s. A large number of religious leaders and antislavery and women's rights advocates passed through the house while visiting the family. She conceived the idea of her famous abolitionist novel *Uncle Tom's Cabin* when she visited a plantation across the river in Kentucky and observed slavery firsthand. The house today serves as a black history education and cultural center.

Harriet Beecher Stowe House
2950 Gilbert Avenue, Cincinnati, Ohio 45206
513-751-0651
http://ohsweb.ohiohistory.org/places/sw18/index.shtml

Poet Yolanda "Nikki" Giovanni (1943–   ), who was elected to the Ohio Women's Hall of Fame in 1985, grew up in Lincoln Heights, a suburb of Cincinnati. In 1967, she organized the first Black Arts Festival in Cincinnati. Her first published book of poetry, *Black Feeling, Black Talk* (1967) emerged from her response to the deaths of Martin Luther King, Jr., Medgar Evers, and Robert Kennedy, and the need to raise awareness of the injustices done to black people. Her poetry is often militant and uncompromising, but some of it is intensely personal. She also has published a number of books for children and has taught since 1987 at Virginia Tech.

▶ Meigs County

Ambrose Bierce was born in Meigs County, east of Cincinnati, on June 24, 1842. One of the most popular writers of the nineteenth century, Bierce served in the Union Army for most of the Civil War, leaving the army with the rank of major. He is known for his sarcastic stories and for his writings about ghosts and other supernatural topics. His best-known book is the humorous *Devil's Dictionary*. His most famous story is the Civil War drama "An Occurrence at Owl Creek Bridge." In 1913, he moved to Mexico to seek out the

A poster from a theatrical production of *Uncle Tom's Cabin*

revolutionary Pancho Villa and join his army. At this point, he disappears from the historical record; it is believed that he died in 1914 while with Villa's army, but his true fate is a mystery.

Harriet Beecher Stowe

▶Lebanon

If you're traveling on I-71 between Columbus and Cincinnati, be sure to stop to eat at a place with a literary history: the Golden Lamb Inn. This is the oldest hotel in Ohio, first built in 1803. The current structure dates to 1815.

Because the inn is strategically located between Columbus and Cincinnati and is close to the National Road, it has attracted numerous illustrious guests, including Harriet Beecher Stowe and Daniel Webster. No fewer than twelve U.S. presidents have signed the register. Mark Twain stayed here when he performed at the Lebanon Opera House in the late nineteenth century. The most expensive guest room is named for Charles Dickens, who was distressed during his 1842 visit that no spirits were served. Legend has it that he walked down the street to a tavern where he had his drink and an

Ambrose Bierce

argument with the owner. (Times have changed; the current menu at the Golden Lamb includes an extensive wine list.)

Golden Lamb Inn
27 South Broadway, Lebanon, Ohio 45036
513-932-5065
www.goldenlamb.com

▶Wilberforce

This town near Xenia, Ohio, is home to the National Afro-American Museum and Cultural Center. It has a permanent exhibit titled *From*

Victory to Freedom: Afro-American Life in the Fifties. The museum includes manuscripts and other publications of interest to researchers.

National Afro-American Museum and Cultural Center
1350 Brush Row Road, Wilberforce, Ohio 45384
937-376-4944
http://ohsweb.ohiohistory.org/places/sw13/index.shtml

▶ Lucas

Malabar Farm State Park is a bit off the beaten path, but it's well worth turning off I-71 at Exit 173 and exploring it. Located in beautiful rolling country in the middle of the state, this is the home and farm of author Louis Bromfield. Bromfield (1896–1956) is barely known today, but he was a successful novelist and screenwriter in the middle of the twentieth century. He won the Pulitzer Prize in 1926 for his second novel, *Early Autumn*, and every one of his thirty books was a best seller. A number of his novels were adapted for the screen. After achieving success with fiction and in film, Bromfield focused on his farm and began to write nonfiction about progressive farming methods and conservation.

His farm attracted lots of famous Hollywood friends, including William Powell, Errol Flynn, Dorothy Lamour, and Shirley Temple. Humphrey Bogart and Lauren Bacall were married there and stayed around for the honeymoon. If you take the tour of the house, you can see the desk that Bromfield had custom built with fancy drawers … but actually he worked at a card table that he had set up behind it.

I arrived too late in the day for a guided tour, but I still enjoyed my visit. I drove up the path and to the right of the park entrance to view the house where the famous wedding of Bogart and Bacall took place. I also drove to a scenic overlook with the poetic name of Mount Jeez (that's what people are inclined to say if they walk up it) just in time for a beautiful sunset.

Malabar Farm State Park
4050 Bromfield Road, Lucas, Ohio 44843
419-892-2784
www.malabarfarm.org

►Mansfield

Pulitzer Prize–winning author Louis Bromfield (1896–1956) was born here. So was John Sherman (1823–1900), who was the author of the Sherman Anti-Trust Act (as well as the brother of General William T. Sherman). But there are other attractions that put the "awww" in "awesome."

For example: the Living Bible Museum. To get to the first unbelievable site, take Exit 176 off I-71 and go west on U.S. 30. Watch for the Living Bible Museum signs. I'll try to describe a little of what happens next, but it's something you have to see for yourself. If you are a devout Christian, this place is a must-see. If you are a book lover, you'll be interested in the collection of rare Bibles, as well as the Bible Walk itself, which, of course, is based on the best-selling book of all time. If you're none of these, you'll still find plenty to amuse and amaze you as you walk down a dark corridor past a series of seventy Bible scenes that are illustrated by more than three hundred life-size wax figures. Members of the adjacent Diamond Hill Cathedral sewed the costumes and constructed the scenes. The wax figures were reportedly purchased from an old wax museum; look closely and you might recognize a celebrity or two among them. (Elizabeth Taylor's figure appears in Solomon's Temple.)

There are four separate Bible Walks; the Old and New Testament walks each take an hour. The Museum of Christian Martyrs and Heart of the Reformation each take half an hour. How much time is required to recover from the experience is up to each individual.

Living Bible Museum
500 Tingley Avenue, Mansfield, Ohio 44905
419-524-0139
www.livingbiblemuseum.org

Don't miss the old Ohio State Reformatory building outside the Bible Walk off OH Highway 545/Olivesburg Road. It's truly one of the scariest-looking buildings I have ever seen, and I'm not alone in my opinion. A group of actors has created the Ohio State Reformatory's Haunted Prison Experience for your entertainment—if you dare. Find out more at www.hauntedx.com.

You may recognize the building from movies like *The Shawshank Redemption* (based on the novella by Stephen King) and *Air Force One*. This facility was slated to be torn down, but a group of smart citizens realized its potential and saved it. Today, you can take tours of the building, such as a Tower Tour and Dungeon Tour, including a special Hollywood Tour that leads you to spots where movie scenes were filmed. Of course, there's a gift shop.

Ohio State Reformatory
Reformatory Road, Mansfield, Ohio 44905
419-522-2644
www.mrps.org

When you're in Mansfield, you may want to check out the Stuffed Animal Scenes and Elektro the Robot, some truly strange attractions located at 34 Park Avenue West.

I-75: From the Old Mill Stream to the Elizabethan Poet

▶ Findlay

Findlay was named to honor the officer in charge of a fort erected on its site as a local outpost in the War of 1812. It's still the headquarters of the Cooper Tire and Rubber Company, but during the 1880s it was a booming center of oil and natural gas production. The *Findlay Jeffersonian* published the fictitious Civil War letters of "Petroleum Vesuvius Nasby," a stupid Copperhead whose arguments made the Confederacy appear ridiculous.

James Purdy—novelist, short story writer, poet, and playwright—was born in Hicksville, Ohio, but his family moved to Findlay when Purdy (1914–2009) was very young, and he lived here for many years in later life. Despite critical praise and respect within the literary community, Purdy never achieved the stature his devoted followers felt he deserved, though he won numerous awards. He is best known for his first two novels, *Malcolm* (1959) and *The Nephew* (1961).

The American classic song "Down by the Old Mill Stream" was composed here by popular songwriter Tell Taylor (1876–1937), who was raised in Findlay and who is buried here.

But the main reason I recommend a stop in Findlay is to visit the Mazza Museum. This is the first and largest museum devoted to the art of children's picture books with a three-thousand-piece collection that includes Marcia Brown's illustrations from "Cinderella" and several drawings by Randolph J. Caldecott, for whom the Caldecott Medal is named.

Mazza Museum
1000 North Main Street, Findlay, Ohio 45840
Wednesday through Friday, noon to 5, Sunday, 1 to 4 p.m.
419-434-5521
www.findlay.edu/offices/resources/mazza/default.htm

▶Sidney

This town was named for poet and courtier Sir Philip Sidney (1554–1586). It's not clear why. The land was donated to local authorities by an Irish immigrant, Charles Starrett, who may have had enthusiasm for Sidney. The William A. Ross Jr. Historical Center includes a research library and much information about the town and Shelby County.

I-77: From the Canterbury Tales to the Signal House

▶Akron

The formal dining room of the Stan Hywet Hall and Gardens, a sixty-five-room mansion, boasts an oil-on-canvas mural depicting Geoffrey Chaucer's *The Canterbury Tales*. The estate hosts Shakespeare plays each July.

Stan Hywet Hall and Gardens
714 North Portage Path, Akron, Ohio 44303
330-836-5533; 888-836-5533
www.stanhywet.org

▶Canton

Canton is probably best known as the home of the Pro Football Hall of Fame, but if you want a completely different type of experience, costumed docents provide tours of the First Ladies National Historic Site. This facility preserves the site of the home of Ida Saxton McKinley, wife of U.S. President William McKinley. It's now focused on first ladies. It includes museum exhibits, a Victorian the-

First Lady Ida Saxton McKinley

ater, and a library. There is also an educational center adjacent in a former bank building. A collection of books replicates the first White House library created by Abigail Fillmore. If you can't make it in person, you can still check out their online bibliographic database.

National First Ladies Library
205 and 331 Market Avenue South, Canton, Ohio 44702
330-452-0876
www.firstladies.org

▶Kirtland

Okay, this is a stretch, but Joseph Smith (1805–1844) wrote much of the doctrine of the Church of Latter Day Saints while he and other Mormon settlers lived here. I'm not related to the Holden who established the Holden Arboretum, but I'm sure you'll love their reference library. And, hey, you can't blame a guy for touting his own name whenever he gets a chance.

First Ladies National Historic Site in Canton

▶ Oxford

William Holmes McGuffey established his first reading audience while a professor at Miami University in the 1830s. He became famous for writing the *McGuffey Readers*, among the first and most popular school textbooks ever used. His home in Oxford is now a National Historic Landmark and part of the campus of Miami University in Ohio.

William Holmes McGuffey Museum
410 E. Spring Street, Oxford, Ohio 45056
513-529-8380
www.units.muohio.edu/mcguffeymuseum

The Education and Resource Center, part of the National First Ladies' Library

▶ Ripley

The Rankin House State Memorial in Ripley is the restored home of Reverend John Rankin (1793–1886), an early Ohio abolitionist. You can see some of his possessions, including a 1793 Bible, plus many of his letters that were published in 1826. A station on the Underground Railroad, the house is reputedly the one in which Eliza, a character in *Uncle Tom's Cabin*, found refuge after crossing the ice on the

Ohio River. In fact, some say that Reverend Rankin told Harriet Beecher Stowe the story of Eliza, which led her to write her famous book using Eliza as the basis. If you want to sleep with history, book a room in the nearby bed and breakfast called the Signal House. It earned its name because its occupants would signal those in the Rankin House that the waterfront was clear of bounty hunters, dogs, and slave owners.

Rankin House State Memorial
6152 Rankin Road (northeast of State Route 52), Ripley, Ohio 45167
937-392-1627
www.ripleyohio.net/htm/rankin.htm

The Signal House
234 North Front Street, Ripley, Ohio 45167
937-392-140

chapter eight

Wisconsin

Driving Tours

1. I-94: From the Liar's Club to the Western Gateway
2. I-90/94: From Wilhelm Tell to Storybook Gardens
3. I-43 north: From Ten Chimneys to the Friend of the Prairie Chicken
4. I-39: Rocks, Rivers, and Frontiers
5. I-41: Edna Ferber Meets Harry Houdini

*T*he natural beauty of the state of Wisconsin has inspired many writers, from Laura Ingalls Wilder, who wrote her book *Little House in the Big Woods* about her family's time in the state, to journalist Don Johnson, who wrote a series of articles on pesticide pollution that led to the passage of important environmental legislation.

You, too, will be inspired as you drive through the state, passing over rivers and lakes, marshes and green forests. There are hills here—a natural feature that's often in short supply in the Midwest. *The Glacier Stopped Here* is a moving anthology of poems published by the Dane County Cultural Affairs Commission that sing the praises of this part of the Wisconsin terrain.

Madison, the state capital as well as home to the University of Wisconsin, is a center for bookstores and writers, not to mention readers. The book *The Insiders' Guide to Madison* claims that "there are at least 165 registered book clubs here with more than 2,000 members." Other parts of the state were home to writers as illustrious as Carl Sandburg, Thornton Wilder, John Muir, and Edna Ferber. And if you time your visit just right, you'll be able to attend festivals that commemorate the work of local writers such as Hamlin Garland, Zona Gale, and August Derleth.

I-94: From the Liar's Club to the Western Gateway

If you're traveling between Chicago and Milwaukee, chances are you'll take I-94. This highway also stretches northwest all the way to the Minneapolis area. Along the way, you'll pass the lake towns of Kenosha, Racine, and Oconomowoc, and historic small towns like Hudson and Pepin.

▶Burlington

If you like books and stories, you probably like tall tales, and that's no lie. The Burlington Liars Club, which has been around for more than seventy-five years, holds an annual contest to find the greatest lie told in the preceding year. No matter when you arrive, be sure to stop in at the Chamber of Commerce Office to pick up a map so you can walk the Tall Tales Trail. As the trail leads you past businesses and stores throughout the town, keep an eye out for the bronze plaques that commemorate this brand of American humor. Burlington is just west of I-94 on WI 11, so you don't need much of a map to get to the town itself.

Burlington Liars Club
www.burlingtonliarsclub.com

Burlington Chamber of Commerce
113 East Chestnut Street, Burlington, Wisconsin 53105
262-763-6044
www.burlingtonchamber.org

You might be tempted to call a Liars Club competitor a yo-yo, but if you want to look at the real thing among a collection that includes tops and gyroscopes, head for the Spinning Top & Yo-Yo Museum. Don't be surprised if you end up playing one of the thirty-five hands-on games.

Spinning Top & Yo-Yo Museum
533 Milwaukee Avenue, Burlington, Wisconsin 53105
262-763-3946
www.topmuseum.org
Must schedule a tour time

▶Kenosha

Orson Welles (1915-1985), director of *Citizen Kane* and other notable movies, was born in the upstairs flat at 6116 Seventh Avenue
on May 6, 1915. With the director Peter Bogdonovich, Welles wrote
one autobiography, *This Is Orson Welles*. In the book, he makes a
vague reference to his
hometown when talking
about his flat Midwestern
accent. He calls it "my own
little touch of Kenosha." A
timeline in the back of the
book describes his mother,
Beatrice Ives Welles, as a
"pianist, champion rifle
shot, and suffragette who
once served a prison term
for her radical views," and
his father Richard Head
Welles as "a sometime
inventor from a wealthy
Virginia family."

You might not be able to
tour his birthplace, which
is a private home, but once

Director and actor Orson Welles

you find this town on the Lake Michigan shore just north of WI Highway 50, you'll have trouble deciding which attraction to see first.

Just get on the vintage Kenosha Transit Electric Streetcar to
sample quaint shops, galleries, an outdoor market, and eateries. The
lakefront museum campus features the Kenosha Public Museum,
Dinosaur Discovery Museum, Kenosha History Center, and the Civil
War Museum. Or go a little south to pick up a free bag of Jelly Belly
beans at the Jelly Belly Center in Pleasant Prairie. Yum, my favorite!

▶Racine

"I remember a lad in Racine," journalist, author, and screenwriter
Ben Hecht (1894-1964) says about his hometown. Hecht was actually born in New York but grew up in Racine before leaving for Chicago after high school. In his memoir *A Child of the Century*, Hecht
reminisces about being surrounded by remnants of circus life. An

old round circus barn stood in front of his residence, which was, in fact, a rooming house for retired circus people. The name of the landlady was Frances Castello, and her husband, Dan, had been a partner of P. T. Barnum. Young Ben only had to cross the street to to play in the barn or on the trapeze. He called the barn "one of the five hills of my youth."

As an adult, Hecht wrote, collaborated, or was a consultant on several movie scripts that focused on circus stories. Perhaps he was trying to recall his days growing up with the carnival performers or the barn overlooking Lake Michigan. He worked on *Trapeze* starring Burt Lancaster, *Jumbo* starring Doris Day and Jimmy Durante, *At the Circus* starring the Marx Brothers, and *7 Faces of Dr. Lao*, starring Tony Randall.

The house where the Hecht family lived was torn down in the 1960s, but the house where Mrs. Castello lived at 827 Lake Avenue still remains.

▶Pepin

"Once upon a time, sixty years ago, a little girl lived in the Big Woods of Wisconsin, in a little house made of logs."

So begins one of the most popular books ever set in Wisconsin—*Little House in the Big Woods* by Laura Ingalls Wilder. Laura tells you more or less where the house was:

"It was seven miles to town. The town was named Pepin, and it was on the shore of Lake Pepin."

Today, you can visit The Laura Ingalls Wayside and Cabin, which includes a replica of the "Little House in the Big Woods." You can have a picnic on the shore of Lake Pepin, picking up pretty pebbles just as young Laura did. Pepin is also her birthplace. There are Laura Ingalls Wilder Days in September, and other displays and memorabilia of Laura and her work can be found year-round at the Pepin Historical Museum. If you're into railroads and steamboats or would like to be, check out the historical displays at the Pepin Depot Museum.

But if you come for Laura, you may end up hanging around for a few extra days after you see the scenic beauty provided by bluffs, rivers, and prairies. No less a person than William Cullen Bryan stated: "Lake Pepin ought to be visited by every poet and painter in the land." It was a favorite of Mark Twain, although he might not have had the privilege of staying at—drum roll please—the Holden Campground.

Laura Ingalls Wilder Museum

306 Third Street, WI Highway 35, Pepin, Wisconsin 54749

800-442-3011

May 15 through October 15 , 10 a.m. to 5 p.m.

Laura Ingalls Wayside and Cabin

N3238 City Road CC, Pepin, Wisconsin 54749

800-442-3011

April 15 through November 15, 10 a.m. to 5 p.m.

Pepin Depot Museum

800 Third Street, WI Highway 35, Pepin, Wisconsin 54759

715-442-6501, 800-442-3011

▶Milwaukee

Don Johnson, who served as outdoor writer for the Milwaukee
Sentinel, grew up in the Milwaukee area and hunted and fished on
family farms in the area. His series on the effect of pesticide pollution on the environment led to Wisconsin becoming the first state
to ban DDT.

Although Carl Sandburg was born in Galesburg, Illinois, he
moved to Milwaukee in the early twentieth century. He joined the
Social Democratic Party there and served as secretary to the mayor
of Milwaukee. He met his wife, Lilian Steichen, in the Social Democratic Party office at 344 Sixth Street in 1907 and, after a six-month
exchange of letters, they were married in 1908. During his time in
Milwaukee, he began writing poems in free verse about what were
then unconventional subjects, such as working men, women, and
children—the people he encountered at the mayor's office. His Milwaukee years were the start of his life as a poet. He later wrote:

> Ah, Milwaukee . . . I got my bearings there.
> The rest of my life has been the unrolling
> Of a scene that started up in Wisconsin.[1]

In 1907, while recruiting members to the Social Democratic
Party, he lived in Oshkosh at 248 Wisconsin Avenue. In 1908, he
and his young family lived in a house on Hawley Road.[2]

Milwaukee is the hometown of mystery writer Peter Straub, who
was born here in 1943. On his Web site (www.peterstraub.net), he
writes in an entertaining way about his childhood. He taught him-

self to read in kindergarten, and he recalls "ransacking" the school library while his classmates were laboring over Dick, Jane, and Spot. He attended Milwaukee Country Day School and later the University of Wisconsin.

Yet another Milwaukee literary light—science fiction and thriller writer Jack Finney, who was born here in 1911. He is best remembered for his 1955 novel *The Body Snatchers*, which was adapted for film as *Invasion of the Body Snatchers*, a cult classic. The movie has been remade three times, most recently in 2007.

Bookstores

Boswell Book Company
2599 N. Downer Avenue, Milwaukee, Wisconsin 53211

New Chapter Bookshop
10976 N. Port Washington Road, Mequon, Wisconsin 53092

▶Oconomowoc

This town was long a summer home and tourist stop for prominent families from Milwaukee, Chicago, and St. Louis. Perhaps because of its interesting and poetic name, Oconomowoc pops up occasionally in different novels and television shows. In Theodore Dreiser's novel *The Titan*, the protagonist, Cowperwood, encounters a woman he is interested in, a Mrs. Hand, who tells him she is going to visit friends in Oconomowoc. The two are later seen together in various locales, including Oconomowoc.

In *You Shall Know Our Velocity*, the first novel by Dave Eggers, the main character is beaten up by a resident of Oconomowoc.

Oconomowoc isn't just home to vacationers and local toughs. Booklovers flock to Books & Company, an independent bookstore that has been in business for more than a quarter century. Authors from around the country stop here to do readings and signings. Live music is often staged on Saturday nights. The store's Web site includes a list of more than sixty-five local book groups, some of which meet on the premises.

Books & Company
1039 Summit Avenue, Whitman Park Shopping Center
Oconomowoc, Wisconsin 53066
262-567-0106
www.booksco.com

▶ Hudson

This town of less than twelve thousand is situated on the St. Croix River and considers itself the "Western Gateway to Wisconsin." It has a historic downtown area that is becoming a tourist attraction. That area includes some good independent bookstores. Back to Books says it has been in business, under one name or another, since 1866. Local authors who sometimes visit to sign their books include William Kent Kreuger, author of *Mercy Falls*, poet Aasha Sunar, and novelists Louise Erdrich and Amy Timberlake. The staff of Back to Books was planning a local TV show as this book was being written.

Back to Books
520 Second Street, Hudson, Wisconsin 54016
715-381-1199
Backtobooks.booksense.com

Hudson was also one of the locations for a film called *Rachel River*. The film, about a young female journalist who returns to her hometown in Minnesota and examines her life, was based on stories contained in writer Carol Bly's collection *Backbone* (1985).

I-90/94: From Wilhelm Tell to Storybook Gardens

This highway leads you through the heart of Wisconsin past some of its most populated and popular areas. Tourists flock to the towns near the Wisconsin River, Lake Wisconsin, and other lakes, such as the Wisconsin Dells and Baraboo. Writers and booklovers flock here too, drawn to natural areas or to the many bookstores in Madison.

▶ New Glarus

For someone who may or may not have actually existed, William Tell (otherwise known as Wilhelm Tell) has been quite an influential character. The legend about Tell is that his punishment for failing to bow before the hat of a local bigwig was that he either had to shoot an apple perched on the head of his son or else both would be executed. Luckily, Tell was an expert marksman, and he was able to split the fruit with a single shot from his crossbow.

Tell was purported to live in Switzerland, and the New Glarus area is heavily into Swiss culture and heritage. So it's only appropriate that the Wilhelm Tell Festival is held each Labor Day weekend. The festival includes a children's lantern and a not-to-be-missed yodeling contest.

Wilhelm Tell Festival
P.O. Box 456, New Glarus, Wisconsin 53574
www.wilhemtell.org

▶Baraboo

After plenty of time in the water parks at the Wisconsin Dells, I convinced my daughters to take a detour to visit a tiny shack. Why? "The Shack," as his family called it, was actually the laboratory of conservationist Aldo Leopold, author of the *Sand County Almanac* and *Sketches Here and There*. Believe it or not, this book sells more copies today than when it was first published in 1949—2.5 million and counting. Leopold also literally wrote the book on game management, while virtually single-handedly creating the academic discipline of wildlife ecology.

Aldo Leopold's peaceful forest shack

Finding The Shack is an adventure in itself. As you drive deep into the beautiful countryside, you begin to understand why Leopold loved this part of Wisconsin. The roads get smaller and smaller, until you are on a tiny road in the forest. Keep going until you see signs directing you to the Aldo Leopold Legacy Center on the right. Pull into the parking area, and you'll see the big wooden building. You can stay for a tour or to view a video about Leopold. If you pay a small extra fee, you can visit The Shack itself. Now the fun begins. You are given a map of the surrounding area and discover that, in fact, you've already driven past the unmarked entrance leading to The Shack.

By this time in our excursion, my kids were chafing to get home. But I persevered by herding them down the prescribed path—one of the most beautiful walks I have ever seen, surrounded by flowers with bees buzzing and birds singing all around. At the end of the path, you come to The Shack. You can easily imagine that Leopold himself has just stepped outside to admire the view. It's a beautiful and peaceful place, and I highly recommend it.

Aldo Leopold Legacy Center
138 First Street, Baraboo, Wisconsin 53913
608-355-0279
www.aldoleopold.org/legacycenter
May 1–November 1, Monday through Saturday, 10:00 a.m. to 4:30 p.m.

The Aldo Leopold Legacy Center

There are plenty of books for sale in the gift shop of the nearby International Crane Foundation. After all, every culture where they appear has ancient tales and myths about cranes. But wait to crack open your new book until you get home. While you're on the premises you'll mostly want to enjoy the beauty of these magnificent creatures and learn about what the foundation is doing to keep their presence part of our future by protecting and displaying a mating pair of each of the world's fifteen crane species.

International Crane Foundation
E13701 Levee Road. Baraboo, Wisconsin 53913
608-356-7309
www.savingcranes.org
Seasonal hours

▶Edgerton

Sterling North (1906–1974), who spun yarns about his pet raccoon, Rascal, was born on a farm in Edgerton, which he renamed Brailsford Junction in several of his books. His bestseller *So Dear to My Heart* was translated into twenty-six languages and filmed by Walt Disney. But for his final book, *The Wolfling*, he returned to the theme of wild animals. This time it was his father and neighbor naturalist Thure Kumlien who were raising a wolf pup near Busseyville. The Kumlien and North homesteads, as well as North's birthplace, are private property, but the Sterling North Home and Museum serves as a literary center and museum. The property has been restored to its 1917 setting by the Sterling North Society, and displays North's desk and typewriter, as well as many other family artifacts, photos, books, and memorabilia.

Sterling North Home and Museum
409 West Rollin Street, Edgerton, Wisconsin 53534
608-884-3731 or 608-884-3870
www.sterlingnorth.com
April–December, Sunday, 1:00 p.m. to 4:30 p.m.

Sterling North's older sister, Jessica Nelson North (1891–1988), was born in Madison but grew up with her younger brother in Edgerton. She became a novelist and poet in her own right; her novel *Morning in the Land* is set in Wisconsin during the pre-Civil War era.

►Fort Atkinson

The stereotype of the solitary, poverty-stricken poet who dies unrecognized has some vestige of truth in the life of at least one Wisconsin poet. Lorine Niedecker (1903–1970) was born on the Black Hawk Island near Fort Atkinson. When she was young, her family moved to Riverside Drive in Fort Atkinson, where she attended school. Later, her fisherman-father moved the family back to the island.

Aside from a few brief trips, Niedecker lived much of her life on the island or in Fort Atkinson in isolation and often in poverty. The world of birds, trees, and marshes around Fort Atkinson informed her poetry, and she was associated with the Objectivist poets. Her unpublished manuscripts were found after her death in 1970, and it was only then that she received recognition for her *Collected Works*. In 2002, a centennial celebration was held to commemorate her life and work. Visits were made to her two homes on the edge of the Rock River on Black Hawk Island.

The Lorine Niedecker cabin is located a few miles southwest of Fort Atkinson on Black Hawk Island Road. You'll find a map at www.lorineniedecker.org/map.html.

Fireside Dinner Theatre has presented theater in the round for the past forty-four years, and if you're around when a performance is being held, be sure to buy a ticket.

Fireside Dinner Theatre
1131 Janesville Avenue, Fort Atkinson, Wisconsin 53538
920-563-9505
www.firesidetheatre.com

►Madison

Culture vultures and book hunters alike will have a field day in Madison with venues too numerous to cover completely. But what you really need to know is that it has been recognized as one of the country's top canoe towns by *Paddler* magazine and one of the ten best bicycling cities by *Bicycling* magazine.

The Wisconsin Book Festival is held annually in the fall—late September or early October—and is one of the largest book fairs in the country. The event features poetry readings, entertainment stages, and an auction of autographed books. Learn more at www.wisconsinbookfestival.org.

Ronald Wallace

Poet Ronald Wallace is a professor in the
creative writing program at the University of
Wisconsin in Madison. His collection of poems
called *The Makings of Happiness* draws on the
people and landscape of the state.

"I've always thought of myself as a
Midwestern writer—I was born in Iowa, grew
up in St. Louis, attended college in Ohio and
university in Michigan, and have lived and
taught in Wisconsin for the past thirty-seven
years. So, I've spent my life circling the upper
Midwest, and the flora and fauna and people
of the region have been central to my poetry and fiction. In 1984, my wife, Peg, and
I bought a forty-acre farm in Bear Valley, Wisconsin, in the "driftless," or unglaciated,
part of the state. We have a carpenter-built old farmhouse (with no indoor plumbing
or central heat), a couple of sheds, and a lovely barn. When my two daughters were
growing up, we lived about half the year at the farm, gardening, restoring prairie,
raising chickens and goats, and generally coming to know the birds and foxes and
coyotes and deer and groundhogs and moles and field mice fairly intimately.

"All of this was fodder for my writing, and my book *The Makings of Happiness*
is mostly set in this place. Although we no longer spend as much time at the farm
(winters with an outhouse and without central heat no longer seem as appealing), we
still spend time during the summer there, and the quiet and serenity and rhythms of
country life, along with our neighbors (small farmers and a retired country carpenter)
continue to provide inspiration for my writing.

"My office at the University of Wisconsin, tucked behind a small conference room
where only the intrepid can find it, with its view of Lake Mendota and Picnic Point,
also provides a place rich with potential for writing and reflection. And Picnic Point
itself, a protected wooded finger of land that juts out into the lake and is managed
by the University, has afforded me the space for my four-mile runs and their rhythms
that also have engendered poems. To the north, Door County, surrounded by Lake
Michigan and Green Bay, is a further favorite retreat. Although I grew up in a big city,
I've found that my muse is most responsive in the contexts of a smaller university
town with surrounding rural space."

At the risk of forgetting a worthy author, here's a list of some notables who live in Madison or lived here in the past:

Kelly Cherry (1940–) is the author of seventeen books of fiction, nonfiction, and poetry. A native of Louisiana, she hold the position of Eudora Welty Professor Emerita of English and Evjue-Bascom Professor Emerita in the Humanities at the University of Wisconsin-Madison.

Merle Curti (1897–1995) taught in the history department at the University of Wisconsin-Madison from 1942 to 1968. During that time he published *The Growth of American Thought*, which won the Pulitzer Prize in History in 1944.

Jacquelyn Mitchard (1957–   ) lives south of Madison. Her book *The Deep End of the Ocean* was Oprah Winfrey's first choice for her book club.

Lorrie Moore (1957–   ) teaches at the University of Wisconsin-Madison and is an acclaimed writer of novels and short stories.

Thornton Wilder (1897–1975) was born in Madison but the family lived in numerous places due to his father's job as a government diplomat. Wilder is one of the most highly regarded American writers of the 20th century, for such novels as *The Bridge of San Luis Rey* (which won the Pulitzer Prize in 1928) and *The Eighth Day* (which won the National Book Award in 1967). He is perhaps remembered even more as a playwright, especially for *Our Town*, which won the Pulitzer Prize in 1938 and has been staged countless times in theaters across the country.

If all the literary activity tires you out, check in at the Canterbury Inn Apartments bed-and-breakfast, where each room has been painted to represent a chapter of Geoffrey Chaucer's *Canterbury Tales*.

Canterbury Inn Apartments
315 West Gorham Street
Madison, Wisconsin 53703
608-663-4872

The Reeve's Tale room includes images of the bed-swapping characters described in the tale. And you'll find a copy of *The Canterbury Tales* on the bedside table.

The Canterbury is only half a block from State Street, the long commercial street in Madison that is lined with quirky stores, many

The Canterbury Inn bed-and-breakfast

of them bookstores. Just how many bookstores are there in Madison? Scan the following list and you'll get an idea.

- Booked for Murder (mystery books).
- A Room of One's Own (travel, contemporary women's fiction, lesbian literature) 307 West Johnson Street, 608-257-7888.
- Avol's Bookstore, 240 West Gilman Street, 608-255-4730
- Bookworks, 109 State Street, 608-255-4848, does book restoration.
- McDermott Books, 449-D State Street, 608-284-0744, 3,000 secondhand books on two levels connected by spiral staircase.
- Paul's Book Store, 670 State Street, rare and out-of-print bookstore.
- Pic-A-Book, 506 State Street, 608-256-1125.
- Rainbow Bookstore Cooperative, 426 West Gilman.
- Shakespeare's Books, 18 North Carroll Street, 608-255-5521.

Madison Bookstores
Ronald Wallace recommends the local Borders Books, which, he says, "has tried to retain the feel of a smaller place." Avol's Bookstore is the best place for used books in town, and has a very active series of readings by both local and nationally known writers. You might hear Wallace read his own poetry at The Froth House, which hosts readings by neighborhood poets.

Literary Groups in Madison

Cheap At Any Price Poets' Collective
317 North Brearly Street, Madison
Council for Wisconsin Writers
608-233-2484

Madison Storytellers' Guild
3126 Buena Vista Street, Madison
608-249-5030
Meetings held September through May on the third Saturday of the month. The Guild sponsors storytelling concerts and events. Call Susan Gilchrist.

The Writers' Place
7 North Pinckney Street
Street, J, Madison
608-255-4030
Nonprofit literary center offering creative writing workshops and classes, a newsletter, readings, and an annual literary contest.

- State Street, which runs from the Capitol to Bascom Hill, is a favorite haunt for used book hunters.

- University Book Store, 711 State Street, Madison, 608-257-3784. "The mother of all Madison bookstores." Actually has four locations in all, two on State Street, two at Hilldale Shopping Center.

- The Book Rack, Market Square 6648 Odana Road, 608-829-3191.

- Booked for Murder Ltd., Lakepoint Commons, 2701 University Avenue, 608-238-2701.

- Borders Book Shop, 3416 University Avenue, 608-232-2600.

- Borders Books Music & Café, 2173 Zeier Road, 608-240-0080.

▸Maple Bluff

This town near Madison was the home of one of Wisconsin's most famous politicians, Robert La Follette, Sr., known to his supports as Fightin' Bob. La Follette (1855–1925) served three terms as senator from Wisconsin and was governor from 1901 to 1906. His autobiography is called, appropriately enough, *La Follette's Autobiography: A Personal Narrative of Political Experiences*. In it, he speaks of his decision to run for public office for the first time:

> I was born in Primrose Township, Dane County, only twenty miles from Madison, where my father, a Kentuckian by birth, had been a pioneer settler from Indiana. I knew farm ways and farm life, and many of the people who were not acquainted with me personally knew well from what family I came—and that it was an honest family. The people of the county were a mixture of New Englanders, Norwegians, and Germans. I had been raised among the Norwegians and understood the language fairly well, though I could speak it only a little—but even that little helped me.[3]

Wisconsin Senator and Governor Robert La Follette

La Follette and his family moved to this rural town just east of Madison in 1905. He unsuccessfully ran for president in 1912 and 1924 but remained one the most formidable politicians of his day. The home where this progressive politician lived is privately owned at 733 Lakewood Boulevard, but is on the National Register of Historic Places.

▶Sauk City

Sauk City is the home of Wisconsin's most prolific writer—author of 150 books as well as articles, short stories, and poetry—August Derleth (1909–1971). He sold his first story to the magazine *Weird Tales* when he was sixteen. From 1941 to 1960 he was the literary editor of the *Capital Times* newspaper in Madison. In many of his books, he told the stories of Sauk City and its twin village, Prairie du Sac.

Sauk City is still closely intertwined with Derleth's life and legacy. If you dine at Leystra's Restaurant, you can eat in "Augie's Room." You can visit his home and, afterwards, visit the resting place of the author himself in nearby St. Aloysius Cemetery. When you pass over the Wisconsin River in the town of Sauk

City, you are passing over the August Derleth Bridge. Derleth himself frequently mentioned the trestle bridge over the Wisconsin River in his writings.

Every second Sunday in October, the August Derleth Society hosts the Walden West Festival, which includes music, speeches, and other events for fans of Derleth. You can take a drive through the countryside and tour his birth site, where he hiked, and settings mentioned in his books. There's even an evening poetry reading at his grave.

The August Derleth Society maintains a substantial amount of information about the writer at www.derleth.org.

Sauk City is also the birthplace of Mark Schorer (1908–1977). A scholar and critic, he was the author of works about other authors, such as his biography *Sinclair Lewis: An American Life*.

►Wisconsin Dells

Before waterparks captivated kids there was Storybook Gardens. There's a one-room schoolhouse plus exhibits depicting fairytales, nursery rhymes, and books such as *Alice in Wonderland*. Live animals are also friendly. A ride on the train and carousel will make your day complete. For a souvenir, pick out a book at the gift shop.

Timbavati Wildlife Park at Storybook Gardens
1500 Wisconsin Dells Parkway
Wisconsin Dells, Wisconsin 53965
www.storybookgardens.net

►Richland Center

This is the birthplace (in 1956) of Lynda J. Barry, who created the comic strip "Ernie Pook's Comeek." She is also the author of several novels. These include *The Good Times Are Killing Me*, which described an interracial friendship between two girls, *Cruddy*, and *One Hundred Demons*.

I-43 North: From Ten Chimneys to the Friend of the Prairie Chicken

The scenic area north of Milwaukee takes you past some beautiful small towns, including Genesee Depot. You'll also pass some rural farm country that has inspired one best-selling local novelist.

▶Genesee Depot

Many literary figures gathered at Ten Chimneys, the summer home of theater legends Alfred Lunt (1892–1977) and Lynn Fontanne (1887–1983), but Noël Coward was a special friend who had his own accommodations, although he shocked the staff with his sarcasm and habit of forgetting to wear his bathrobe. Tours of the house and grounds are available, and there are many exhibits and special events. Among the objects on display are inscribed first edition books from Edna Ferber and Alexander Woollcott. There are two tours offered, and I found it well worth the extra money to get to see the grounds and outbuildings as well as the main house.

Ten Chimneys
S43 W31575 Depot Road, Genesee Depot, Wisconsin 53127
Ten Chimneys Foundation: 262-968-4161
Tour Reservations: 262-968-4110

▶Menomonee Falls

If you're passing through this town, be sure to stop at Village Bookstore, a local independent bookseller.

Village Bookstore
N88W 16521 Main Street, Menomonee Falls, Wisconsin 53051
262-253-0883

▶Rochester

This is the home of novelist Jane Hamilton (1957–), who was born in Illinois and educated at Carleton College in Minnesota. Nearly all of her novels are set in Wisconsin. Her first novel, *The Book of Ruth*, was a selection of the Oprah Winfrey book club in 1996, bringing a large audience to Hamilton's work. Other books include *The Short History of a Prince* and *A Map of the World*. In the latter book, she describes the Wisconsin farm country vividly:

> I have thought a fair amount about our farm, about our house that was built in 1852. It was still a good house, even though it didn't look like much. There are thousands of those houses across the Midwest. White clapboard houses with old windmills in their yards, many of them standing empty now on the prairies of Kansas and Nebraska. They are a series of squares,

built according to need. Ours are deceptively strong houses, stronger than the winds of a twister, determined against insects and drought and long winters, determined against time, against all of the generations that have passed through them.[4]

In 2000, the Wisconsin Library Association named Hamilton a Notable Wisconsin Author.

I-39: Rocks, Rivers, and Frontiers

▶ Castle Rock

I'm not sure of the royalty arrangement, but the hieroglyphs at Roche-A-Cri have attracted visitors for centuries. Even the graffiti is interesting, as some of the carvings made from the mid-1800s to the 1950s record the family names of Adams County's earliest settlers. At three hundred feet, this remnant of Wisconsin's glacial history is considered to be the steepest hill in the state.

Roche-A-Cri State Park
1767 WI 13, Friendship, Wisconsin 53934
888-947-2757 or 608-339-6881

▶ Portage

Portage was important because the Fox and Wisconsin rivers are separated by a narrow neck of land that had to be portaged over. French explorers Marquette and Joliet were among the first whites to portage in 1673. Portage is also the home of one of Wisconsin's most notable writers, Zona Gale (1874–1938).

Zona Gale (1874–1938) began her career as a journalist, but turned to fiction writing soon after. She built the Zona Gale House for her parents on the banks of the Wisconsin River after the publication of her first novel, *Romance Island*, in 1906. Its classical Greek revival exterior is in contrast to the rustic craftsman interior. In 1932, it was given to the Women's Civic League. In 1980, it was listed on the National Register of Historic Places.

The Zona Gale Breese House, built in 1912, is at 804 MacFarlane at the corner of West Franklin. It was donated to the city in 1946 to house the public library. When the library moved to a new location in 1994, it was renovated to house the Museum at the Por-

Novelist Zona Gale

tage, run by the Portage Historical Society. Her study is preserved just as it was when she lived in the house.

On the east side of Pauquette Park, you can see a bridal arch that was created when a couple on their honeymoon missed the turn and drowned in the pond. Zona Gale wrote a short story "Bridal Pond" in memory of the couple.

In 1920, the Zona Gale novel *Miss Lulu Bett* shared bestseller honors with *Main Street* by Sinclair Lewis (see the chapter on Minnesota). She adapted the story for the stage, and the play won the Pulitzer Prize in 1921.

Friendship Village takes its name from a series of popular "Friendship Village" stories by Gale. Her home in Friendship Village is now known as the Museum at the Portage. The area commemorates Zona Gale as dramatist and social activist in August during a Zona Gale festival. Activities held at various locations around Portage often include poetry readings, tours of two houses, and an ice cream and pie social. Other ways to remember her include a Zona Gale Young People's Theater and also a community choir called the Gale Singers.

Museum at the Portage
804 MacFarlane, Portage, Wisconsin 53901
608-742-6700
www.portagewi.com/v_areattr.asp#pcfa

John Harris Kinzie was the Indian agent to the Ho-Chunk Nation (Winnebago) at Portage before he played a major role in founding Chicago. His wife, Juliette Magill Kinzie (1806–1870), published an engaging account of their adventures, *Wau-Bun, The Early Day in the Northwest*, which is well worth reading even if you can't stop by the Historic Indian Agency House, though I recommend taking the short extra drive to enjoy the location and exhibits. A side note is that John and Juliette were grandparents of Juliette Gordon Low, the founder of the Girl Scouts, so you'll learn more about that also. The Agency House and surrounding 233 acres are owned and administered by the National Society of the Colonial Dames of America. The house, which is listed on the National Register of Historic Places, is furnished with American antiques no later than 1833 (the year the Kinzies left for Chicago).

Historic Indian Agency House
1490 Indian Agency Road, Portage, Wisconsin 53901
608-742-6362

Another writer from Portage who earned the Pulitzer was a historian: Frederick Jackson Turner (1861–1932). He believed the study of the role of the frontier in American history would illuminate the broader story of America. His father, Andrew Jackson Turner, who served in the state assembly and senate and also was on the State Railroad Commission between 1878 and 1882, began the Wisconsin State Register in 1861 with a strongly Republican/ Abolitionist perspective. In 1922, Fredrick wrote to C. C. Skinner: "I spent my youth in a newspaper office in contact with practical politics . . . where as local editor my father reported the community life, which I helped to 'set up.'"

Turner is best known for his lecture "The Significance of the Frontier in American History," a reflection on the closing of the American frontier, which he gave in 1893 to a gathering of historians in Chicago. His essays were collected into a book with the same title, winning the Pulitzer Prize in History in 1933.

►Whitewater

Writer and historian Stephen Ambrose (1936–2002) was born in Illinois, but his family moved to Whitewater when he was young. He graduated from Whitewater High School and was educated at the University of Wisconsin-Madison. He was the author of many nonfiction books that had to do with different periods of American history. His books about World War II include *Band of Brothers*, *The Victors*, and *Citizen Soldiers*. He is perhaps best remembered for his book *Undaunted Courage* (1996) about the Lewis and Clark expedition. One of the most popular writers of history in the final decades of the twentieth century, Ambrose was also the target of controversy in his final years when accusations of plagiarism arose.

►Plainfield

Writer Fran Hamerstrom (1907–1998) lived in an 1850s-era home in Plainfield that lacked indoor plumbing. She wrote about wildlife, particularly the prairie chicken, which she and her husband, Frederick, are credited with saving from extinction in Wisconsin. In later years, the house was opened to hundreds of volunteers who came to help with annual prairie chicken counts. Hamerstrom's books include *Walk When the Moon is Full*, *Memoirs of a Lady Hunter*, and *An Eagle to the Sky*. To reach the house, take I-30 to WI Highway 73. Head west on WI 73 1.5 miles, then turn north on Third Avenue.

Historic Hamerstrom Home
N6789 Third Avenue, Plainfield, Wisconsin 54966

►Ellison Bay

This idyllic, unincorporated town in the vacation area of Door County is home to Norbert Blei, a writer who divides his time between Chicago and Wisconsin. He wrote a trilogy of books exploring a life spent in this rural area and in urban Chicago: *Door Way* (1981), *Door Steps* (1983), and *Door to Door* (1985). The books are full of character studies of fishermen, farmers, poets, and painters who live in a part of Wisconsin that is changing its economic base from agriculture to tourism.

▸Three Lakes

In far northern Wisconsin, well after I-39 turns into state highway 51, you come to Three Lakes, which is part of the Nicolet National Forest. The Sam Campbell Memorial Trail in the forest commemorates the writer, photographer, and naturalist who was called "The Philosopher of the Forest." Campbell's (1895–1962) popular writings included stories about animals, including a porcupine called Inky. The beautiful 1.75-mile trail leads to Vanishing Lake, which is mentioned in Campbell's writings.

I-41: Edna Ferber Meets Harry Houdini

I defy you to say "Oshkosh" without adding "By Gosh" or maybe "The Genuine Article." Lake Winnebago is huge, and so is the beauty of the views of the countryside near it. But in addition to being picturesque, the philanthropy of paper barons (where would we be without paper?) made sure to add some big-city appeal from Oshkosh to Appleton.

▸Appleton

Pulitzer Prize-winning author Edna Ferber (1885–1968) was born in Michigan, but the family moved to Appleton when she was twelve years old and used it as the setting for her early stories, including "The Homely Heroine," the first one she published in a national magazine in 1910. At age nineteen she was the first female reporter for the *Appleton Crescent*. When she encountered Harry Houdini, another Appleton resident born here in 1874 as Erich Weiss, in a drugstore on College Avenue, she wrote a profile that was published July 23, 1904. A collection of her papers is housed in the Seeley G. Mudd Library of Lawrence University.

Magician Harry Houdini

Though now somewhat forgotten, largely because her novels are not taught in schools, Ferber was one of the most popular novelists of her era. In 1924 she won the Pulitzer Prize for her novel *So Big*, followed up by *Show Boat* (1926) and *Cimarron* (1929), both of which were adapted successfully for the film, as were her later novels *Giant* (1952) and *Ice Palace* (1958). *Show Boat* was also made into a classic Broadway musical.

Ferber also published two memoirs—*A Peculiar Treasure* (1939) and *A Kind of Magic* (1963).

Other Appleton literary notables include: Heima Korth, whose life in the Arctic National Wildlife Refuge is the subject of *The Final Frontiersman*, by James Campbell of Lodi. The bestselling book *Flags of Our Fathers* was written by James Bradley about his father and the other five men raising the flag in the famous photo from Iwo Jima. Still others include: Gladys Taber (books, magazine columns), Lan Samantha Chang (director of the University of Iowa's Writers' Workshop), RachelleB (blogger), Mark Dintefass (author, Lawrence University English professor, reviewer for the *New York Times*), and Mike Lowe (editor in chief of the original *Onion*).

Appleton is also home to several good independent bookstores:

Conkey's
226 East College Avenue
920-735-6223

Shenandoah Books
133 East Wisconsin Avenue
920-832-9525

Children's Bookshop
226 East College Avenue
920-735-6223

▶ Southwest Wisconsin

"A river runs through it" could be the theme of this part of the state. Sites to visit range from Villa Louis, a Victorian country estate with one of the nation's finest collections of late nineteenth-century decorative arts, to the Prairie du Chien Museum at Fort Crawford that celebrates all things military. But there are also literary spots of interest.

►Spring Green

Don't miss a chance to tour Taliesin, the home and studio of Frank Lloyd Wright (1867–1959), who wrote an autobiography among other books. Plenty of other ink has been spilled regarding the other inhabitant of this house, Mamah Borthwick Cheney, who had been the wife of one of Frank's clients. I predict you'll leave the Visitor's Center with a purchase from its good bookstore, as well as a ticket to tour Taliesin where you can admire Wright's own well-stocked bookshelves.

Another reason to come here during the summer is to take in a top-notch play in a lovely outdoor setting at the American Players Theatre. Shakespeare's plays are regularly performed, as well as others by classic playwrights such as Eugene O'Neill.

Taliesin Visitor Center
WI Highway 23 and County Road C, Spring Green, Wisconsin 53588
www.taliesinpreservation.org/visitorsguide/index.htm

American Players Theatre
5950 Golf Course Road, Spring Green, Wisconsin 53588
608-588-7401
www.playinthewoods.org

Frank Lloyd Wright's home anad studio, Taliesin

▶Platteville

Speaking of Shakespeare, the Wisconsin Shakespeare Festival is held from early July to early August, and the University of Wisconsin at Platteville hosts a Heartland Festival each summer—a six-week celebration of the performing arts. In the way of other attractions, The Mitchell Roundtree Stone Cottage is a historic 1837 home that contains many original furnishings, and you can ride a mine train before you descend into the old Bevins Mine at the Mining Museum-Rollo Jamison Museum. There's another hand-dug 1827 lead mine you can visit at the Badger Mine and Museum in nearby Shullsburg. Or go to Belmont to see the 1836 Capitol of the Wisconsin Territory.

▶West Salem

A trip to West Salem was one of the first excursions that alerted me to the power certain regional writers still hold on the areas where they once lived. Novelist and memoirist Hamlin Garland (1860–1940), still a staple in college literature courses but otherwise virtually forgotten, provides a good example. His home is lovingly preserved and a festival is held in his honor each fall.

Garland lived in his home in West Salem only during the summer months and spent the winters in an apartment in Chicago. When I made an appointment to see the house, I was greeted by a man named Errol Kindschy, who said he regularly dressed as Garland and portrayed him in local schools. A visit to Garland's house shows the attention he lavished on his daughters. Their toys are still visible in a second-floor alcove, along with their dolls and some clothing, and their beds can be seen in a screened porch where they slept on hot nights. A large dining room table and furniture made by the author himself shows his proficiency at carpentry. The two bathrooms in the house were the first in town. One is located in the carefully designed suite he lovingly provided for his invalid mother.

For some writers, the location of their house takes on not only geographic significance (because of the location in the midpoint of the United States) but a psychic significance as well. Garland continually wrote about the area where he grew up, even after he moved to upstate New York and, later, to California. His memoirs *Son of the Middle Border*, *Daughter of the Middle Border*, and *Trailblazers of the Middle Border* and others show him returning time and again to the place of his birth. He died in California, but had his body shipped back to West Salem for burial.

Today's West Salemites ignore the fact that Hamlin Garland was notably rude to his neighbors during his lifetime and they, in turn, were scandalized by his politics. Nevertheless, the Hamlin Garland Society keeps his memory alive, and merchants are only too happy to welcome culture seekers each year to Hamlin Garland Days.

A tour visits a number of other sites, including:

- A historical marker erected in 1960 points to the accomplishments of Garland and the fame he brought to this region.
- The original farmhouse has been replaced, but Garland's grandparents lived on the Gills Coulee Farm. His parents were married here in 1859, and it's the setting for *Rose of Dutcher's Coolly* and several stories in *Main-Travelled Roads*, the book for which he is best remembered.
- Molasses Gap, which is now named Quackenbush Road, appears in a number of short stories.
- Green's Coulee is the first farm and home of Richard and Isabel. Hamlin was a year old when they moved here. The only remaining building from that farm is the spring house. "Return of a Private" is Garland's story of his father's return to this site from the Civil War.
- Garland wanted his ashes spread over the hillside, but local officials insisted that he be buried in Neshonoc Cemetery along with his parents, wife, and daughters. Other Garlands are buried in the Onalaska Oaklawn Cemetery.

Hamlin Garland House
357 West Garland Street, West Salem, Wisconsin 54669
Memorial Day through Labor Day, 1 p.m. to 4 p.m.

▶La Crosse

Author and historian John Toland (1912–2004) was born here. He won the 1971 Pulitzer Prize in history for *The Rising Sun*, his book about the military regime in Japan in the late 1930s until the end of World War II. He is best remembered for *Adolf Hitler: The Definitive Biography* (1976), which remains a cornerstone work for historians. His family moved to Connecticut when he was seven years old, and the town has no museum or birthplace to visit.

Endnotes

1   Quoted on the Wisconsin Electronic Reader Web site, www.library.wisc
    .edu/etext/wireader/WER0131.html.

2   Op cit.

3   La Follette, Robert M. *La Follete's Autobiography: A Personal Narrative of
    Political Experiences* (Madison, WI: The Robert La Follette Company,
    1913), 7–8

4   Hamilton, Jane. *A Map of the World* (New York: Anchor Books/Doubleday,
    1994), 153.

Appendix

Independent Bookstores

►ILLINOIS

After-Words Books
23 E. Illinois
Chicago, IL 60611
312-464-1110

Anderson's Bookshop
5112 Main St.
Downers Grove, IL
60515
630-963-2665

Anderson's Bookshop
123 W. Jefferson
Naperville, IL 60540
630-355-2665

Azizi Books
134 Lincoln Mall Dr.
Matteson, IL 60443
708-283-9850

Book Bin, Inc.
1151 Church St.
Northbrook, IL 60062
847-498-4999

Book Cellar
4736-38 N. Lincoln Ave.
Chicago, IL 60625
773-293-2665

Book Mouse
820 LaSalle St.
Ottawa, IL 61350
815-433-7323

Book Shelf
252 South Side Square
Carlinville, IL 62626
217-854-4040

Book Stall at Chestnut Court
811 Elm St.
Winnetka, IL 60093
847-446-8880

BookBundlz
1419 W. Byron St. #1FF
Chicago, IL 60613
773-726-3509

Book World
300 S. Main St.
Galena, IL 61036
815-776-1060

The Bookstore, Inc.
475 N Main St.
Glen Ellyn, IL 60137
630-469-2891

Books on First
202 W. First St.
Dixon, IL 61021
815-285-2665

Books on Vernon
664 Vernon
Glencoe, IL 60022
847-835-5180

Burke's Books of Park Ridge
116 Main St.
Park Ridge, IL 60068
847-692-2300

Café Book
395 Lake St.
Antioch, IL 60002
847-395-2223

Cherry Hill Bookstore Center
2505 E. Washington St.
Joliet, IL 60433
815-722-0166

Chicago-Main Newsstand
860 Chicago Ave.
Evanston, IL 60202
847-425-8900

Christian Pages
PO Box 957384
Hoffman Estates, IL
60169
800-939-7922

City Newsstand
4018 N Cicero
Chicago, IL 60641
773-545-7377

Da Book Joint
8134 S. Burnham
Chicago, IL 60617
773-978-3555

Great Debate Books
535 Maine #3
Quincy, IL 62301
217-221-9673

I Know You Like a Book,
LLC
4707 N Prospect Rd.
Peoria Heights, IL
61616
309-685-2665

Illinois Prairie Book
Sellers
427 Court St.
Pekin, IL 61554
309-347-3600

Lake Forest Book Store
680 N. Western Ave.
Lake Forest, IL 60045
847-234-4420

Little Bird Books
1809 Kenilworth Ave.
Berwyn, IL 60402
708-370-9819

Magic Tree Bookstore
141 N. Oak Park Ave.
Oak Park, IL 60301-
1303
708-848-0770

Read Between the
Lynes
129 Van Buren St.
Woodstock, IL 60098
815-206-5967

Sly Fox
123 N Springfield
Virden, IL 62690
217-965-3641

Town House Books
105 N. Second Ave.
St. Charles, IL 60174-
1912

630-584-8600

Women & Children First
5233 N. Clark St.
Chicago, IL 60640-
2122
773-769-9299

▶INDIANA

4 Kids Books & Toys
8654 E. 96th St.
Fishers, IN 46037-9626
317-570-0715

4 Kids Books, Inc.
4450 Weston Pointe Dr.
Ste. 120
Zionsville, IN 46077
317-733-8710

Bookmamas, Inc.
9 Johnson Ave.
Indianapolis, IN 46219

Bookshelf-Batesville
101 N Walnut St.
Batesville, IN 47006
812-934-5800

Bookworm Inc.
114 N. Michigan, City
Center
Plymouth, IN 46563
574-935-9674

Don's Books
815 N Washington St.
Kokomo, IN 46901
765-459-4901

Imagination Station
26 E. Jefferson St.
Franklin, IN 46131
317-736-9636

Kids Ink Children's
Bookstore
5619 N. Illinois
Indianapolis, IN 46208
317-255-2598

Mitchell Books
6360 W. Jefferson Blvd.
Fort Wayne, IN 46804
260-432-2665

MJ's Bookmark
414 S. Main
Auburn, IN 46706
260-925-2330

Mudsock Book &
Curiosity Shoppe
11631 N. Fishers
Station Dr.
Fishers, IN 46037
317-579-9822

Mystery Company
233 Second Ave. SW
Carmel, IN 46032
317-705-9711

Next Page Bookstore &
More
208 W. Monroe St.
Decatur, IN 46733
260-724-9027

Page by Page the
Bookstore
1801 N Wayne St.
Angola, IN 46703
260-665-9841

Reader's World
4027 Franklin St.
Michigan City, IN 46360
219-872-1882

Summer's Stories
131 S. Main St.
Kendalville, IN 46755
260-349-1745

The Wild
884 Logan St.
Noblesville, IN 46060
317-773-0920

Three Sisters Books &
  Gifts
7 Public Square
Shelbyville, IN 46176
317-392-2270

Viewpoint Books
548 Washington St.
  Columbus, IN 47201
  812-376-0778

Village Lights Bookstore,
110 E. Main St.
Madison, IN 47250
812-265-1800

Von's Book Shop
315 W. State St.
West Lafayette, IN
  47906-3591
765-743-1915

Wabash College
  Bookstore
301 W. Wabash Ave.
Crawfordsville, IN
  47933
765-361-6095

►IOWA

Basically Books
212 Edgewood Rd. NW
Cedar Rapids, IA 52405
319-396-8420

Beaverdale Books, LLC
2629 Beaver Ave, Ste 1
Des Moines, IA 50310
515-279-5400

Body & Soul Wellness
  Center & Spa
2728 Asbury Rd.
 - Ste 777
Dubuque, IA 52003
563-556-9642

Book People
Marketplace
Sioux City, IA 51104
712-258-1471

Book Vault
105 S. Market St.
Oskaloosa, IA 52577
641-676-1777

Book Vine
204 W. Main St.
Cherokee, IA 51012
712-225-2445

Bookends & Beans, LLC
309 E. Water St.
Decorah, IA 52101
563-382-0100

Courtyard Books
415 Main St,
PO Box 71
Keokuk, IA 52632
319-524-4605

Guzzardo's Book Nook
236 Fifth Ave. S.
Clinton, IA 52732
563-242-6632

Iowa Books, LLC
8 S. Clinton St.
Iowa City, IA 52240
319-337-4188

Iowa State University
  Book Store
2229 Lincoln Way, ISU
  Mem. Union

Ames, IA 50011
515-294-0245

The Learning Post
2761 100th St.
Urbandale, IA 50322
515-331-8008

Mattingly Music & Books
113 W. Second St. N.
Newton, IA 50208
641-792-3250

Next Chapter
202 E. Robinson St.
Knoxville, IA 50138
641-828-7323

Paper Moon
206 A St.
McGregor, IA 52157
563-873-3357

Prairie Moon Books
916 Third Ave.
Sheldon, IA 51201
712-324-3624

River Lights Bookstore,
  2nd Edition
1098 Main St.
Dubuque, IA 52001
563-556-4391

Savereide Books, LTD.
2227 Greenwood Ave.
Cedar Falls, IA
  50613
319-277-5084

►MICHIGAN

2nd Glance Books, LLC
1001 Welch Rd., #110
Commerce Twp, MI
  48390
248-960-1030

Another Look Books
22263 Goddard Rd.
Taylor, MI 48180
734-374-5665

Archives Book Shop
517-519 W. Grand River
East Lansing, MI 48823
513-332-8444

Aria Booksellers
216 W. Grand River
Howell, MI 48843
517-548-5577

As the Page Turns, LLC
149 N. Center St.,
  Ste 102
Northville, MI 48167
248-912-0085

Best Books
1204 Jackson Crossing
Jackson, MI 49202
517-780-0024

Bestsellers Bookstore &
  Coffee Co
360 S. Jefferson
Mason, MI 48854
517-676-6648

Between The Covers
152 E. Main St.
Harbor Springs, MI
  49740-1510
231-526-6658

Black River Books
330 Kalamazoo St.,
  Ste 2
South Haven, MI 49090
269-637-7374

Book Beat Ltd
26010 Greenfield
Oak Park, MI 48237
248-968-1190

Book Nook
42 S. Monroe St.
Monroe, MI 48161-
  2238
734-241-2665

Book Nook & Java Shop
8726 Ferry St.
Montague, MI 49437
231-894-5333

Book Shoppe
316 N State St.
Alma, MI 48801
989-463-1667

Bookbug
3019 Oakland Dr.
Kalamazoo, MI 49008
269-385-2847

Bookman
715 Washington St.
Grand Haven, MI
  49417-1487
616-846-3520

Book World
112 E. Aurora St.
Ironwood, MI 49938
906-932-5787

Book World
515 Sheldon Ave.
Houghton, MI 49931
906-482-8192

Book World
Delta Plaza Mall
Escanaba, MI 49829
906-786-3973

Book World
136 W. Washington St.
Marquette, MI 49855
906-228-9490

Book World
407 Bridge St.
Charlevoix, MI 49720
231-547-2005

Book World
404 Ashmun St.
Sault Ste. Marie, MI
  49783
906-632-0559

Book World
52 N State St.
St. Ignace, MI 49781
906-643-7569

Book World
Midtown Mall
Iron Mountain, MI
  49801
906-779-1416

North Wind Books at
  Finlandia University
601 Quincy St.
Hancock, MI 49930
906-487-7309

Snowbound Books
118 N. Third St.
Marquette, MI 49855
906-228-4448

Books & More
119 N. Superior St.
Albion, MI 49224
517-629-7560

Books Connection
19043 Middlebelt
Livonia, MI 48152
248-471-4742

Boyne Country Books
125 Water St.
Boyne City, MI 49712
231-582-3180

Brilliant Books
305 St. Joseph St.
Suttons Bay, MI 49682
231-271-7323

Cabbages & Kings
36 Center
Douglas, MI 49406
269-857-1950

Carol's Paperbacks Plus
5947 Highland Rd.
  (M59)
Waterford, MI 48327
248-674-8179

Cottage Book Shop
5989 Lake St.
Glen Arbor, MI 49636
231-334-4223

Cranesbill Books
108 E. Middle St.
Chelsea, MI 48118
734-433-2665

Crazy Wisdom Bookstore
114 S. Main St.
Ann Arbor, MI 48104
734-665-2757

Curious Book Shop
307 E. Grand River
East Lansing, MI
  48823-4324
517-332-0112

Everybody Reads Books
  & Stuff
2019 E. Michigan Ave.
Lansing, MI 48912
517-346-9900

Fireside Books
1110 W. Michigan Ave.,
  Ste C
Marshall, MI 49068
269-781-3800

Fitz's Booknook
114 Newman
East Tawas, MI 4873

Forever Books
312 State St.
St. Joseph, MI 49085
269-982-1110

Grandpa's Barn
S. Fourth St.
Copper Harbor, MI
  49918
906-289-4377

Great Lakes Book &
  Supply
840 Clark St.
Big Rapids, MI 49307
231-796-1112

Great Northern Bookstore
209 S. State
Oscoda, MI 48750
989-739-7960

Hidden Room Book
  Shoppe
518 Phoenix St.
South Haven, MI 49090
877-637-7222

Horizon Books, Inc.
317 E. Mitchell
Petoskey, MI 49770
231-347-2590

Horizon Books, Inc.
243 E. Front St.
Traverse City, MI 49684
231-946-7290

Hostetter's News Agency
135 Washington St.
Grand Haven, MI 49417
616-842-3920

I.H.S. Christian Books,
  Gifts & More

36103 Plymouth Rd.
Livonia, MI 48150
734-422-9998

Island Bookstore
7372 Main St.
Mackinac Island, MI
  49757-1298
906-847-6202

Island Bookstore &
  Coffee Shop
215 E. Central Ave.
Mackinaw City, MI
  49701-1006
231-436-2665

Kazoo Books
407 N. Clarendon
Kalamazoo, MI 49006
800-516-2665

Kazoo Books II
2413 Parkview Ave.
Kalamazoo, MI 49008
269-553-6506

Ladels
1413 Brooklyn
Detroit, MI 48226
313-963-8550

Leelanau Books
109 N. Main
Leland, MI 49654-0035
231-256-7111

Literary Life Bookstore
  & More, Inc.
758 Wealthy St. SE
Grand Rapids, MI 49503
616-458-8418

Little Professor Book
  Center
105 W. Shiawassee Ave.
Fenton, MI 48430
810-513-2393

Local Flavor
125 Water St.
Boyne City, MI 49712
231-582-7499

Log Mark Bookstore
334 N Main St.
Cheboygan, MI 49721
231-627-6531

Lowry's Books
22 N. Main St.
Three Rivers, MI 49093-1532
269-273-7323

Lowry's Books and More
118 W. Chicago Rd.
Sturgis, MI 49091-1708
269-651-6817

Marwil Bookstore
4870 Cass
Detroit, MI 48201-1204
313-832-3078

McLean & Eakin
Booksellers
307 E. Lake St.
Petoskey, MI 49770
231-347-1180

Michigan News Agency
308 W. Michigan
Kalamazoo, MI 49007
269-343-5958

Nicola's Books
2513 Jackson Rd.
Ann Arbor, MI 48103
734-662-0600

North Shore Books
315 Center St.
North Muskegon, MI 49445
231-981-0606

North Wind Books
601 Quincy St.
Hancock, MI 49930
906-487-7217

Page One Bookstore &
Café
7331 Old Mission Dr.
Rockford, MI 49341
616-916-5294

Paperback Book
Exchange
1811 S. Mission
Mount Pleasant, MI 48858
989-772-5473

Partners Book
Distributing Inc.
2325 Jarco Ave.
Holt, MI 48842
517-694-3205

Pooh's Corner
1886½ Breton Rd. SE
Grand Rapids, MI 49506
616-942-9887

Read It Again Books
39733 Grand River
Novi, MI 48375
248-474-6066

Reading & Rhythm
110 E. Huron Ave.
Bad Axe, MI 48413
989-269-6300

Reading Tree
5300 Northland Dr. NE
Grand Rapids, MI 49525
616-363-1051

Research Unlimited
4546 Merkel Lane

Oscoda, MI 48750
989-739-3294

Rivertown Bookstore
126 E. Bridge St.
Portland, MI 48875
517-647-5743

Robbins Book List
320 S. Lafayette St.
Greenville, MI 48838
616-754-4354

Round Lake Book Store
107 Mason Ave. Ste. 102
Charlevoix, MI 49720
231-547-2988

Safe Harbor Books
16 E. M-134
Cedarville, MI 49719
906-484-3081

Saturn Booksellers
133 W. Main St.
Gaylord, MI 49735
989-732-8899

Schuler Books & Music
Downtown
40 Fountain St. NW
Grand Rapids, MI 49503
616-459-7750

Schuler Books & Music
- Alpine
3165 Alpine Ave. Ste C
Grand Rapids, MI 49544

Schuler Books & Music
2660 28th St. SE
Grand Rapids, MI 49512
616-942-2561

Self Esteem Shop
32839 Woodward
Royal Oak, MI 48073
248-549-9900

Singapore Bank
  Bookstore
317 Butler St.
Saugatuck, MI 49453
269-857-3785

Snowbound Books
118 N. Third St.
Marquette, MI 49855
906-228-4448

Source Booksellers
4201 Cass Ave. @ Willis
Detroit, MI 48201
313-832-1155

Third Mind Books
123 N. Ashley, Ste. 208
Ann Arbor, MI 48104
734-994-3241

Tree House Books
37 E. Eighth St.
Holland, MI 49423
616-494-5085

Tuesday Books
137 W. Grand River Ave.
Williamston, MI 48895
517-655-9700

Uncommon Threads
  Expresso Café
111 Locust St.
Allegan, MI 49010
269-686-2348

Voorhees Books
1370 Yorktown
Grosse Pointe, MI
  48236
313-881-1598

▶MINNESOTA
Beagle Books
112 Third St. W
Park Rapids, MN 56470
218-237-2665

Bear Books and Gifts
27 W. Main St.
Isanti, MN 55040
763-444-4600

Best of Times
  Bookstore, Ltd.
425 W. Third St.
Red Wing, MN 55066
651-388-1003

Bev's Book Nook
126 W. Main St.
Perham, MN 56573
218-346-2556

Birchbark Books
  and Gifts
11 First Ave. W
Grand Marais, MN
  55604
218-387-2315

Birds Books
13484 Dellwood Way
Rosemount, MN 55068
651-423-6444

Book Break
20 Central Ave.
Buffalo, MN 55313
763-682-6790

The Book Shelf
162 W. Second St.
Winona, MN 55987
507-474-1880

The Book Wagon
419 Toronto St.

St. Paul, MN 55102
651-227-1942

Book World
Northbridge Mall
Albert Lea, MN 56007
507-377-6090

Book World
15528 Edgewood Dr.
Baxter, MN 56401
218-855-0054

Book World
Kandi Mall
Willmar, MN 56201
320-214-0555

Book World
Winona Mall
Winona, MN 55987
507-452-1317

Book World
211 S. Main Ave.
Park Rapids, MN 56470
218-732-0770

Book World
PO Box 250
Walker, MN 56484
218-547-2743

Book World
Viking Plaza
Alexandria, MN 56308
320-759-7236

Book World
815 Washington Ave.
Detroit Lakes, MN 56502
218-847-0133

Book World
316 Beltrami Ave. NW
Bemidji, MN 56601
218-444-5523

The Bookcase
607 E. Lake St.
Wayzata, MN 55391
952-473-8341

Bookin' It Bookstore
104B Second St. SE
Little Falls, MN 56345
320-632-1848

Bookrealm
10840 Rockford Rd.
#310
Plymouth, MN 55442
612-360-9131

Books Revisited
607 W. St. Germain
St. Cloud, MN 56301
320-259-7959

The Bookstore at Fitger's
600 E. Superior St.
Duluth, MN 55802
218-727-9077

Buffalo Books & Coffee
6 Division St.
Buffalo, MN 55313
763-682-3147

Carleton College
   Bookstore
Carleton College
Northfield, MN 55057
507-646-4153

Central Ave. Bookstore
229 Central Ave.
Faribault, MN 55021
507-334-4500

Cherry St. Books
503 Broadway St.
Alexandria, MN 56308
320-763-9400

CLN Store
13570 Grove Dr. #353
Maple Grove, MN
   55311
763-416-5385

Common Good Books
165 Western Ave. N.
   #14
St. Paul, MN 55102
651-225-8989

Creative Kidstuff
4313 Upton Ave. S
Minneapolis, MN 55410
612-927-0653

DreamHaven Books
2301 E. 38th St.
Minneapolis, MN 55406
612-823-6161

Drury Lane Books
PO Box 998
Grand Marais, MN
   55604
218-387-3370

Excelsior Bay Books, Inc.
36 Water St.
Excelsior, MN 55331
952-906-1180

Gustavus Adolphus
   College
St. Peter, MN 56082
507-933-6017

Hamblin House Books
923 Second Ave. NE
Byron, MN 55920
507-775-7405

Harris Communications
Retail Store
Eden Prairie, MN 55344
952-906-1180

Howard St. Booksellers
115 E. Howard St.
Hibbing, MN 55746
218-262-5206

Inspiration Hollow
106 Center St. W
Roseau, MN 56751
218-463-1002

Inver Hills Community
   College Bookstore
2500 80th St. E
St. Paul, MN 55076
651-450-8534

Lake Country
   Booksellers
4766 Washington
   Square
White Bear Lake, MN
   55110
651-426-0918

Lake Wobegon USA
350 E. Broadway, MOA
Bloomington, MN
   55425
952-854-3795

Lisa's Second-Floor
   Bookstore
Piragis Northwoods Co.
Ely, MN 55731
218-365-6745

Little Professor Book
   Center MN
110 W. Park Square
Owatonna, MN 55060
507-455-0969

Lundeen, Victor Co.
126 W. Lincoln Ave.
Fergus Falls, MN 56537
218-736-5433

Magers & Quinn
  Booksellers
3038 Hennepin Ave.
Minneapolis, MN 55408
612-822-4611

Many Voices Bookseller
  & Coffeehouse
12805 Lake Blvd.
Lindstrom, MN 55045
651-213-6604

Micawbers
Milton Square
2238 Carter Ave.
St. Paul, MN 55108
651-646-5506

Minneapolis Institute
  of Arts
2400 Third Ave. S
Minneapolis, MN 55404
612-870-3285

Minnesota History
  Center Museum Store
345 Kellogg Blvd. W
St. Paul, MN 55102
651-259-3012

Minnesota/UMD Stores
1120 Kirby Dr, 175 KSC
Duluth, MN 55812
812-726-7286

Minnesota University
  Bookstore
Coffman Memorial
  Union, Room G054
Minneapolis, MN 55455
612-626-1896

Monkey See, Monkey
  Read
425 Division St.
Northfield, MN 55057
507-645-6700

Nancy's Book Nook
103 W. Seventh St.
Red Wing, MN 55066
651-388-6421

Normandale Community
  College Bookstore
9700 France Ave. S
Bloomington, MN
  55431
952-487-7010

Northern Lights Books
  and Gifts
307 Canal Park Dr.
Duluth, MN 55802
218-722-5267

Oleanna Books
PO Box 141020
Minneapolis, MN 55414
612-722-5267

Once Upon a Crime
604 W. 26th St.
Minneapolis, MN 55405
612-870-3785

OrderPoint, Inc.
3405 W. 44th St.
Minneapolis, MN 55410
612-920-4171

Paperback Exchange
2227 W. 50th St.
Minneapolis, MN 55419
612-929-8801

Paperbacks and Pieces
429 Mankato Ave.
Winona, MN 55987
507-452-5580

Rainy Days
25491 Main St.
Nisswa, MN 56468
218-963-4891

The Red Balloon
  Bookshop
891 Grand Ave.
St. Paul, MN 55105
651-224-8320

Saint Benedict Saint
  John's
Highway 94, Sexton
  Commons
Collegeville, MN 56321
320-363-3081

Saint Kate's Bookstore
St. Paul Campus
St. Paul, MN 55105
651-690-6855

Saint Olaf College
  Bookstore
St. Olaf College
Northfield, MN 55057
507-786-3048

Saint Thomas University
1000 LaSalle Ave, Ste
  TMH 105
Minneapolis, MN 55403
651-962-4343

Scout and Morgan
  Books
114 Buchanan St. N.
Cambridge, MN 55008
763-689-2474

Sister Wolf Books
20471 State 226
Park Rapids, MN 56470
218-732-7565

The Source Comics &
  Games
1601 W. Larpenteur Ave.
Falcon Heights, MN
  55113
651-645-0386

The Book Cliffs
161 Pembroke Ave.
Wabasha, MN 55981
651-565-5312

The Tree House
33632 Lavern Rd. NE
Cambridge, MN 55008
763-689-6992

True Colors Bookstore
4755 Chicago Ave. S
Minneapolis, MN 55407
612-821-9630

Uncle Edgar's Mystery
   Bookstore
2864 Chicago Ave. S
Minneapolis, MN 55407
612-824-9984

Uncle Hugo's Science
   Fiction Bookstore
2864 Chicago Ave. S
Minneapolis, MN 55407
612-824-6347

Valley Bookseller
217 N Main St.
Stillwater, MN 55082
651-430-3385

Village Bookstore
Central Square Mall
Grand Rapids, MN
   55744
218-326-9458

Walker Art Center Shops
Walker Art Center
Minneapolis, MN 55403
612-375-7638

Wild Rumpus
2720 W. 43rd St.
Minneapolis, MN 55410
612-920-5005

Wonderment, Inc.
4306 Upton Ave. S.
Minneapolis, MN 55410
612-929-2707

Woodward's
Thunderbird Mall
Virginia, MN 55792
218-741-1744

▶MISSOURI

Cate's Books and Stuff
   LLC
1216 S. Third St.
Louisiana, MO 63353
573-754-5388

Dog Eared ½ Price
   Books
3625 S. Noland Rd.
Independence, MO
   64055
816-833-8889

Forest Park Bookstore
5600 Oakland Ave.
St. Louis, MO 63110
314-644-9146

Main St. Books MO
307 S. Main
St. Charles, MO 63301
636-949-0105

Pudd'nhead Books
37 S. Old Orchard
Webster Groves, MO
   63119
314-918-1069

River Reader LLC
1010 Main St.
Lexington, MO 64067
660-259-4996

▶OHIO

Appletree Books Inc.
12419 Cedar Rd.
Cleveland Heights, OH
   44106-3155
216-791-2665

Ashland Univ Bookstore
Hawkins-Conard
   Student Center
Ashland, OH 44805
419-289-5301

Athens Book Center, Inc
74 E. State
Athens, OH 45701
740-592-4865

Beehive Books
25 N. Sandusky St.
Delaware, OH 43015
740-363-2337

Blue Manatee Children's
   Bookstore
3054 Madison
Cincinnati, OH 45209
513-731-2665

Book Loft of German
   Village
631 S. Third St.
Columbus, OH 43206
614-464-1774

Book Shelf LLC
152 E. Aurora Rd.
Northfield, OH 44067
330-468-3736

Books & Co.
4453 Walnut St.
Beavercreek, OH 45440
937-429-2169

Books 'N' More
28 W. Main St.
Wilmington, OH 45177
937-383-7323

Books of Aurora
PO Box 305
Aurora, OH 44202
330-995-3228

Bookshelf
7754 Camargo Rd.
Cincinnati, OH 45243-
 2661
513-271-9140

Cleveland Museum of
 Natural History
Museum Store
Cleveland, OH 44106
2162314600x3239

EarthWords-Cleveland
 Metroparks
4524 E. 49th St.
Cuyahoga Heights, OH
 44125
216-206-1003

Fireside Book Shop
29 N Franklin St.
Chagrin Falls, OH
 44022-3050
440-247-4050

Florence O. Wilson
 Bookstore
College of Wooster-
 Lowry Center
Wooster, OH 44691
330-263-2421

Frogtown Books, Inc.
2131 N. Reynolds Rd.
Toledo, OH 43615
419-531-8101

Fundamentals
25 W. Winter St.
Delaware, OH 43015
740-363-0290

Jay & Mary's Book
 Center
1201-C Experiment
 Farm Rd.
Troy, OH 45373
937-335-1167

Kenyon College
 Bookstore
106 Gaskin Ave.
Gambier, OH 43022
740-427-5710

Learned Owl Book Shop
204 N. Main
Hudson, OH 44236
330-653-2252

Mack Bookstore &
 Office Supply
1373 Stone Dr.
Harrison, OH 45030
513-367-7243

Mac's Backs Books on
 Coventry
1820 Coventry Rd.
Cleveland Heights, OH
 44118
216-321-2665

Mind Fair Books
13 W. College St.
Oberlin, OH 44074
440-774-6463

Nanna's Bookstore
26597 N. Dixie Hwy
Perrysburg, OH 43551
419-873-0030

National Underground
 Railroad Freedom Ctr
50 E. Freedom Way
Cincinnati, OH 45202
513-333-7738

New & Olde Pages Book
 Shop
856 Union Blvd.
Englewood, OH 45322
937-832-3022

News-Readers Inc.
4 W. Main St.
Fairborn, OH 45324
937-879-4444

Ole' Book Nook
1637 E. Rt 36
Urbana, OH 43078
937-652-1531

Page by Page--The
 Bookstore
840 S. Main St.
Bowling Green, OH
 43402-4601
419-354-2402

Paragraphs Bookstore
105 S. Main St.
Mount Vernon, OH
 43050-3418
740-392-9290

Sacred Path Books &
 Art
2242 Euclid Ave.
Cleveland, OH 44115
216-774-0470

Stately Raven Bookstore
1315 N. Main St.
Findlay, OH 45840
419-427-2814

Sugden Book Store
282 Front St.
Marietta, OH 45750
740-373-0347

Village Bookworm
435 N. Whitewoman St.
Coshocton, OH 43812
740-623-6564

Wooster Book Company
205 W. Liberty St.
Wooster, OH 44691
330-262-1688

▶WISCONSIN

Apple Blossom Books
513 N Main St.
Oshkosh, WI 54901
920-230-3395

Back to Books
520 Second St.
Hudson, WI 54016
715-381-1188

Book Heads
216 E. Mill St.
Plymouth, WI 53073
920-892-6657

Book Look
2724 Post Rd.
Stevens Point, WI 54481
715-341-2665

Book World
30 N Third Ave.
Sturgeon Bay, WI 54235
920-743-3159

Boswell Book Company
2559 N Downer Ave.
Milwaukee, WI 53211
414-332-1181

Book World
10580 Country Walk
   Dr. #11
Sister Bay, WI 54234
920-854-4248

Book World
134 S. Main St.
Shawano, WI 54166
715-524-3837

Book World
10553 Main St.
Hayward, WI 54843
715-634-6007

Book World
121 N Main St.
Waupaca, WI 54981
715-256-9393

Book World
211 W. North Water St.
New London, WI 54961
920-982-5267

Book World
85 S. Main St.
Fond du Lac, WI 54935
920-922-2980

Book World
1136 Main St.
Stevens Point, WI 54481
715-344-5311

Book World
1723 Main St.
Marinette, WI 54143
715-735-5188

Book World
907 S. Eighth St.
Manitowoc, WI 54220
920-682-9202

Book World
320 Watson St.
Ripon, WI 54971
920-748-7680

Book World
414 S. Central Ave.
Marshfield, WI 54449
715-387-6667

Book World
Taylor Heights
Sheboygan, WI 53081
920-694-0011

Book World
58 N Brown St.
Rhinelander, WI 54501
715-369-2627

Book World
116 Front St.
Beaver Dam, WI 53916
920-887-8711

Book World
522 Oneida St.
Minocqua, WI 54548
715-356-7071

Book World
725 Fifth Ave.
Antigo, WI 54409
715-623-2500

Book World
114 E. Wall St.
Eagle River, WI 54521
715-479-7094

Book World
253 W. Grand Ave.
Wisconsin Rapids, WI
   54495
715-421-2570

Book World
317 Broadway
Wisconsin Dells, WI
 53965
608-254-2425

Book World
135 Third St.
Baraboo, WI 53913
608-356-5155

Book World
105 N Main St.
Rice Lake, WI 54868
715-234-8038

Book World
120 W. Cook St.
Portage, WI 53901
608-742-1989

Book World
300 E. Main St.
Watertown, WI 53094
920-206-9705

Book World
921 E. Main St.
Merrill, WI 54452
715-539-9557

Book World
301 W. Main St.
Ashland, WI 54806
715-685-9998

Bookends LLC
214 E. Main St.
Menomonie, WI 54751
715-233-6252

Bookfinders
1001A Brilowski Rd.
Stevens Point, WI
 54481
715-341-8300

Bookland, Inc. – Book
 World
224 W. Wisconsin Ave.
Neenah, WI 54956
920-725-6550

Boswell Book Company
2559 N. Downer Ave.
Milwaukee, WI 53211
414-332-1181

Books & Company
Libris, Inc.
Oconomowoc, WI
 53066
262-567-0106

Bramble Bookstore
117 S. Main St.
Viroqua, WI 54665
608-637-8717

Brown St. Books
25 S. Brown St.
Rhinelander, WI 54501
715-362-5111

Butterfly Books
118 N Broadway
DePere, WI 54115
920-339-1133

Camelot Corner Books
303 Winneconne Ave.
Neenah, WI 54956
608-469-7790

Chequamegon Book Co.
2 E. Bayfield St.
Washburn, WI 54891
715-373-2899

Conkey's Book Store
226 E. College Ave.
Appleton, WI 54911
920-735-6223

Cover to Cover Books
 & Gifts
202 W. Wisconsin Ave.
Tomahawk, WI 54487
715-453-0727

Creekside Books
W62 N596 Washington
 Ave.
Cedarburg, WI 53012
262-546-0004

Dragonwings Bookstore
108 N. Main St.
Waupaca, WI 54981
715-256-9186

Fireside Books and Gifts
1331 W. Paradise Dr.
West Bend, WI 53095
262-334-1444

HelpWithCancer.org
137 Red Fox Trail
St. Croix Falls, WI
 54024
715-271-5037

IslandTime Books &
 More
1885 Detroit Harbor Rd.
Washington Island, WI
 54246
920-847-2565

Jabberwocky
711C Highway 45 N.
Eagle River, WI 54521
715-479-4425

Janke Book Store
505 Third St.
Wausau, WI 54403
715-845-9648

LaDeDa Books &
Beans, Inc.
1624 New York Ave.
Manitowoc, WI 54220
920-682-7040

The Little Read Book
7603 W. State St.
Wauwatosa, WI 53213
414-774-2665

MHS Bookstore
Memorial High School
Eau Claire, WI 54701
715-852-6301

Next Chapter Bookshop
10976 N Port
  Washington Rd.
Mequon, WI 53092
262-241-6220

Northwind Book & Fiber
205 Walnut St.
Spooner, WI 54801
715-635-6811

Novel Ideas
8085 Highway 57
Baileys Harbor, WI
  54202
920-839-1300

Ocooch Books &
  Libations LLC
145 W. Court St.
Richland Center, WI
  53581
608-647-8826

Pages & Pipes – Book
  World
322 W. College Ave.
Appleton, WI 54911
920-734-2821

Pages & Pipes
748 W. Northland Ave.
Appleton, WI 54914
920-830-0309

Paper Tiger Book Store –
  Book World
100-D City Center
Oshkosh, WI 54901
920-321-0800

Pastimes
PO Box 396
Princeton, WI 54968
920-295-4801

Prairie Bookshop
117 E. Main St.
Mount Horeb, WI 53572
608-437-4118

Rainbow Bookstore
  Cooperative
426 W. Gilman St.
Madison, WI 53703
608-257-6050

Reader's Loft
2069 Central Court –
  Ste. 44
Green Bay, WI 45311
920-406-0200

Redbery Books, Inc.
43455 Kavanaugh Rd.
Cable, WI 54821
715-798-5014

A Room of One's Own
307 W. Johnson St.
Madison, WI 53703
608-257-7888

Thyme Worn Treasures
30 N Main St.
Rice Lake, WI 54868
715-736-0233

The Velveteen Rabbit
  Bookshop & Guest
  House
20 E. Sherman Ave.
Fort Atkinson, WI 53538
920-568-9940

Wisconsin Milwaukee
  UWM Bookstore
2200 E. Kenwood Blvd.
Milwaukee, WI 53211
414-229-4201

Barnes & Noble

►ILLINOIS

The Annex of Arlington
  Shopping Ctr
13 W. Rand Rd.
Arlington Heights, IL
  60004
847-259-5304

200 S. Gary Ave.
Bloomingdale, IL
60108
630-671-9760

1701 E. Empire
Bloomington, IL 61704
309-662-1506

The Promenade
Bolingbrook
631 E. Boughton Rd.
Ste. 100
Bolingbrook, IL 60440
630-783-0009

Water Town Plaza
1577 N. State Route 50
Bourbonnais, IL 60914
815-935-2209

1300 E. Main St.
Carbondale, IL 62901
618-351-0404

Marketview Shopping
Center
65 E. Market View Dr.
Champaign, IL 61820
217-355-2045

The Merchandise Mart
Ste. #204
222 The Merchandise
Mart
Chicago, IL 60654
312-329-1881

1130 N. State St.
Chicago, IL 60610
312-280-8155

Webster Place
1441 W. Webster Ave.
Chicago, IL 60614
773-871-3610

Bohl Farm Market Place
5380 Route 14
Crystal Lake, IL 60014
815-444-0824

Deer Park Town Center
20600 N. Rand Rd.
Deer Park, IL 60010
847-438-7444

Deerfield Square
728 N. Waukegan Rd.
Deerfield, IL 60015
847-914-9293

Oakland Place
Shopping Center
2439 Sycamore Rd.
Dekalb, IL 60115
815-787-3234

1550 W. 75th
Downers Grove, IL
60516
630-663-0181

Sherman Plaza
1630 Sherman Ave.
Evanston, IL 60201
847-424-0848

Shoppes at St. Clair
Square
6510 N.Illinois St.
Fairview Heights, IL
62208
618-624-4361

102 Commons Dr.
Geneva, IL 60134
630-262-8568

2621 Plainfield Rd.
Joliet, IL 60435
815-254-2253

Lincolnshire Commons
920 N. Milwaukee Ave.
Lincolnshire, IL 60069
847-793-8740

Times Square Mall
42nd & Broadway
Mt Vernon, IL 62864
618-244-4400

47 E. Chicago Ave.
Ste. #132
Naperville, IL 60540
630-579-0200

North Riverside Park
Mall
7501 W. Cermak Rd.
North Riverside, IL
60546
708-442-9383

297 Oakbrook Center
Oak Brook, IL 60523
630-684-0586

Orland Park Place
160 Orland Park Place
Orland Park, IL 60462
708-226-9092

5001 N. Big Hollow Rd.
Peoria, IL 61615
309-693-9408

Kensington Center
12700 S. IL Route 59
Plainfield, IL 60544
815-609-8233

Cherryvale Mall
7200 Harrison Ste. 5
Rockford, IL 61112
815-332-3069

Woodfield Plaza
Shopping Center
590 E. Golf Rd.
Schaumburg, IL 60173
847-310-0450

Old Orchard
55 Old Orchard Center
Skokie, IL 60077
847-676-2230

Village Crossing
Shopping Center
5405 Touhy Ave.
Skokie, IL 60077
847-329-8460

3111 S. Veterans Pkwy
Springfield, IL 62704
217-546-9440

720 Hawthorne Center
Vernon Hills, IL 60061
847-247-1157

Spring Hill Mall
1468 Springhill Mall
  Blvd.
West Dundee, IL 60118
847-426-5614

351 Town Sq Wheaton
Wheaton, IL 60189
630-653-2122

INDIANA

Avon Commons
10269 E. US 36
Avon, IN 46123
317-271-5857

2813 E. Third St.
Bloomington, IN 47408
812-331-0669

Greyhound Plaza
14709 US Hwy 31 N.
Carmel, IN 46032
317-844-2501

624 S. Green River Rd.
Evansville, IN 47715
812-475-1054

Glenbrook Square Mall
4201 Coldwater Rd.
  Ste. B-01
Fort Wayne, IN 46805
260-482-3720

Jefferson Pointe
  Shopping Center
4140 W. Jefferson Blvd.
  Bldg. J
Ft. Wayne, IN 46804
260-432-3343

1251 US 31 N.
Greenwood, IN 46142
317-859-8089

Clearwater Crossing
3748 E. 82nd St.
Indianapolis, IN 46240
317-594-7525

2323 Sagamore
  Parkway S.
Lafayette, IN 47905
765-449-4330

2240 E. 80th Ave.
Merrillville, IN 46410
219-736-7788

South Bend
4601 Grape Rd.
Mishawaka, IN 46545
574-277-9482

University Park Mall
6501 N. Grape Rd.
Mishawaka, IN 46545
574-247-0864

Stony Creek Marketplace
17090 Mercantile Blvd.
Noblesville, IN 46060
317-773-7952

Metropolis LifeStyle
  Center
2540 Futura Pkwy. #135
Plainfield, IN 46168
317-838-7941

Valparaiso Marketplace
150 Silhavy Rd. Ste. 120
Valparaiso, IN 46383
219-531-6551

▶IOWA

1315 College Square
  Mall
Cedar Falls, IA 50613
319-277-5466

Northland Square SC
333 Collins Rd. NE
  Bldg 1
Cedar Rapids, IA 52402
319-393-4800

Coral Ridge Mall
1451 Coral Ridge Ave.
  Ste. 1108
Coralville, IA 52241
319-337-3337

Mall of the Bluffs
1751 Madison Ave.
Council Bluffs, IA 51503
712-323-3700

North Park Mall
320 W. Kimberly Rd.
Davenport, IA 52806
563-445-8760

Crossroads Mall C-125
217 S. 25th St.
Fort Dodge, IA 50501
515-955-6083

Southbridge Mall
303 Southbridge Mall
100 S. Federal
Mason City, IA 50401
641-424-1193

Southern Hills Mall
4400 Sergeant Rd. Unit
  550
Sioux City, IA 51106

518 Flammang Dr.
Waterloo, IA 50702
319-232-0475
712-276-5515

Westland Mall 0124
550 S. Gear Ave. #37
W. Burlington, IA 52655
319-753-1681

The Shoppes at Three
Fountains
4550 University Ave.
West Des Moines, IA
50266
515-221-9171

Jordan Creek Town
Center
101 Jordan Creek
Parkway Unit 12170
West Des Moines, IA
50266
515-453-2980

▶MICHIGAN
3120 Fairlane Dr.
Allen Park, MI 48101
313-271-0688

Huron Village
3235 Washtenaw Ave.
Ann Arbor, MI 48104
734-973-0846

Lakeview Square
5701 Beckley Rd.
Battle Creek, MI 49015
269-979-8060

Bay City Mall
4101 Wilder Rd. B215
Bay City, MI 48706
989-686-7799

The Orchards E-24
1800 Pipestone Rd.
Benton Harbor, MI
49022
269-926-8259

Jacobson's Building
333 E. Grand River Ave.
East Lansing, MI 48823
517-324-3926

Genesee Valley Mall
4370 Miller Rd. Unit
E-10
Flint, MI 48507
810-732-0704

4325 24th Ave.
Fort Gratiot, MI 48059
810-385-4849

Green Oak Village
605 Green Oak Village
Place
Green Oak Township, MI
48116
810-225-4670

19221 Mack Ave.
Grosse Pointe, MI 48236
313-884-5220

Felch St. Plaza
3050 Beeline Rd. Ste. 50
Holland, MI 49424
616-994-6015

28th St. Retail
3670 28th St. SE
Kentwood, MI 49512
616-954-2211

Lansing Mall
5132 W. Saginaw Hwy
245
Lansing, MI 48917
517-327-0437

Westwood Mall
3020 US Hwy 41 W.
Marquette, MI 49855
906-228-6495

Midland Mall
6800 Eastman Ave.
Space F630
Midland, MI 48642
989-835-5037

Lake Shore Marketplace
5275 Harvey St.
Muskegon, MI 49444
231-798-4388

17111 Haggerty Rd.
Northville, MI 48167
248-348-0696

Southland SC
6134 S. Westnedge Ave.
Portage, MI 49002
269-324-1433

2800 S. Rochester Rd.
Rochester Hills, MI
48307
248-853-9855

▶MINNESOTA
Fischer Marketplace
14880 Florence Trail
Apple Valley, MN 55124
952-997-8928

Paul Bunyan Mall
Highway 2 W.
Bemidji, MN 56601
218-751-2270

710 County Hwy. 10 NE
Blaine, MN 55434
763-786-0686

Mall of America
118 E. Broadway, Ste.
238
Bloomington, MN 55425
952-854-1455

1353 Brookdale Center
Ste. 1
Brooklyn Center, MN
55430
763-503-0264

Burnhaven Shopping
Center
828 W. County Rd. 42
Burnsville, MN 55337

Miller Hill Mall
1600 Miller Trunk Hwy.
#L25
Duluth, MN 55811
218-786-0710

Eden Prairie Center
3000 Eden Prairie
Center
Eden Prairie, MN 55344
952-944-5683

Galleria Shopping
Center
3225 W. 69th
Edina, MN 55435
952-920-0633

River Hills Mall
1850 Adams St. # 404
Mankato, MN 56001
507-345-3444

8040 Wedgewood Lane
Maple Grove, MN
55369
763-420-4517

Maplewood Mall
3001 White Bear Ave. N.
Ste. 1030
Maplewood, MN 55109
651-779-9999

Calhoun Village
Shopping Center
3216 W. Lake St.
Minneapolis, MN 55416
612-922-3238

Southdale Center
1645 Southdale Center

66th and France Ave. S.
Minneapolis, MN 55435
952-920-2678

Midwest Plaza
801 Nicollet Mall
Minneapolis, MN 55402
612-371-4443

Ridgehaven Mall
13131 Ridgedale Dr.
Minnetonka, MN 55305
952-546-2006

Apache Mall
1201 12th St. SW,
Ste. 425
Rochester, MN 55902
507-281-7950

Chateau Theatre
15 First St. SW
Rochester, MN 55902
507-288-3848

HarMar Mall
2100 N. Snelling Ave.
Roseville, MN 55113
651-639-9256

St. Cloud
St. Cloud Rainbow Village
3940 Division St.
St. Cloud, MN 56301
320-251-4537

Highland Park
2080 Ford Parkway
St. Paul, MN 55116
651-690-9443

Woodbury
Woodbury Village
Shopping Center
7020 Valley Creek Plaza
Woodbury, MN 55125
651-739-7274

▶MISSOURI

Westfield West Park
3049 Williams St.,
Ste 219A
Cape Girardeau, MO
63703
573-335-0522

Chesterfield Oaks
1600 Clarkson Rd.
Chesterfield, MO 63017
636-536-9636

2208 Bernadette Dr.
Columbia, MO 65203
573-445-4080

9618 Watson Rd.
Crestwood, MO 63126
314-843-9480

West County Mall
113 West County Center
Des Peres, MO 63131
314-835-9980

Fenton Commons
Shopping Center
721 Gravois Rd.
Fenton, MO 63026
636-326-4619

Independence
Commons
19120 E. 39th St.
Independence, MO
64057
816-795-9878

Wildwood Shopping
Center
3535 Missouri Blvd.
Jefferson City, MO
65109
573-634-2691

Northpark Mall
101 N. Rangeline Dr.
Joplin, MO 64801
417-623-1813

Zona Rosa
8625 NW Prairie View
   Rd. Spac
Kansas City, MO 64153
816-505-3355

Ladue Crossing
   Shopping Center
8871 Ladue Rd.
Ladue, MO 63124
314-862-6280

3055 S. Glenstone
Springfield, MO 65804
417-885-0026

320 Mid Rivers Center Dr.
St. Peters, MO 63376
636-278-1118

▶OHIO

4015 Medina Rd.
Akron, OH 44333
330-665-5199

The Shoppes of
   Beavercreek
2720 Towne Dr. # 200
Beavercreek, OH 45431
937-429-1660

Sycamore Plaza at
   Kenwood
7800 Montgomery Rd.
Cincinnati, OH 45236
513-794-9440

Waterstone
9891 Waterstone Blvd.
Cincinnati, OH 45249
513-683-5599

Festival @ Sawmill
3685 W. Dublin-Granville
Columbus, OH 43235
614-798-0077

Polaris Fashion Center
1560 Polaris Parkway
Columbus, OH 43240
614-854-0339

Lennox Town
1739 Olentangy River Rd.
Columbus, OH 43212
614-298-9516

Upper Arlington
3280 Tremont Rd.
Columbus, OH 43221
614-459-0921

Easton Town Center
4005 Townsfair Way
Columbus, OH 43219
614-476-8480

Dayton Mall
2619 Miamisburg-
   Centerville Rd.
Dayton, OH 45459
937-433-0750

Findlay Village Mall #MI
1800 Tiffin Ave.
Findlay, OH 45840
419-424-5708

North Lexington-
   Springmill
832 N. Lexington
   Springmill
Mansfield, OH 44906
419-747-7748

The Shops at Fallen
   Timbers
3100 Main St. #1400
Maumee, OH 43537
419-878-0652

Great Lakes Mall
7900 Mentor Ave.
Mentor, OH 44060
440-266-0212

Hunters Run Centre
1738 N. Hill Rd.
Pickerington, OH 43147
614-751-0927

691 Richmond Rd.,
   Ste D30
Richmond Heights, OH
   44143
440-720-0374

Upper Valley Mall
1475 Upper Valley Pike
Springfield, OH 45504
937-325-7316

Franklin Park
4940 Monroe St.
Toledo, OH 43623
419-472-6164

The Streets of
   Westchester
9455 Civic Centre Blvd.
West Chester, OH
   45069
513-755-2258

Crocker Park
198 Crocker Park Blvd.
Westlake, OH 44145
440-250-9233

Eton Collection
28801 Chagrin Blvd.
Woodmere, OH 44122
216-765-7520

381 Boardman-
   Poland Rd.
Youngstown, OH 44512
330-629-9436

▶WISCONSIN

Brookfield Square Mall
95 N. Moorland Rd.,
Unit C-1
Brookfield, WI 53005
262-796-8550

Bayshore Mall
5755 N Bayshore Dr.
Glendale, WI 53217
414-967-1610

Fox River Commons
4705 W. Grande Market Dr.
Grand Chute, WI 54915
920-831-7880

Village of Ashwaubenon
2498 Oneida St.
Green Bay, WI 54304
920-490-1770

4935 S. 76th St.
Greenfield, WI 53220
414-281-8222

Valley View Mall
3800 State Rd. 16
La Crosse, WI 54601
608-785-1330

West Towne Mall
7433 Mineral Point Rd.
Madison, WI 53717
608-827-0809

East Towne Mall
#1 East Towne Mall
Madison, WI 53704
608-241-4695

Southland Center
2710 S. Green Bay Rd.
Racine, WI 53406
262-598-9757

Wausau Shopping Center
3400 Rib Mountain Dr.
Wausau, WI 54401
715-241-6360

2500 N. Mayfair Rd.
Ste. 196
Wauwatosa, WI 53226
414-475-6070

Borders Books

▶ILLINOIS

2216 S- Randall Rd.
Algonquin, IL 60102
847-658-7548

161 N. Weber Rd.
Bolingbrook, IL 60490
630-771-9560

96 River Oaks Center
Calumet City, IL 60409
708-868-2755

802 West Town Center Blvd.
Champaign, IL 61822
217-351-9011

500 W. Madison St.
Chicago, IL 60661
312-627-8334

Beverly
2210 W. 95th St.
Chicago, IL 60643
773-445-5471

Hyde Park
1539 E. 53rd St.
Chicago, IL 60615
773-752-8663

Lincoln Village
6103 N. Lincoln Ave.
Chicago, IL 60659
773-267-4822

830 N. Michigan Ave.
Chicago, IL 60611
312-573-0564

755 W. North Ave.
Chicago, IL 60610
773-334-7338

Ridge Mall
Ridgeland & 95th St.
Chicago, IL 60415
708-424-9190

6000 Northwest Highway
Crystal Lake, IL 60014
815-455-0302

2917 N. Vermilion
Danville, IL 61832
217-442-2708

2520 Sycamore Rd.
DeKalb, IL 60115
815-758-8771

49 S. Waukegan Rd.
Deerfield, IL 60015
618-659-0554

1700 Maple Ave.
Evanston, IL 60201
847-733-8852

601 N. Illinois
Fairview Heights, IL 62208
618-397-6097

Route 51 North
Forsyth, IL 62535
217-877-0293

1660 S. Randall Rd.
Geneva, IL 60134
630-262-8747

6971 W. Grand Ave.
Gurnee, IL 60031
847-249-1845

6170 W. Grand Ave.
Sp. 631
Gurnee, IL 60031
847-855-8426

595 Central Ave.
Highland Park, IL 60035
847-433-9130

3340 Loop Dr.
Joliet, IL 60435
815-439-2025

3333 W. Touhy Ave.
Lincolnwood, IL 60712
847-677-1797

3000 W. Deyoung St.
Marion, IL 62959
618-993-6981

700 E. Broadway
Mattoon, IL 61938
217-235-3441

2221 Richmond Rd.,
Route 31
McHenry, IL 60050
815-578-9330

John Deere Expressway
& 16 St.
Moline, IL 61265
309-797-8140

909 N. Elmhurst Rd.
Mount Prospect, IL
60056
847-342-6421

336 S. Route 59
Naperville, IL 60540
630-637-9700

200A N. Greenbriar Dr.
Normal, IL 61761
309-888-4246

7100 W. Forest Preserve
Ave.
Norridge, IL 60706
708-457-2111

1500 16th St., Ste. D
Oak Brook, IL 60523
630-574-0800

1144 Lake St.
Oak Park, IL 60301
708-386-6927

15260 S. La Grange Rd.
Orland Park, IL 60462
708-460-7566

5201 W. War Memorial
Dr.
Peoria, IL 61615
309-692-3082

4501 War Memorial Dr.
Peoria, IL 61613
309-688-2436

3940 Route 251
Peru, IL 61354
815-223-4910

3382 Quincy Mall
Quincy, IL 62301
217-224-9762

199 Deane Dr.
Rockford, IL 61107
815-399-2898

1540 Golf Rd.
Schaumburg, IL 60173
847-330-0031

3539 E. Main St.
St. Charles, IL 60174
630-443-8160

900 E. Lincolnway
Sterling, IL 61081
815-626-5144

101 Rice Lake Square
Wheaton, IL 60187
630-871-9595

3232 Lake Ave., Ste.
100
Wilmette, IL 60091
847-256-3220

▶INDIANA

109 S. Scatterfield Rd.
Anderson, IN 46016
765-649-3634

2634 E. Third St.
Bloomington, IN 47401
317-843-0450

757 Hwy 131 E.
Clarksville, IN 47129
812-282-4658

2306 25th St.
Columbus, IN 47201
812-372-2144

3701 S. Main St.
Elkhart, IN 46517
574-875-5535

6401 E. Lloyd
Expressway
Evansville, IN 47715
812-402-9300

4320 Coldwater Rd.
Fort Wayne, IN 46805
260-471-5598

1251 US 31 N.
Greenwood, IN 46142
317-882-0270

10135 Indianapolis Blvd.
Highland, IN 46322
219-922-1103

6020 E. 82nd St.
Indianapolis, IN 46250
317-849-8660

11 S. Meridian St.
Indianapolis, IN 46204
317-859-2949

8675 River Crossing
Blvd.
Indianapolis, IN 46240
317-574-1775

Airport
800 Col. H. Weir Cook
Memorial Dr.
Indianapolis, IN 46241
317-481-8161

Kem Rd. & Baldwin Ave.
Marion, IN 46952
765-664-9962

2060 Southlake Mall
Merrillville, IN 46410
219-795-1925

4230 Grape Rd.
Mishawaka, IN 46545
574-271-9930

Noblesville
13145 Levinson Lane
Noblesville, IN 46060
317-770-7030

3801 National Rd. E.
Richmond, IN 47374
765-966-5488

3401 US Hwy 41
Terre Haute, IN 47802
812-232-0271

348 E. State St.
West Lafayette, IN
47906
765-743-7775

▶IOWA

1200 S. Duff
Ames, IA 50010
515-233-2833

555 John F. Kennedy
Rd.
Dubuque, IA 52002
563-585-0085

1650 Sycamore St.
Iowa City, IA 52240
319-351-3677

2060 Crossroads Blvd.
Waterloo, IA 50702
319-232-8423

4100 University Ave.,
Ste.115
West DesMoines, IA
50266
515-223-1620

1551 Valley West Dr.
West Des Moines, IA
50266
515-225-1753

▶MICHIGAN

1357 S. Main
Adrian, MI 49221
517-263-1767

2298 US 23 S.
Alpena, MI 49707
989-356-6488

3527 Washtenaw Ave.
Ann Arbor, MI 48104
734-677-6948

636 Briarwood Circle
Ann Arbor, MI 48108
734-669-0785

3140 Lohr Rd-
Ann Arbor, MI 48108
734-997-8884

612 E. Liberty St.
Ann Arbor, MI 48104
734-668-7652

3924 Baldwin Rd.
Auburn Hills, MI 48326
248-335-5013

4230 Baldwin Rd.
Auburn Hills, MI 48326
248-454-0331

31150 Southfield Rd.
Beverly Hills, MI 48025
248-644-1515

12156 S. Beyer Rd.
Birch Run, MI 48415
989-624-0215

34300 Woodward
Birmingham, MI 48009
248-203-0005

8101 Movie Dr.
Brighton, MI 48116
810-225-1717

43435 Ford Rd.
Canton, MI 48187
734-844-2090

5601 Mercury Dr.
Dearborn, MI 48126
313-271-4441

18900 Michigan Ave.
Dearborn, MI 48126
313-336-7863

Detroit Metro Airport
601 Rogell N. Terminal
Ste. 1132
Detroit, MI 48242
734-955-9344

30995 Orchard Lake
Rd.
Farmington Hills, MI
48334
248-737-0110

4135 Miller Rd.
Flint, MI 48507
810-230-8830

4350 24th Ave.
Ft Gratiot, MI 48059
810-385-1989

17141 Kercheval
Grosse Pointe, MI
48230
313-885-1188

1778 W. Michigan Ave.
Jackson, MI 49202
517-782-3650

37560 W. Six Mile Rd.
Livonia, MI 48152
734-464-2720

2121 N. Monroe St.
Monroe, MI 48161
734-242-3479

43075 Crescent Blvd.
Novi, MI 48375
248-347-0780

Twelve Oaks Mall
27280 Novi Rd.
Novi, MI 48377
248-735-8301

6650 S. Westnedge
Portage, MI 49024
269-323-1095

1122 S. Rochester Rd.
Rochester Hills, MI
48307
248-652-0558

1946 Gratiot Ave.
Roseville, MI 48066
989-793-6291

Southgate Center
13667 Eureka Rd-
Southgate, MI 48195
734-282-4197

Sterling Heights
14600 Lakeside Mall
Sterling Heights, MI
48313
586-247-0420

Southland Mall
Taylor, MI 48180
734-374-5345

2612 Crossings Circle
Traverse City, MI 49684
231-933-0412

Oakland Mall
460 W. 14 Mile Rd.
Troy, MI 48083
248-585-6029

45290 Utica Park Blvd.
Utica, MI 48315
586-726-8555

Westland Mall
35000 W. Warren
Westland, MI 48185
734-421-7724

▶MINNESOTA

3577 River Rapids Dr.
NW
Coon Rapids, MN
55448
763.755-7550

12059 Elm Creek Blvd.
Maple Grove, MN
55369
763-494-0720

1501 Plymouth Rd.
Minnetonka, MN 55305
952-595-0977

800 W. 78th St.
Richfield, MN 55423
612-869-6245

866 Rosedale Center
Roseville, MN 55113
651-633-1344

41St. & Division St.
St. Cloud, MN 56301
320-253-3383

1390 W. University Ave.
St. Paul, MN 55104
651-641-0026

8472 Tamarack Bay
Woodbury, MN 55125
651-578-2931

► MISSOURI

15355-A Manchester
Rd.
Ballwin, MO 63011
636-230-2992

1519 S. Brentwood
Blvd.
Brentwood, MO 63144
314-918-8189

2040 Chesterfield Mall
Chesterfield, MO 63017
636-536-1779

11745 Olive Blvd.
Creve Coeur, MO 63141
314-432-3575

2450 Grand Blvd.
Kansas City, MO 64108
816-474-8774

Northland
8628 N. Boardwalk Ave.
Kansas City, MO 64154
816-741-1787

1664 NW Chipman Rd.
Lees Summit, MO
64081
816-347-0044

1113 St. Louis Galleria
Richmond Heights, MO
63117
314-725-9655

3300 S. Glenstone Ave.
Springfield, MO 65804
417-881-4111

Battlefield Mall
2825 S. Glenstone
Springfield, MO 65804
417-881-4811

5201 N. Belt Highway
St. Joseph, MO 64506
816-279-6111

25 S. County Centerway
St. Louis, MO 63129
314-892-1700

1320 Mid Rivers Mall
St. Peters, MO 63376
636-278-5000

10990 Sunset Hills
Plaza
Sunset Hills, MO 63127
314-909-0300

► OHIO

Chapel Hill Mall -
Brittain Rd.
Akron, OH 44310
330 633 2538

2500 W. State St.
Alliance, OH 44601
330-823-7320

3045 Northridge E.
Ashtabula, OH 44004
440-998-1992

2101 Richmond Rd.
Beachwood, OH 44122
216-292-2660

2727 N. Fairfield Rd.
Beavercreek, OH 45431
937-427-9092

6751 Strip Ave. NW
North Canton, OH
44720
330-494-4776

6139 Glenway Ave.
Cincinnati, OH 45211
513-662-5837

Eastgate Mall
4530 Eastgate Blvd.
Cincinnati, OH 45245
513-943-0068

Northgate Mall
9459 Colerain Ave.
Cincinnati, OH 45251
513-245-9898

230 W. Huron Rd.
Cleveland, OH 44113
216-861-0010

3466 Mayfield Rd.
Cleveland Heights, OH
44118
216-291-8605

5043 Tuttle Crossing
Blvd. #270
Columbus, OH 43017
614-760-8776

1500 Polaris Parkway,
Space 1126
Columbus, OH 43240
614-848-3150

4545 Kenny Rd.
Columbus, OH 43220
614-451-2292

6670 Sawmill Rd.
Columbus, OH 43235
614-718-9099

335 Howe Ave.
Cuyahoga Falls, OH
44221
330-945-7683

2700 Miamisburg
Centerville Rd.
Dayton, OH 45459
937-434-3800

4332 Midway Blvd.
Elyria, OH 44035
440-324-5355

3737 W. Market St,
Unit U
Fairlawn, OH 44333
330-666-7568

771 S. 30th St.
Heath, OH 43056
740-522-3638

8360 Factory Shop
Blvd.
Jeffersonville, OH
43128
740-948-2408

1635 River Valley Cir. S.
Lancaster, OH 43130
740-653-6463

2400 Elida Rd.
Lima, OH 45805
419-331-5131

1445 Marion-Waldo Rd.
Marion, OH 43302
740-389-5557

5105 Deerfield Blvd.
Mason, OH 45040
513-770-0440

4927 Grande Shops
Ave.
Medina, OH 44256
330-723-8270

9565 Mentor Ave.
Mentor, OH 44060
440-350-8168

400 Mill Ave. S.E.
New Philadelphia, OH
44663
330-339-6830

2102 Niles-Cortland
Rd.. SE
Niles, OH 44484
330-652-6184

4650 Great Northern
Blvd.
North Olmsted, OH
44070
440-777-2630

402 Great Northern
Blvd.
North Olmsted, OH
44070
440-734-8892

7793 W. Ridgewood Dr.
Parma, OH 44129
440-845-5911

4314 Milan Rd.
Sandusky, OH 44870
419-626-1173

6025 Kruse Dr.
Solon, OH 44139
440-542-9480

846 Upper Valley Mall
Springfield, OH 45504
937-322-2421

Ohio Valley Mall
St. Clairsville, OH
43950
740-695-5398

100 Mall Dr.
Steubenville, OH 43952
740-264-2594

4248 Kent Rd.
Stow, OH 44224
330-688-2184

17200 Royalton Rd.
Strongsville, OH 44136
440-846-1144

Southpark Center, Unit
Au716
Strongsville, OH 44136
440-846-8890

5001 Monroe St.
Toledo, OH 43623
419-474-3704

30121 Detroit Rd.
Westlake, OH 44145
440-892-7667

3575 Maple Ave.
Zanesville, OH 43701
740-455-3439

▸WISCONSIN

4030 Commonwealth
Ave.
Eau Claire, WI 54701
715-832-2852

833 W. Johnson St.
Fond Du Lac, WI 54935
920-921-6298

8705 N. Port
  Washington
Fox Point, WI 53217
414-540-1427

Green Bay
661 Bay Park Square
Green Bay, WI 54304
920-499-5943

5250 S. 76th St.
Greendale, WI 53129
414-282-0882

5300 S. 76 St.
Greendale, WI 53129
414-421-4290

2500 Milton Ave.
Janesville, WI 53545
608-756-3493

3750 University Ave.
Madison, WI 53705
608-232-2600

2173 Zeier Rd.
Madison, WI 53704
608-240-0080

101 W. Wisconsin Ave.
Milwaukee, WI 53203
414-225-9977

3347 Kohler Memorial
  Dr.
Sheboygan, WI 53081
920-458-9001

A-104 Wausau Center
Wausau, WI 54401
715-848-3463

Index

Chessnutt, Charles W., 219, 229–230
Chopin, Kate, 193, 195, 202
Cisnerso, Sandra, 7
Collier, Andrea King, 155
Collins, Martha, 35
Conroy, Jack, 216
Cooper, James Fenimore, 108
Corey, Paul Frederick, 121–122
Coward, Noel, 265
Crane, Hart (Harold Hart Crane), 227–228
Curti, Merle, 260
Curwood, James Oliver, 156

▸D

Dale, Arizona Stone, 55
Davis, Jim, 86
de Beauvoir, Simone, 38, 94
Debs, Eugene, 78–79
DeJong, David, 153
Derleth, August, 248, 263–264
Dickens, Charles, 7, 27–28, 31, 203, 238
Diller, Phyllis, 208
Disch, Thomas M., 172
Doner, Mary Frances, 161
Dreiser, Theodore, 58, 76–77, 98–100, 106, 253
Dresser, Paul, 76–77
Dubkin, Leonard, 61
Dunbar, Paul Laurence, 221–222, 230

▸E

Eggers, Dave, 253, 253
Eliot, T. S., 39, 135, 192, 193, 195, 196, 209, 217

Elkin, Stanley, 193, 196
Engle, Paul, 111–112
Erdrich, Louise, 177, 186, 254
Erickson, Lori, 116
Etter, Dave, 35

▸F

Farrell, James T., 45, 63
Ferber, Edna, 47, 63, 247, 248, 265, 270
Field, Eugene, 11, 53, 193, 197, 201
Finley, John, 67–68
Finney, Jack, 11, 253
Fitzgerald, Scott F., 171, 173–174
Flanigan, B. P., 139
Frey, James, 13
Frostic, Gwen, 147, 152–153

▸G

Gag, Wanda, 167
Gale, Zona, 248, 266–267
Garland, Hamlin, 2, 248, 273–274
Gass, William H., 83, 193, 197, 226–228
Gerber, Dan, 153–154
Giovanni, Nikki, 219, 236
Godwin, Gail, 113
Goethe, Wolfgang von, 52
Goldman, Emma, 7
Graham, Jorie, 112
Grant, Ulysses S., 16–17, 35
Gray, Alice (Diana of the Dunes), 95
Grey, Zane, 219, 224–226
Gross, Samuel Eberly, 50–51

Vonnegut, Kurt (Jr.), 71, 73–74, 78, 111

About the Author

A lover of literature, travel, and history, Greg Holden has written more than forty books, which have sold more than three-hundred thousand copies since 1996. These include *Literary Chicago: A Book Lover's Tour of the Windy City* (Lake Claremont Press). Many of his books are Internet-related. He is currently Director of Communications at the UIC Jane Addams College of Social Work. A father of two girls and a practicing Buddhist, he also wrote *Karma Kids: Answering Everyday Parenting Questions with Buddhist Wisdom*.

Greg is a Midwesterner born and bred, who started his writing career as a copy boy for the *Chicago Tribune* before moving on to be a reporter and columnist for a group of newspapers in his hometown of Des Plaines, Illinois. He has written his own stories and fiction, having studied with teachers ranging from poet Allen Ginsberg to novelist Molly Daniels.

Although Greg enjoys visiting the places he writes about in this book, he also loves visiting Faulkner's home in Oxford, Mississippi; Zane Grey's ranch in the Sonoma Valley of northern California; and Carl Sandburg's farm in North Carolina.

To learn more about how Greg successfully balances his high-tech expertise with his lifelong love of literature, visit www.greg holden.com or send an e-mail to greg@gregholden.com.